Cinnamon-Chocolate Swirl Coffee Cake, page 109

Lemon-Thy...

Breakfast Fruit Pastries, page 102

Tropical Granola, page 99

Pecan Fudge, page 306

Autumn Sweet Potato Pie, page 204

THE

Redpath

CANADIAN
BAKE BOOK

Lemon–White Chocolate Cupcakes
with Blackberry Buttercream
(recipe page 139)

THE

Redpath

CANADIAN
BAKE BOOK

**Over 200 Delectable Recipes
for Cakes, Breads, Desserts and More**

appetite
by RANDOM HOUSE

Appetite by Random House® and colophon are registered trademarks of Penguin Random House LLC.

Redpath® Sugar is a registered trademark of Redpath Sugar Ltd.

Redpath® Sugar is part of ASR Group.

Library and Archives Canada Cataloguing in Publication is available upon request.

ISBN: 9780147530141
eBook ISBN: 9780147530158

Book design by Kelly Hill
Printed and bound in China

Published in Canada by Appetite by Random House®,
a division of Penguin Random House Canada Limited.

www.penguinrandomhouse.ca

10 9 8 7 6 5 4 3 2 1

appetite
by RANDOM HOUSE | Penguin
Random
House

Nutty Divinity
(recipe page 319)

CONTENTS

Introduction

The pure cane sugar which we craft at Redpath has helped Canadian bakers fill their homes with cheer and happiness for over 160 years; from the majestic Pacific coast to the rugged Maritimes, from the bountiful Great Lakes to our frozen North and anywhere in between.

This book represents a collection of our favourite classic recipes, many of which were originally brought to Canada from all four corners of the world by the families of immigrants who came here looking for a place to call home. There's nothing quite as comforting and tantalizing as the smell of home baking, be it a sheet of simple chocolate chip cookies or an elaborate cake for a special occasion.

The recipes in this collection have been tested and perfected not just in our test kitchen, but also with our own families.

We hope that this book will help you fill your own home with the joy that comes from baking for the people you love for years to come.

Jonathan Bamberger
President, Redpath Sugar

The Story of *Redpath* Sugar

The distinctive style of the "Redpath" name on our packaging is not only instantly recognizable but also a sign of quality. It's the oldest Canadian food-related trademark and the company has a fascinating story.

Canada's first sugar company, the Canada Sugar Refinery, started production in 1854 on the banks of the Lachine Canal in Montreal. It was founded by a 57-year-old entrepreneur and businessman named John Redpath, who had already enjoyed a successful career as a stonemason, building contractor and mercantile trader. John had been involved in the building of the Lachine Canal and saw the opportunity for ships that were carrying raw sugar from the tropics to be unloaded at the company's own wharf.

The CANADA SUGAR REFINING Co. LIMITED.
MONTREAL, CANADA.
1904

Humble Beginnings

He may have grown up to be successful, but John was certainly not born with a silver spoon—sugar or otherwise—in his mouth. The son of a farm worker, he came into the world in the Scottish border village of Earlston in 1796. He was orphaned at an early age and brought up by an older sister's family.

When he was 13, John became an apprentice stonemason. Seven years later, he found himself newly qualified . . . and unemployed.

In 1816, he chose to spend what little money he had saved to emigrate to the British colony of Lower Canada. Arriving in Quebec City and finding no work, he walked—mostly barefoot to save his only pair of shoes—to seek his fortune in Montreal, over 150 miles away.

Redpath's Rising Fortunes

When John arrived in Montreal, it was a town of around 16,000 people—a small city by the standards of the time—and a good place to find success.

John started working as a general labourer, but within two years he had the funds to start his own construction business. By the age of 40, he was one of Canada's most successful building contractors, and Montreal had become Canada's largest city and its economic engine.

As well as the Lachine Canal in Montreal, John Redpath's building company was involved in the construction of the Notre-Dame Basilica, the Montreal General Hospital, the headquarters of the Bank of Montreal, parts of McGill University and many more buildings we now consider landmarks.

He was also one of the main contractors of the Rideau Canal in Upper Canada (now known as Ontario).

When John opened the Canada Sugar Refinery, sugar was processed in large conical pots. The resulting purified sugar was then dried in the pots, creating rock-hard "sugar cones," which became the standard retail product. At its start, John's company produced around 15 tons of these sugar cones each day, as well as 30 tons of lower-grade sugars and molasses, which were then sold across Quebec, the Maritimes and Ontario.

Meanwhile, John gained a reputation as a philanthropist committed to civic duty. He was a Montreal city councillor and alderman, and established and supported many educational and religious institutions as well. He also sat on the management boards for many social agencies dedicated to helping those in need.

John spent the last years of his life living at Terrace Bank, a grand home he had built on the side of Mount Royal. He died in 1869, leaving his second wife, Jane, and 12 surviving children. Following an elaborate civic funeral, he was laid to rest in the family plot at the Mount Royal cemetery.

Sweet Innovations

John had run the company as a family business, taking his sons, Peter and John James, as well as his son-in-law (who was also his brother-in-law) George A. Drummond as partners in the renamed John Redpath & Son, Canada Sugar Refinery. This continued until 1880, when the company went public as The Canada Sugar Refining Company Ltd. Over the next decades, the Montreal plant was constantly expanded and modernized to meet the changing needs of the Canadian market.

In 1871, Redpath was the first company to introduce boxes and barrels of loose granular sugar to the Canadian market, replacing the earlier sugar cones. In 1880, John Redpath's signature was officially registered as the brand's trademark. At this point, the company's range of products included granulated, extra-ground, powdered and confectioner's sugars; Paris lumps (the precursor of today's sugar cubes); yellow and demerara sugars; light, golden and dark syrups; and black molasses.

By the late-1800s, granulated sugar was being shipped to grocery stores in barrels from which grocers scooped sugar for their customers. In 1896, Redpath started to include a selection of 5- and 20-pound blue paper bags in each barrel into which the grocers could package the sugar.

In 1912, pre-packaged 1- and 2-pound cartons of sugar were introduced to the Canadian market. This innovation coincided with women starting to work in Redpath's packaging department.

CUTTING AND PACKING REDPATH PARIS LUMPS.

Redpath's Expansion

The Lachine Canal was closed to shipping in 1940, which made deliveries of the raw cane sugar difficult, but production continued at Redpath's Montreal location until 1980. Warehousing and distribution services remained there until the property was sold in 1986 and later redeveloped. Today, some of the original buildings of the historic Redpath factory are now luxury condominiums.

In 1950, the company bought a parcel of land on Toronto's waterfront to build a warehouse and distribution building. In 1957, construction of a new production plant began in Toronto, with its opening scheduled to coincide with the inauguration of the brand-new St. Lawrence Seaway. On June 29, 1959, the new Redpath plant was opened by Her Majesty Queen Elizabeth II and His Royal Highness the Duke of Edinburgh.

Since then, the Toronto facility has been continually expanded and upgraded with cutting-edge technologies to create one of the most up-to-date, efficient and environmentally conscious sugar manufacturing plants in North America.

Toronto's waterfront remains Redpath's home, and it's where we continue to produce the highest-quality sugar to sweeten the lives of Canadians from coast to coast to coast.

How *Redpath* Crafts Sugar

Sugar cane cannot be transported any distance before it spoils, so its natural sucrose juice must be extracted and concentrated as raw sugar before shipping. At Redpath Sugar we ship raw sugar from sugar cane mills in the tropics to Canada, then craft the different types of sugars we make at our plant on Toronto's waterfront.

Raw sugar is a natural product, but it needs to be cleaned up before it's fit for human consumption. Crafting sugar involves a series of steps designed to remove everything that isn't sugar— like plant residue and waxes—from the sucrose crystals.

Cleaning the Sugar

First we soften the sucrose crystals. We then remove the layer of residue surrounding them through a process called affination. The raw sugar is mixed with a warm, concentrated sugar syrup, then spun in a centrifuge to separate the crystals. This removes most of the impurities, leaving behind only some colour, and very fine particles, gums and resins from the sugar cane plant.

Filtering Out the Small Stuff

Next we add tiny particles of natural chalk to the second stage of liquid sugar. These chalk particles cling to the tiny particles of residue still left in the sugar, making them large enough to be filtered out by cloth filters.

After the chalk and residue have been filtered out, we remove all remaining waxes through even finer filtration, leaving behind nothing but pure

sugar. This fine-liquor, as the pure sugar is called, is now ready to be turned back into crystals.

Boiling the Sugar

The fine-liquor is boiled in sugar pans until an expert known as a Master Sugar Boiler decides that the conditions are right for sugar crystals to grow. To initiate crystal formation, we add some very fine sugar crystals to the sugar pans. Once the crystals have grown, the resulting mixture of sugar crystals and liquid is spun in a centrifuge (similar to washing being spun dry) to separate the two. The crystals are then given a final drying with hot air before being packed.

The Final Destination

We craft many different sugars at Redpath, from granulated sugar to ultra-fine icing sugar and various brown sugars. Once we've packed them all up, they're delivered to their final destinations: grocery stores, professional bakers, and food and drink manufacturers across Canada.

The Baker's Kitchen

Stock up your kitchen with pantry staples and you'll always be ready for baking day. Having all the ingredients you need on hand means you can prepare lots of different treats without having to go grocery shopping first.

In the Redpath test kitchen, you'll always find the pantry items listed here. Most of these keep well for many months, but ingredients such as spices and raising agents (baking powder, baking soda and yeast, for instance) should be replaced after 6 months.

IN THE PANTRY

SUGAR

dark brown
demerara-style
golden yellow
granulated
icing
instant-dissolving
turbinado

Store sugars in airtight containers in a cool, dry, dark place for up to 6 months. Make sure the containers are wide enough to fit a measuring cup so you can scoop the sugar easily. Adding a piece of apple or a slice of bread to containers of golden yellow and dark brown sugar helps prevent them from drying out and clumping.

FLOUR

all-purpose
bread
cake-and-pastry
whole wheat

Store flours in airtight containers in a cool, dry, dark place for up to 6 months. Make sure the containers are wide enough to fit a measuring cup so you can scoop the flour easily.

Other types of flour we like to bake with include corn flour, quinoa flour, oat flour, arrowroot flour and white and brown rice flour. We also use almond meal (also called almond flour) in some recipes. Almond meal is made from very finely ground almonds.

BAKING POWDER & BAKING SODA

Baking powder and baking soda are both raising agents. They help make treats like cakes and biscuits light and fluffy.

Baking powder is baking soda with an acidic element (cream of tartar) and a drying element (usually starch) added.

A cake batter needs to contain acidic ingredients, such as lemon juice, vinegar or buttermilk, to activate the baking soda.

As soon as baking powder or baking soda come in contact with liquids, the rising process starts, so make sure to add them to the dry ingredients in a recipe before adding any liquid.

Buy baking powder and baking soda in small quantities, as they lose their potency after 6 months. (See page 14 for our Baking Powder and Baking Soda Freshness Tests.)

DRIED FRUIT; CANDIED ORANGE & LEMON PEEL; CRYSTALLIZED GINGER

Store dried fruit, candied peel and crystallized ginger in airtight containers in a cool, dry, dark place for up to 2 months. For longer storage (especially if you want to stockpile dried fruit ahead of the holidays when it can be in short supply), refrigerate dried fruit for up to 6 months or freeze for up to 1 year.

VANILLA
beans
extract

Buy the best-quality vanilla extract you can find, and check that the label features the word "extract" and not "flavouring." Vanilla extract is one of the few pantry items that improve with time. If tightly capped and stored in a cool, dry, dark place, it will keep for up to 3 years.

Store vanilla beans, tightly wrapped in plastic wrap or in an airtight container to prevent them from drying out, in a cool, dry, dark place for up to 1 year.

OTHER EXTRACTS & FLAVOURINGS

Among the other flavourings we have on hand are almond, peppermint, coconut, lemon, orange, rum and anise extracts. We also like to use rose water, an aromatic flavouring made from distilling rose petals (look for it in specialty or Middle Eastern grocery stores, or baking supply stores).

FOOD COLOURING

We prefer gel food colouring rather than the liquid kind because you need to use less gel to achieve a bright colour. But either can be used in our recipes.

SPICES

Store all ground spices in airtight containers in a dark cupboard, and replace them every 6 months. For the best flavour, instead of using ground nutmeg, buy whole nutmegs and a nutmeg grater and grate the nutmeg you need for a recipe just before adding it.

UNSWEETENED COCOA POWDER

Cocoa powder comes from cocoa beans. After harvesting, the beans are fermented, dried, roasted and cracked. After grinding the nibs to extract cocoa butter, a paste called chocolate liquor is left behind. This is dried and then ground into unsweetened cocoa powder.

Store cocoa powder in an airtight container at room temperature for up to 2 years.

INSTANT ESPRESSO POWDER

This is useful for adding strong coffee flavour to cakes, puddings and frostings.

MOLASSES

Molasses is a must-have during the holidays for making gingerbread and other spiced goodies. It's a by-product of sugar production and adds a sweet, almost smoky flavour to baked goods. Molasses works in harmony with many spices, such as cinnamon, ginger or nutmeg.

We prefer to cook with fancy molasses but, if you want a more pronounced molasses flavour, substitute blackstrap molasses.

CHOCOLATE & CHOCOLATE CHIPS

The more cocoa solids a chocolate contains, the more intense its flavour. Here are the varieties we like to use, along with their approximate cocoa solids content:

dark (at least 70% cocoa solids)
bittersweet (at least 60% cocoa solids)
semi-sweet (at least 40% cocoa solids)
milk (at least 20% cocoa solids)
white (0% cocoa solids)

Store chocolate and chocolate chips in a cool, dry, dark place for up to 3 months.

SALT
coarse sea salt
fine sea salt
fleur de sel
sea salt flakes

We like to use fine sea salt in all our baking, and reserve the coarser salts, such as fleur de sel (a coarse French sea salt) and sea salt flakes, for garnish.

Keep salt in a cool, dry place. It will last almost indefinitely. If you wish, add a few uncooked grains of white rice to the salt to prevent it from clumping.

IN THE PANTRY CONTINUED

OIL

Oils can turn rancid if stored for too long, and just to make things extra complicated, different oils have different shelf lives. Canola oil, for example, lasts for about 1 year in the pantry and olive oil for up to 3 years, but oils made from seeds, nuts or coconut have only a 3-month shelf life and should be stored in the fridge.

CORN SYRUP

Corn syrup can be stored in a cool, dark place for up to 4 months. We use both white (colourless) and golden corn syrup in our baking. White corn syrup has a more delicate flavour than golden.

UNFLAVOURED POWDERED GELATIN

Gelatin is essential for helping puddings to set and become firm. Store gelatin in a cool, dry, dark place for up to 4 months.

VINEGAR

apple cider
white

White vinegar has a stronger flavour than apple cider vinegar, but the two can be used interchangeably in baking.

HONEY

Honey is one of the few foods that doesn't spoil. In fact, honey from the graves of ancient Egyptians was found to be still safe to eat.

After long storage, honey might crystallize, but you can return it to its liquid state by warming it gently: set the opened jar in a saucepan of hot water over low heat until the honey melts.

CANNED MILK

condensed
evaporated
unsweetened coconut

Canned milk keeps for several months, but always check the use-by date on the can. Don't confuse evaporated and condensed milk. The former is runny and unsweetened, the latter thick, sticky and sweet.

SPRINKLES & CANDIES

These are an easy way to personalize your home-baked cakes, cookies and cupcakes. There are lots to choose from, so browse the selection at your local bulk or craft store. Most will last indefinitely if stored in a cool, dry place, but always check the use-by date on the package. Among our favourites are sprinkles, dragées, jelly beans, licorice laces and allsorts, and sugar pearl candies.

IN THE FRIDGE & FREEZER

BUTTER

We prefer unsalted butter for baking. Well-wrapped butter can be refrigerated for up to 3 weeks.

MILK

Unless otherwise noted in a recipe, milk for baking should be at room temperature. Use whole milk where stated in a recipe; otherwise, any milk— 2% or skim dairy milk, or almond or soy milk—can be used.

Dairy milk can be refrigerated for up to 3 weeks. Almond milk and soy milk can be refrigerated for up to 1 week after opening. For all types of milk, always check the best-before date on the carton.

BUTTERMILK

We like to use buttermilk in recipes for biscuits and shortcakes as it makes them extra fluffy and light. Buttermilk will keep in the fridge for up to 2 weeks.

If you're out of buttermilk, pour 1 tablespoonful of white vinegar or fresh lemon juice into a 1-cup liquid measure. Add milk (dairy, soy or almond) to come to the 1-cup mark, then let stand for 5 minutes before using. If the recipe requires more than 1 cup of buttermilk, increase the amount of vinegar or lemon juice accordingly.

EGGS

All the recipes in this book use large eggs. For best results, eggs for baking—whether used whole or separated—should be at room temperature.

Eggs in the shell can be refrigerated for up to 3 weeks but always check the best-before date on the carton. Raw shelled whole eggs and egg yolks can be refrigerated for up to 2 days; raw egg whites for up to 4 days.

CREAM CHEESE

Unflavoured, brick-style cream cheese is best for baking. We also like to use mascarpone (a rich Italian cream cheese) in dessert recipes, like our Bellissimo Tiramisu (page 292).

Unopened packages of cream cheese can be refrigerated for up to 1 month; opened packages for up to 10 days.

CREAM & YOGURT
whipping cream (35%)
sour cream (14%)
half-and-half cream (10%)
plain yogurt (3%)
plain Greek yogurt (2%)

The percentage numbers on cartons of cream and milk denote the milk fat content; the higher the percentage, the richer the product.

Sour cream will keep for up to 2 weeks; other types of cream should be used within 4 days. Yogurt will keep for up to 1 week.

For the fluffiest whipped cream, put your bowl and beaters in the freezer for 30 minutes, and make sure the whipping cream is used straight from the fridge before whipping it.

NUTS

Nuts can turn rancid quickly when kept at room temperature. Freeze walnuts, pecans and pistachios for up to 1 year, or refrigerate them for up to 6 months.

Almonds should not be frozen—they tend to soften—but can be refrigerated for up to 6 months.

COCONUT
sweetened flaked coconut
unsweetened shredded
   coconut

As with nuts, coconut can go rancid quickly if stored at room temperature. Freeze coconut for up to 1 year, or refrigerate it for up to 6 months.

SEEDS

Because of their high oil content, seeds can go rancid quickly. Store them in an airtight container in the fridge for up to 6 months.

YEAST
active dry
instant

Unopened jars or packages of active dry or instant yeast should be stored in a cool, dry place. Yeast is very perishable when exposed to air, moisture and/or heat, so, once opened, refrigerate or freeze the yeast in an airtight container. We recommend using yeast within 4 months if refrigerated, or 6 months if frozen.

For best results, active dry or instant yeast should be at room temperature when added to a recipe. When you're ready to bake, take out only the amount of yeast needed for your recipe and let it sit at room temperature for 30 to 45 minutes before using.

Yeast is a living organism and will lose potency over time, even if the package is unopened. If you're unsure of your yeast's freshness, perform the Yeast Freshness Test (page14) before using it.

PEANUT & OTHER NUT BUTTERS

Once opened, all nut butters should be refrigerated to prevent them turning rancid. Use nut butters within 3 months.

MAPLE SYRUP

Maple syrup is a Canadian staple and will last for several years in an unopened glass bottle. Once opened, store maple syrup in the fridge and use within 1 year. For longer storage, freeze the maple syrup for up to 1 year (it will remain liquid in the freezer).

MUST-HAVE EQUIPMENT

For most of the recipes in this book, you don't need any fancy kitchen equipment, but there are some basic tools that will make your baking day go more smoothly.

BAKING PANS & DISHES

Baking pans and dishes come in a wide range of shapes and sizes, from large Bundt pans to dainty mini muffins pans. For best results, always use the shape and size of pan called for in a recipe. If you use too large a pan, the batter will cook too quickly; use too small a pan and the batter will take longer to bake.

These are the pans and dishes you need to bake all the recipes in this book:

BASIC PANS & DISHES:

Round pans
  6-inch
  8-inch
  9-inch
  10-inch
Deep round pans
  8-inch
  9-inch
Square and rectangular pans
  8-inch
  9-inch
  13- x 9-inch pan
  13- x 9-inch dish
Loaf pans
  8- x 4-inch
  9- x 5-inch
Muffin pans
  regular
  mini
Shallow roasting pan
Springform pans
  8-inch
  9-inch
  10-inch
Bundt pans
  8-inch
  9-inch
Tart pans with removable base
  9-inch
  10-inch

Tart pan
  14- x 4-inch
Tart pans (individual)
  3-inch
  5-inch
Pie dish
  9-inch
Deep pie dish
  9-inch
Jelly roll pans
  17- x 11-inch
  15- x 10-inch
Baking sheets
  rimmed
  unrimmed
Soufflé dish
  10-cup
Ovenproof skillets
  10-inch
  12-inch
Ramekin
  ¾-cup

SPECIALIST PANS:

Madeleine pan
Cannelé moulds
Panettone mould

BASIC UTENSILS

Few of these utensils are expensive but all are handy to have in your kitchen when the baking bug hits:

Box grater
Citrus reamer
Cookie cutters
Disposable gloves (handy for prepping items like pomegranate which can stain)
Dry and liquid measuring cups
Hand-held mixer
Ice cream scoop
Kitchen twine
Measuring spoons
Microplane or other fine zester
Mixing bowls
Muffin/cupcake liners
Nutmeg grater
Offset spatulas (small and large)
Parchment paper
Pastry blender
Pastry brush
Pastry cutter/wheel (straight or fluted)
Pastry scraper
Piping bags
Piping tips
Rolling pin
Rubber spatulas (make sure they're heat-resistant)
Thermometers
  candy
  instant-read
Tongs
Whisk
Wire cooling rack (at least one)

UTENSILS THAT ARE HANDY TO HAVE BUT NOT ESSENTIAL

Butane kitchen torch
Deep-fryer
Food processor and/or blender
Griddle
Stand mixer

TESTING RAISING AGENTS FOR FRESHNESS

It's so disappointing if baked goods don't rise because they were made with stale raising agents (yeast, baking powder or baking soda). Here's how to check the potency of those ingredients you may have had in your cupboard for too long.

YEAST FRESHNESS TEST

Follow these steps if you're unsure of the freshness of your yeast. If the yeast passes the test, you can use it in a recipe. Remember to deduct ½ cup liquid from the recipe to adjust for the water used in the test.

1. Using a small glass or ceramic bowl, dissolve 1 teaspoonful of granulated sugar in ½ cup warm tap water (110°F to 115°F). (If you don't have an instant-read thermometer, the tap water should be warm, not hot, to the touch.)
2. Stir in 2 ¼ teaspoonfuls of room-temperature active dry yeast or instant yeast.
3. Let stand for 10 minutes. After 3 to 4 minutes, the yeast should start to form tiny bubbles. After 10 minutes, the yeast mixture should be foamy and have a rounded top. If so, the yeast is active and can be used immediately. If not, your yeast has little or no potency and should be discarded.

BAKING POWDER FRESHNESS TEST

Pour ¼ cup of warm water into a small bowl. Add ½ teaspoonful baking powder. The mixture should fizz moderately if the powder is fresh. If there's no reaction, replace the baking powder.

BAKING SODA FRESHNESS TEST

Pour ¼ cup of warm water into a small bowl. Add ½ teaspoonful baking soda. The mixture should fizz and bubble furiously if the soda is fresh. If there's no reaction (or only a weak reaction), replace the baking soda.

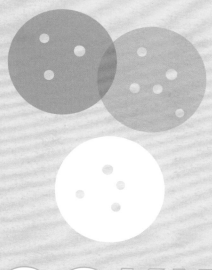

COOKIES

Browned-Butter Triple-Chocolate
Chip Cookies (recipe opposite)

Bittersweet Chocolate
Cookies (recipe on
page 18)

Classic Chocolate Chip
Cookies (recipe on page 19)

Browned-Butter Triple-Chocolate Chip Cookies

Browned butter—made by cooking butter very slowly until it takes on a lovely dark hue—has a fabulous nutty flavour that takes humble chocolate chip cookies to a whole new level of deliciousness. These cookies are particularly rich, and go best with a tall glass of cold milk.

Makes about 36 cookies
Prep time: 20 minutes
Chilling time: at least 1 hour
Cooking time: about 13 minutes

1 cup unsalted butter, softened

2 ¼ cups all-purpose flour

1 tsp baking soda

1 tsp fine sea salt

1 ¼ cups lightly packed golden yellow sugar

¼ cup granulated sugar

1 large egg

1 large egg yolk

2 Tbsp whole milk

1 Tbsp vanilla extract

¾ cup dark chocolate chips

¾ cup semi-sweet or milk chocolate chips

¾ cup white chocolate chips

1. In a small, heavy-bottomed saucepan, melt the butter over medium heat. Cook slowly, stirring constantly, until the butter has browned and smells like toasted nuts, about 5 minutes. Remove from the heat and let cool.

2. In a medium bowl, whisk together the flour, baking soda and salt. Set aside.

3. In a large bowl, stir together both sugars. Add the cooled browned butter to the sugar and beat with a mixer until creamy.

4. Add the egg, egg yolk, milk and vanilla extract to the sugar mixture. Beat until well combined.

5. Slowly add the flour mixture to the sugar mixture, stirring until thoroughly combined. Stir in the dark, semi-sweet and white chocolate chips.

6. Cover the bowl tightly with plastic wrap and refrigerate the dough for at least 1 hour, or preferably overnight.

7. When ready to bake, preheat the oven to 375°F. Line two large baking sheets with parchment paper, then set aside.

8. Using a small ice cream scoop or spoon, scoop tablespoonfuls of the dough and roll it into a ball. Place the balls, 2 inches apart, on the prepared baking sheets.

9. Bake until the cookies are golden brown, about 8 minutes, rotating the baking sheets after 5 minutes for even browning.

10. Remove the cookies to wire racks and let cool completely. (The cookies can be stored in an airtight container at room temperature for up to 4 days, or frozen, with parchment paper between the layers, for up to 2 months.)

BAKING DAY SECRET

If you only have one baking sheet and want to bake a lot of cookies, let the baking sheet cool completely before reusing it to bake each batch.

Bittersweet Chocolate Cookies

These cookies, with their brownie-like texture, are so packed with deep, dark chocolatey goodness, the chocoholics in your life will love you forever if you bake up a batch. Use whatever nuts you like: hazelnuts or almonds are our faves.

Makes about 24 cookies
Prep time: 20 minutes
Cooking time: 11 to 14 minutes

¼ cup all-purpose flour

¼ tsp baking powder

Pinch of fine sea salt

8 oz bittersweet chocolate, finely chopped

2 Tbsp unsalted butter, softened

½ cup granulated sugar

2 large eggs

1 tsp vanilla extract

6 oz dark chocolate, cut into chunks

2 cups nuts, coarsely chopped (see note above)

1. Preheat the oven to 350°F. Line two large baking sheets with parchment paper, then set aside.

2. In a small bowl, whisk together the flour, baking powder and salt. Set aside.

3. In a medium saucepan, combine the bittersweet chocolate and butter. Melt over low heat, stirring occasionally, until smooth. Scrape the melted chocolate into a separate small bowl. Set aside.

4. In a large bowl, whisk together the sugar, eggs and vanilla extract.

5. Whisking vigorously, add a little of the melted chocolate to the sugar mixture. Gradually whisk in the remaining melted chocolate.

6. Stir in the flour mixture just until combined. Stir in the dark chocolate and nuts.

7. Drop the batter by heaping tablespoonfuls, about 2 inches apart, onto the prepared baking sheets. Bake until the edges are crisp but the centres are still shiny-looking, 11 to 14 minutes.

8. Remove the cookies to wire racks and let cool completely. (The cookies can be stored in an airtight container at room temperature for up to 4 days, or frozen, with parchment paper between the layers, for up to 2 months.)

SWEET HISTORY

According to the mythology of the south Pacific nation of the Solomon Islands, the first humans sprouted from a stalk of ripe sugar cane.

Classic Chocolate Chip Cookies

What would the world be without chocolate chip cookies? Pair a couple of these with a glass of milk and you'll be in heaven.

Makes about 50 cookies
Prep time: 15 minutes
Cooking time: 30 minutes

2 ½ cups all-purpose flour

1 tsp baking soda

1 tsp fine sea salt

1 cup unsalted butter, softened

1 cup lightly packed golden yellow sugar

½ cup granulated sugar

2 large eggs

1 tsp vanilla extract

2 cups semi-sweet chocolate chips

1. Preheat the oven to 350°F. Line two large baking sheets with parchment paper, then set aside.

2. In a medium bowl, whisk together the flour, baking soda and salt. Set aside.

3. In a large bowl and using an electric mixer, beat the butter until smooth. Add both sugars and beat until the mixture is pale and fluffy.

4. Beat in the eggs one at a time, beating well after each addition. Beat in the vanilla extract.

5. Add the flour mixture to the butter mixture, stirring just until combined. Stir in the chocolate chips.

6. Using a small ice cream scoop or spoon, scoop tablespoonfuls of the dough and roll it into balls. Place the balls, 1 inch apart, on the prepared baking sheets. Bake until lightly golden around the edges, 10 to 12 minutes.

7. Let the cookies cool slightly on the baking sheets, then remove to wire racks to cool completely. (The cookies can be stored in an airtight container at room temperature for up to 4 days, or frozen, with parchment paper between the layers, for up to 2 months.)

GET A HEAD START

Be ready for unexpected guests by prepping the dough in advance:

1. Form the dough into balls on the baking sheets.

2. Freeze the unbaked dough on the baking sheets until hard, then pack the balls in freezer bags and freeze for up to 2 months.

3. When ready to bake, place the frozen dough balls on parchment-paper-lined baking sheets and bake as described, adding 2 to 3 minutes to the baking time.

Chocolate & Vanilla Sandwich Cookies (recipe on page 23)

Chocolate-Hazelnut Sandwich Cookies (recipe on page 22)

Dulce de Leche Sandwich Cookies (*Alfajores*) (recipe opposite)

Dulce de Leche Sandwich Cookies (*Alfajores*)

These melt-in-the-mouth shortbread sandwich cookies, known as *alfajores*, originated in Spain and are now popular throughout Latin America. Our version features a dulce de leche filling and a finishing coating of coconut, a popular addition in Mexico. If you're short of time, substitute store-bought dulce de leche.

Makes about 16 sandwich cookies
Prep time: 20 minutes
Chilling time: 1 hour
Cooking time: 12 to 15 minutes

1 cup unsalted butter, softened

1 cup icing sugar, sifted

½ tsp fine sea salt

2 cups all-purpose flour

Dulce de Leche (recipe follows)

¼ cup unsweetened shredded coconut (optional)

1. For the shortbread cookies, in a large bowl and using an electric mixer, wooden spoon or spatula, beat together the butter, icing sugar and salt until pale and fluffy.

2. Stir in the flour. The dough will be stiff, so you may have to use your hands to incorporate all the flour.

3. Turn out the dough onto a large piece of plastic wrap. Pat it into a disc about ½ inch thick. Wrap the dough tightly in the plastic wrap, then refrigerate until firm, about 1 hour. (The dough can be refrigerated for up to 3 days. Remove the dough from the fridge about 1 hour before rolling it out.)

4. When ready to bake, preheat the oven to 350°F. Line two large baking sheets with parchment paper, then set aside.

5. Dust a large piece of parchment or wax paper with a little flour. Unwrap the dough and place it on the paper. Using a lightly floured rolling pin, roll it out to about ⅛-inch thickness. (If the dough cracks, let it stand at room temperature until it softens enough to roll.)

6. Using a 2-inch cutter, cut out 32 cookies, rerolling the dough scraps once. (Rerolling the scraps more than once makes the cookies tough.) If the dough becomes too soft to roll, rewrap it and return it to the fridge for about 15 minutes.

7. Place the cookies, 1 inch apart, on the prepared baking sheets. Bake until just beginning to brown around the edges, 12 to 15 minutes. Remove the cookies to wire racks and let cool completely.

8. Spread half of the cookies with dulce de leche, using about 1 teaspoonful per cookie. (You won't need the full recipe of dulce de leche if you opt to make your own.) Top with the remaining cookies, squeezing them together gently. Spread the coconut (if using) on a large plate. Roll the edges of the cookie sandwiches in the coconut to coat them. (The cookies can be stored in an airtight container at room temperature for up to 4 days.)

Dulce de Leche

Makes about 1 ⅓ cups
Prep time: 5 minutes
Cooking time: 1 to 1 ½ hours

2 cups whole milk

1 ½ cups granulated sugar

2 tsp vanilla extract

¼ tsp cornstarch

¼ tsp baking soda

1. In a large, heavy-bottomed saucepan, whisk together all of the ingredients. Bring to a boil over medium heat, whisking constantly.

2. Hook a candy thermometer over the side of the saucepan. Turn down the heat to low so the milk mixture boils gently. Cook, stirring occasionally, until it's a deep caramel colour and very thick, and the candy thermometer registers 225°F, 1 to 1 ½ hours. If the dulce de leche starts to catch on the bottom of the saucepan and looks like it might scorch, turn down the heat a little more.

3. Remove from the heat and let cool to room temperature.

Chocolate-Hazelnut Sandwich Cookies

We love dainty cookie sandwiches. These chocolate-hazelnut ones are not only cute but also simple to make.

Makes about 12 sandwich cookies
Prep time: 20 minutes
Chilling time: about 1 hour
Cooking time: 7 to 12 minutes

Cookies

2 cups all-purpose flour

½ tsp baking powder

¼ tsp fine sea salt

½ cup unsalted butter, softened

1 cup granulated sugar

1 large egg

2 Tbsp 2% milk

½ tsp vanilla extract

Filling

½ cup chocolate-hazelnut spread

3 Tbsp toasted hazelnuts (see sidebar), finely chopped

Additional finely chopped toasted hazelnuts (optional)

1. For the cookies, whisk together the flour, baking powder and salt in a medium bowl. Set aside.

2. In a large bowl and using an electric mixer, beat the butter with the sugar until pale and fluffy. Beat in the egg, milk and vanilla extract.

3. Add the flour mixture to the sugar mixture, stirring just until combined.

4. Turn out the dough onto a large piece of plastic wrap. Pat into a disc about ½ inch thick. Wrap the dough tightly in the plastic wrap, then refrigerate until firm, about 1 hour. (The dough can be refrigerated for up to 3 days. Remove the dough from the fridge about 1 hour before rolling out if refrigerating for this length of time.)

5. When ready to bake, preheat the oven to 350°F. Line a large baking sheet with parchment paper, then set aside.

6. Dust a large piece of parchment or wax paper with a little flour. Unwrap the dough and place it on the paper. Using a lightly floured rolling pin, roll it out to about ⅛-inch thickness. (If the dough cracks, let it stand at room temperature until it softens enough to roll.)

7. Using a 2-inch cutter (we used a flower-shaped one), cut out cookies, rerolling the dough scraps once. (Rerolling the scraps more than once makes the cookies tough.) If the dough becomes too soft to roll, rewrap it and return it to the fridge for about 15 minutes.

8. Using a ½-inch round cutter, cut a circle out of the centre of half of the cookies. Place the cookies, 1 inch apart, on the prepared baking sheet. Bake until just beginning to brown around the edges, 7 to 12 minutes. Remove the cookies to wire racks and let cool completely.

9. For the filling, stir together the chocolate-hazelnut spread and hazelnuts in a small bowl. Spread the hole-less cookies with the chocolate-hazelnut spread, using about 1 teaspoonful per cookie. Top with the cookies with the holes, squeezing them together gently. Sprinkle with additional chopped hazelnuts (if using). (The cookies can be stored in an airtight container at room temperature for up to 4 days.)

BAKING DAY SECRETS

To toast hazelnuts, spread them out on a rimmed baking sheet and toast in a 350°F oven until fragrant and the skins are blistered, 10 to 15 minutes. Immediately tip the nuts onto a clean tea towel. Enclose them in the towel and rub vigorously to remove most of the skins.

Chocolate & Vanilla Sandwich Cookies

These sandwich cookies are perfect for dunking into a tall glass of milk, or even a cappuccino.

Makes 20 sandwich cookies
Prep time: 30 minutes
Chilling time: at least 3 hours, 30 minutes
Cooking time: 30 to 40 minutes

Cookies

1 ¼ cups all-purpose flour

½ cup unsweetened cocoa powder

1 tsp baking soda

Pinch of fine sea salt

¾ cup granulated sugar

¼ cup lightly packed golden yellow sugar

1 large egg

1 tsp vanilla extract

¾ cup unsalted butter, softened

Filling

½ cup unsalted butter, softened

1 ¾ cups icing sugar, sifted

1 tsp vanilla extract

1. For the cookies, whisk together the flour, cocoa powder, baking soda and salt in a large bowl. Set aside.

2. In a medium bowl and using an electric mixer, beat together both sugars, the egg and vanilla extract. Add the butter and beat until the mixture is pale and fluffy, about 2 minutes.

3. Add the sugar mixture to the flour mixture and stir to combine. Refrigerate the dough, covered, for 30 minutes.

4. Scrape the dough out of the bowl onto a clean surface and form it into a log, about 10 inches long and 1 ¼ inches in diameter. Wrap it tightly in plastic wrap, then refrigerate for at least 3 hours, or overnight.

5. When ready to bake, preheat the oven to 350°F. Line two large baking sheets with parchment paper, then set aside.

6. Unwrap the log, square it off and cut it into forty ¼-inch slices. Arrange the slices, 2 inches apart, on the prepared baking sheets. Bake until dry to the touch, 6 to 8 minutes. (The cookies will still appear to be soft when done.)

7. Let the cookies cool for 5 minutes on the baking sheets, then remove to wire racks and let cool completely.

8. For the filling, in a small bowl and using an electric mixer on high speed, beat the butter until creamy, about 1 minute.

9. Add the icing sugar and vanilla extract. Beat on low speed for 1 minute. Increase the speed to high and beat until creamy and combined, 1 minute. (The filling will be thick.)

10. Spread half of the cookies with the filling. Top with the remaining cookies, squeezing them together gently. (The cookies can be stored in an airtight container at room temperature for up to 4 days.)

GET A HEAD START

It's easiest to prepare the filling while the cookies are cooling, but if you're in a time crunch you can prepare it up to two days ahead. Refrigerate in an airtight container, then bring to room temperature before using.

BAKING DAY SECRETS

Icebox cookies are a baker's best friend. You prepare the dough ahead of time, form it into a log and store it in the freezer until you're ready to bake. (If securely wrapped, the dough will keep for up to 2 months.) When you want fresh cookies, remove the dough from the freezer and then simply slice and bake.

Checkerboard Icebox Cookies

With these easy icebox cookies in your freezer, you'll be ready to bake up a batch of homemade treats any time. Their checkerboard pattern makes them a stunning addition to a cookie plate. For more on icebox cookies, check out the sidebar (page 24).

Makes about 42 cookies
Prep time: 30 minutes
Freezing time: about 1 ½ hours
Cooking time: 10 to 14 minutes

---

5 cups all-purpose flour

1 tsp baking powder

½ tsp fine sea salt

1 cup unsalted butter, softened

2 cups granulated sugar

2 large eggs

2 large egg whites

2 tsp vanilla extract

6 Tbsp unsweetened cocoa powder

---

1. In a large bowl, whisk together the flour, baking powder and salt. Set aside.

2. In a large bowl and using an electric mixer, beat the butter with the sugar until pale and fluffy. Beat in the eggs, egg whites and vanilla extract until well combined.

3. Add the flour mixture to the sugar mixture, then stir just until the dough comes together.

4. Turn out the dough onto a clean surface and form it into a ball. Divide the dough in half.

5. Sprinkle the cocoa powder over one half of the dough. Knead the cocoa into the dough until fully incorporated.

6. Form each piece of dough into a 10 ½-inch-long log. Square up the sides of the logs so they're shaped like long bricks that each measure 2- x 2- x 10 ½ inches. Wrap these bricks of dough tightly in plastic wrap, then freeze until firm, about 30 minutes.

7. Using a large, sharp knife and a ruler, slice each piece of dough lengthwise into three even-sized pieces. You will end up with three chocolate and three vanilla strips, each 10 ½ inches long.

8. Using a pastry brush, lightly brush a little water onto one 2-inch-wide side of one vanilla strip. Place a chocolate strip on top of the vanilla strip and press down gently. Lightly brush the chocolate strip with a little water and top with another vanilla strip, pressing down gently. Wrap it tightly in plastic wrap, then freeze until firm again, at least 30 minutes.

9. Repeat the layering process with the remaining strips of dough, starting with a chocolate strip.

10. Remove the chilled layered pieces of dough from the freezer. Lay the dough on your worktop so that the stripes are visible. Again, using a large, sharp knife and a ruler, cut each layered piece lengthwise into three even-sized pieces. You should now have six pieces of striped dough.

11. Place one piece of dough with the stripes facing up, then brush lightly with a little water. Making sure the colours alternate, top with another piece of dough and press down gently. Lightly brush this piece with water and place a third piece on top, alternating the colours again. Wrap it tightly in plastic wrap, then freeze again for at least 30 minutes. (The dough can be frozen for up to 2 months.)

12. Repeat the layering process with the remaining pieces of dough, making sure to alternate the colours again.

13. When ready to bake, preheat the oven to 350°F. Line a large baking sheet with parchment paper.

14. Remove one log of dough from the freezer. Unwrap the log and, with a large, sharp knife, cut it crosswise into ½-inch slices. Place the slices, about ½ inch apart, on the prepared baking sheet. Bake until the cookies are lightly golden, 10 to 14 minutes. Let the cookies cool on the baking sheet for 5 minutes. Remove the cookies to a wire rack and let cool completely. Repeat with the remaining log, if liked (or freeze until needed). (The cookies can be stored in an airtight container at room temperature for up to 4 days, or frozen, with parchment paper between the layers, for up to 2 months.)

Caramel-Pecan Cheesecake Cookies

We love cookies; we love cheesecake. So, we thought, why not combine the two? With its chocolatey pecan dough, cream cheese filling and drizzles of caramel sauce and chocolate, this is one decadent, over-the-top cookie!

Makes about 16 cookies
Prep time: 30 minutes
Cooking time: 10 to 13 minutes

Cookies

1 ½ cups all-purpose flour

½ cup unsweetened cocoa powder

½ tsp baking soda

½ tsp fine sea salt

½ cup granulated sugar

½ cup lightly packed golden yellow sugar

½ cup unsalted butter, softened

¼ cup smooth peanut butter

1 large egg

1 tsp vanilla extract

¼ cup finely chopped pecans

Cream Cheese Filling

4 oz full-fat brick-style cream cheese, at room temperature (half of one 8 oz/250 g package)

2 Tbsp granulated sugar

1 tsp vanilla extract

Additional granulated sugar for coating

Delectable Caramel Sauce (page 298)

Melted chocolate for drizzling (optional)

Pecan pieces for garnish (optional)

1. For the cookies, whisk together the flour, cocoa powder, baking soda and salt in a medium bowl. Set aside.

2. In a large bowl and using an electric mixer, beat together both sugars, the butter and peanut butter until light and fluffy. Beat in the egg and vanilla extract.

3. Add the flour mixture to the sugar mixture, stirring just until combined. Stir in the pecans. (The dough will be crumbly.) Set aside.

4. For the cream cheese filling, in a medium bowl and using an electric mixer, beat together the cream cheese, sugar and vanilla extract until smooth and creamy. Set aside.

5. Preheat the oven to 350°F. Line a baking sheet with parchment paper, then set aside. Spread additional sugar out on a large plate.

6. Using a small ice cream scoop or spoon, scoop 1 tablespoonful of the dough and shape it into a ball. With your index finger, create a depression in the centre of the ball. Carefully spoon 1 to 2 teaspoonfuls of the cream cheese filling into the depression.

7. Take about 1 teaspoonful of the remaining dough and gently press it over the top of the cream cheese filling. Gently seal the dough by pressing and rolling the ball in your hand.

8. Roll the ball of dough in the additional sugar, then place on the prepared baking sheet. Repeat with the remaining dough, arranging the balls 1 inch apart.

9. Bake until the cookies have spread a little and darkened slightly, 10 to 13 minutes. Let cool completely on the baking sheet.

10. Drizzle the cooled cookies with caramel sauce and melted chocolate (if using), then sprinkle with pecan pieces (if using). (The cookies can be stored in an airtight container at room temperature for up to 4 days, or frozen, with parchment paper between the layers, for up to 2 months.)

Coffee, Orange & Fennel Biscotti (recipe on page 31)

Almond Fig Biscotti (recipe opposite)

Chocolate-Ginger Biscotti (recipe on page 30)

Almond-Fig Biscotti

Biscotti, the elegant, coffee-shop favourite, are so easy to make—and they keep for weeks in the cookie jar.

Makes about 30 biscotti
Prep time: 30 minutes
Cooking time: 50 minutes
Cooling time: 15 minutes

2 ½ cups all-purpose flour

1 tsp baking powder

1 tsp fine sea salt

1 cup granulated sugar

2 large eggs

¼ cup unsalted butter, melted

1 tsp vanilla extract

1 tsp almond extract

1 cup coarsely chopped almonds

1 cup coarsely chopped dried figs

1 large egg white

1 Tbsp water

1. Preheat the oven to 350°F. Line two large baking sheets with parchment paper, then set aside.

2. In a large bowl, whisk together the flour, baking powder and salt. Set aside.

3. In a large bowl and using an electric mixer, beat together the sugar, eggs, butter and vanilla and almond extracts until pale and thickened, about 3 minutes.

4. Stir the flour mixture into the sugar mixture until no streaks of flour remain. Stir in the almonds and figs.

5. Divide the dough in half and shape each piece into a log, about 3 inches wide and ¾ inch thick. Place the logs on the prepared baking sheets and square them off.

6. In a small bowl, beat together the egg white and water. Brush the egg white mixture all over the logs of dough.

7. Bake for 30 minutes. Remove from the oven and let the logs cool on the baking sheets for 15 minutes. Turn down the oven temperature to 325°F.

8. Using a sharp, serrated knife, cut the cooled dough into ½-inch slices, cutting slightly on the diagonal. Arrange the slices, on their sides, on the baking sheets.

9. Bake until the biscotti are lightly toasted and dry to the touch, about 20 minutes. Let the biscotti cool completely on the baking sheets. (The biscotti can be stored in an airtight container at room temperature for up to 1 month.)

SWEET HISTORY

In the 1600s, drinking tea, coffee and chocolate became popular. Since all these beverages are relatively bitter in their raw state, sugar became the favoured way to sweeten them. Drinking clubs sprang up where members—usually men—met to drink their favourite sweetened beverage while discussing political, social and business matters. Many now-famous enterprises—the London Stock Exchange, the London-based insurance company Lloyd's, and the Hudson's Bay Company, for instance—can trace their origins to these once-trendy clubs.

Chocolate-Ginger Biscotti

If you enjoy the marriage of chocolate and ginger, you'll love these rich biscotti.

Makes about 30 biscotti
Prep time: 30 minutes
Cooking time: 50 minutes
Cooling time: 15 minutes

2 cups plus 2 Tbsp all-purpose flour

⅓ cup unsweetened cocoa powder

1 tsp baking powder

1 tsp fine sea salt

1 cup granulated sugar

2 large eggs

¼ cup unsalted butter, melted

1 tsp vanilla extract

½ cup dark chocolate chips or coarsely chopped dark chocolate

¼ cup finely chopped crystallized ginger

1 large egg white

1 Tbsp water

1. Preheat the oven to 350°F. Line two large baking sheets with parchment paper, then set aside.

2. In a large bowl, whisk together the flour, cocoa powder, baking powder and salt. Set aside.

3. In a large bowl and using an electric mixer, beat together the sugar, eggs, butter and vanilla extract until pale and thickened, about 3 minutes.

4. Stir the flour mixture into the sugar mixture until no streaks of flour remain. Stir in the chocolate and ginger.

5. Divide the dough in half and shape each piece into a log, about 3 inches wide and ¾ inch thick. Place the logs on the prepared baking sheets and square them off.

6. In a small bowl, beat together the egg white and water. Brush the egg white mixture all over the logs of dough.

7. Bake for 30 minutes. Remove from the oven and let the logs cool on the baking sheets for 15 minutes. Turn down the oven temperature to 325°F.

8. Using a sharp, serrated knife, cut the cooled dough into ½-inch slices, cutting slightly on the diagonal. Arrange the slices, on their sides, on the baking sheets.

9. Bake until the biscotti are lightly toasted and dry to the touch, about 20 minutes. Let the biscotti cool completely on the baking sheets. (The biscotti can be stored in an airtight container at room temperature for up to 1 month.)

Coffee, Orange & Fennel Biscotti

This variation on the biscotti theme stars an unusual flavour combo that teams perfectly with a shot of espresso.

Makes about 30 biscotti
Prep time: 30 minutes
Cooking time: 50 minutes
Cooling time: 15 minutes

2 ½ cups all-purpose flour

1 Tbsp fennel seeds

1 tsp baking powder

1 tsp fine sea salt

2 Tbsp instant espresso powder

2 tsp hot water

1 cup granulated sugar

2 large eggs

¼ cup unsalted butter, melted

1 Tbsp finely grated orange zest (about 1 orange)

1 tsp vanilla extract

1 large egg white

1 Tbsp water

1. Preheat the oven to 350°F. Line two large baking sheets with parchment paper, then set aside.

2. In a large bowl, whisk together the flour, fennel seeds, baking powder and salt. Set aside.

3. In a small bowl, stir together the espresso powder and water until the powder has dissolved. Set aside.

4. In a large bowl and using an electric mixer, beat together the sugar, eggs, butter, orange zest and vanilla extract until pale and thickened, about 3 minutes. Beat in the coffee mixture.

5. Stir the flour mixture into the sugar mixture until no streaks of flour remain.

6. Divide the dough in half and shape each piece into a log, about 3 inches wide and ¾ inch thick. Place the logs on the prepared baking sheets and square them off.

7. In a small bowl, beat together the egg white and water. Brush the egg white mixture all over the logs of dough.

8. Bake for 30 minutes. Remove from the oven and let the logs cool on the baking sheets for 15 minutes. Turn down the oven temperature to 325°F.

9. Using a sharp, serrated knife, cut the cooled dough into ½-inch slices, cutting slightly on the diagonal. Arrange the slices, on their sides, on the baking sheets.

10. Bake until the biscotti are lightly toasted and dry to the touch, about 20 minutes. Let the biscotti cool completely on the baking sheets. (The biscotti can be stored in an airtight container at room temperature for up to 1 month.)

BAKING DAY SECRETS

Macarons 101

- Avoid making macarons on a humid or rainy day; they may not dry out enough to form a skin before baking.

- Processing the almond meal and sugar helps you achieve a smooth, consistent batter. If you do not have a food processor, buy the finest almond meal available and sift it with the icing sugar before using.

- For the prettiest macarons, match them together in evenly shaped pairs when you're filling them.

Strawberry Macarons

You'll spot pastel-hued macarons in many bakeries these days. These delicate French pastries take some time to prepare but make a lovely addition to any gathering, and are sure to impress.

Makes about 24 macarons
Prep time: 50 minutes
Drying time: about 30 minutes
Cooking time: 15 to 18 minutes
Chilling time: 2 hours

Macarons

2 cups icing sugar, sifted

1 ½ cups almond meal or almond flour

3 large egg whites

¼ tsp fine sea salt

¼ cup granulated sugar

Red gel food colouring

Filling

¾ cup unsalted butter, softened

3 ½ cups icing sugar, sifted

½ cup strawberry jam

¼ tsp fine sea salt

1. Trace twenty-four 2-inch circles on each of two sheets of parchment paper (you'll have a total of 48 traced circles). Flip the paper over and use it to line two large baking sheets. Set aside.

2. For the macarons, combine the icing sugar and almond meal in a food processor fitted with the steel blade. Process for 2 minutes. Tip the almond mixture into a large bowl. Set aside.

3. In a large bowl and using an electric mixer, beat the egg whites and salt on medium until foamy.

4. Increase the speed to high and gradually add the granulated sugar while beating. Continue to beat the egg white mixture until stiff, glossy peaks form, about 2 minutes. Add food colouring, one drop a time, until the mixture is tinted pink.

5. Using a rubber spatula, fold the egg whites, one-third at a time, into the icing sugar mixture.

6. Spoon the macaron batter into a large piping bag fitted with a ½-inch plain round tip. Holding the bag upright and about ½ inch above the centre of one of the traced circles, pipe the batter to almost fill the shape. Stop squeezing the bag and gently pull up. Repeat until all the circles are filled.

7. Let the macarons stand at room temperature until the shiny surface of each is dry and a soft skin forms on the tops of the macarons, about 30 minutes.

8. When ready to bake, preheat the oven to 300°F.

9. Bake the macarons until their tops are completely dry, 15 to 18 minutes. When the macarons are ready, they should lift easily from the parchment paper and have a flat bottom and a puffy crown.

10. Set the baking sheets on a wire rack and let the macarons cool completely on the baking sheets. When cold, gently peel them off the parchment. Their tops are easily crushed, so take care when handling them. (The macarons can be refrigerated in an airtight container for up to 2 days, or frozen for up to 1 month; thaw before filling.)

11. For the filling, in a large bowl and using an electric mixer, beat the butter on low speed until smooth.

12. Gradually add the icing sugar, 1 cup at a time, beating until all the sugar has been added and the mixture is smooth. Add the strawberry jam and salt. Mix on medium speed for 30 seconds.

13. Spoon the filling in a piping bag fitted with a ¼-inch plain round tip. Pipe the filling onto the flat sides of half of the macarons. Top with the remaining macarons, flat sides down.

14. Refrigerate until firm, about 2 hours. Let the macarons come to room temperature before serving. (The filled macarons can be refrigerated in an airtight container for up to 3 days. Let stand at room temperature before serving.)

Raspberry Macaron Hearts

These pretty pink macarons would be perfect for a bridal shower or Valentine's Day celebration.

Makes about 24 macarons
Prep time: 50 minutes
Drying time: about 30 minutes
Cooking time: 15 to 18 minutes
Chilling time: 2 hours

2 cups icing sugar, sifted

1 ½ cups almond meal or almond flour

3 large egg whites

¼ tsp fine sea salt

¼ cup granulated sugar

Red gel food colouring

Raspberry jam or Strawberry Swiss Buttercream (page 156)

1. Use a 2-inch heart-shaped cookie cutter to trace 24 hearts onto each of two sheets of parchment paper (you'll have a total of 48 traced hearts). Flip the paper over and use it to line two large baking sheets. Set aside.

2. For the macarons, combine the icing sugar and almond meal in a food processor fitted with the steel blade. Process for 2 minutes. Tip the almond mixture into a large bowl. Set aside.

3. In a large bowl and using an electric mixer, beat the egg whites and salt on medium until foamy.

4. Increase the speed to high and gradually add the granulated sugar while beating. Continue to beat the egg white mixture until stiff, glossy peaks form, about 2 minutes. Add food colouring, one drop a time, until the mixture is tinted pink.

5. Using a rubber spatula, fold the egg whites, one-third at a time, into the icing sugar mixture.

6. Spoon the macaron batter into a large piping bag fitted with a ½-inch plain round tip. Holding the bag upright and about ½ inch above the centre of one of the traced hearts, pipe the batter to almost fill the shape. Stop squeezing the bag and gently pull up. Repeat until all the shapes are filled.

7. Let the macarons stand at room temperature until the shiny surface of each is dry and a soft skin forms on the tops of the macarons, about 30 minutes.

8. When ready to bake, preheat the oven to 300°F.

9. Bake the macarons until their tops are completely dry, 15 to 18 minutes. When the macarons are ready, they should lift easily from the parchment paper and have a flat bottom and a puffy crown.

10. Set the baking sheets on a wire rack and let the macarons cool completely on the baking sheets. When cold, gently peel the macarons off the parchment. Their tops are easily crushed, so take care when handling them. (The macarons can be refrigerated in an airtight container for up to 2 days, or frozen for up to 1 month; thaw before filling.)

11. Spread the flat sides of half of the macarons with raspberry jam or buttercream. Top with the remaining macarons, flat sides down. Refrigerate until firm, about 2 hours. Let come to room temperature before serving. (The filled macarons can be refrigerated in an airtight container for up to 3 days. Let stand at room temperature before serving.)

Black & White Cookies

These stunning cookies, with their chocolate and vanilla glaze, have more of a cake-like texture than most cookies. They don't keep for as long as crisper cookies, but they're delicious dunked in coffee or tea if they go a little stale.

Makes about 18 cookies
Prep time: 40 minutes
Cooking time: about 20 minutes
Setting time: 1 hour

Cookies

2 ½ cups all-purpose flour

1 tsp baking powder

1 tsp fine sea salt

¼ tsp baking soda

2/3 cup unsalted butter, softened

1 cup granulated sugar

2 large eggs

1 Tbsp finely grated lemon zest (1 to 2 lemons)

1 tsp vanilla extract

¼ tsp lemon extract

6 Tbsp buttermilk (see page 11)

Glaze

3 to 3 ¼ cups icing sugar, sifted

¼ cup whole milk

1 Tbsp freshly squeezed lemon juice

2 tsp white corn syrup

½ tsp fine sea salt

½ tsp vanilla extract

5 Tbsp unsweetened cocoa powder, sifted

2 Tbsp hot water

1. Preheat the oven to 350°F. Line two large baking sheets with parchment paper, then set aside.

2. For the cookies, whisk together the flour, baking powder, salt and baking soda in a medium bowl. Set aside.

3. In a large bowl and using an electric mixer, beat the butter with the sugar until pale and fluffy, about 4 minutes, scraping down the sides of the bowl once or twice.

4. Beat in the eggs one at a time, beating well after each addition. Beat in the lemon zest and the vanilla and lemon extracts.

5. Add the flour mixture to the sugar mixture alternately with the buttermilk, making three additions of flour and two of buttermilk, and beginning and ending with the flour. Stir until well combined.

6. Using an ice cream scoop or spoon, drop 3 tablespoonfuls of dough for each cookie, 3 inches apart, onto the prepared baking sheets. With your dampened palm, gently press down on each heap of dough to flatten it slightly.

7. Bake until the tops spring back when pressed and the edges of the cookies are light golden, about 20 minutes. Let the cookies cool on the baking sheets for 5 minutes, then remove to wire racks cool completely.

8. For the glaze, whisk together 3 cups of the icing sugar, the milk, lemon juice, corn syrup, salt and vanilla extract in a large bowl until smooth and well combined. Spoon half of the mixture into another bowl. Set aside.

9. If the glaze in the large bowl is too thin to spread, whisk in a little more icing sugar until it's spreadable. Using a small offset spatula, carefully spread the glaze over half of the flat side of each cookie. Place the cookies, glazed side up, on wire racks. Refrigerate the cookies while you prepare the chocolate glaze.

10. In a small bowl, stir together the cocoa and hot water until smooth and free of lumps. Add the cocoa mixture to the reserved glaze and whisk to combine. If the chocolate glaze is too thin to spread, whisk in a little more icing sugar until the glaze is spreadable.

11. Spread the chocolate glaze over the unglazed half of the flat side of each cookie. Set aside at room temperature until the glaze has set, about 1 hour. (The cookies can be stored in an airtight container at room temperature for up to 4 days, or frozen, with parchment paper between the layers, for up to 2 months.)

Cinnamon-Spice Haystacks

Crunchy, spicy and with the rich flavour of chocolate and peanut butter, these cookies offer something for everyone. And they're so easy to prep—baking up a batch of haystacks makes a great project for older children.

Makes about 44 cookies
Prep time: 20 minutes
Cooking time: 15 to 20 minutes
Cooling time: about 1 hour

1 cup slivered almonds

¾ cup large-flake rolled oats

⅓ cup firmly packed dark brown sugar

3 Tbsp unsalted butter, melted

2 tsp vanilla extract

1 tsp unsweetened cocoa powder

1 tsp ground cinnamon

½ tsp ground cayenne

2 cups broken pretzel sticks or twists

1 ½ cups sweetened flaked coconut

½ tsp fine sea salt

1 ½ cups dark chocolate chips

2 Tbsp smooth or crunchy peanut butter

1. Preheat the oven to 350°F.

2. Combine the almonds and oats on a large rimmed baking sheet.

Bake until lightly browned, 5 to 7 minutes. Set aside to cool. Leave the oven on.

3. In a small bowl, stir together the sugar, butter, vanilla extract, cocoa, cinnamon and cayenne. Set aside.

4. In a large bowl, toss together the almonds, oats, pretzels and coconut until well combined.

5. Add the sugar mixture to the almond mixture. Mix until evenly coated. Spread the mixture out onto the baking sheet you used to toast the almonds and oats. Bake until the mixture is crisp and the sugar begins to bubble, 8 to 10 minutes.

6. Remove from the oven, sprinkle with the salt and let cool completely.

7. Break the almond mixture into large pieces and place in a large bowl. Set aside.

8. In a medium heatproof bowl set over a saucepan of gently simmering water, melt the chocolate chips and peanut butter together. Remove from the heat and stir until smooth. Let cool for about 5 minutes.

9. Line two large baking sheets with parchment paper, then set aside.

10. Pour the chocolate mixture over the almond mixture. Stir until all the ingredients are evenly coated with chocolate.

11. Using a small ice cream scoop or spoon, drop tablespoonfuls of the mixture onto the prepared baking sheets. Let cool completely at room temperature until hardened, about 1 hour. (The haystacks can be stored, with parchment or wax paper between the layers, in an airtight container at room temperature for up to 1 week. In warm weather, store them in the fridge in the same way.)

Gingersnaps

Ginger-lovers will go crazy for these old-fashioned gingersnaps. They pack a double whammy of ginger—both ground and fresh—for a perfect, dunkable hit of spice.

Makes about 36 cookies
Prep time: 15 minutes
Chilling time: 30 minutes
Cooking time: 11 to 13 minutes

1 ¼ cups all-purpose flour

1 cup whole wheat flour

2 tsp ground ginger

1 tsp baking powder

½ tsp baking soda

½ tsp ground cloves

½ tsp fine sea salt

¼ tsp freshly ground black pepper

¾ cup unsalted butter, softened

1 cup lightly packed golden yellow sugar

1 large egg

¼ cup fancy molasses

1 Tbsp finely grated fresh ginger

¾ cup turbinado sugar

1. In a medium bowl, whisk together both flours, the ground ginger, baking powder, baking soda, cloves, salt and pepper. Set aside.

2. In a large bowl and using a wooden spoon or spatula, beat the butter with the sugar until smooth, about 1 minute. Beat in the egg, molasses and fresh ginger until well combined.

3. Add the flour mixture to the sugar mixture and stir just until no streaks of flour remain. Cover the bowl tightly with plastic wrap and refrigerate the dough for 30 minutes.

4. When ready to bake, preheat the oven to 350°F. Line two large baking sheets with parchment paper.

5. Measure the turbinado sugar into a small bowl. Using a small ice cream scoop or spoon, scoop tablespoonfuls of the dough and roll it into balls. Roll the balls in the turbinado sugar, then place, 2 ½ inches apart, on the prepared baking sheets.

6. Using the bottom of a heavy drinking glass, gently press each ball to make a ¾-inch cookie. Bake the cookies until lightly browned around the edges and dry to the touch in the centre, 11 to 13 minutes.

7. Let the cookies cool on the baking sheets for 10 minutes, then remove to wire racks to cool completely. (The gingersnaps can be stored in an airtight container at room temperature for up to 4 days, or frozen, with parchment paper between the layers, for up to 2 months.)

BAKING DAY SECRETS

Frozen ginger grates more easily and is less stringy than unfrozen ginger. Buy fresh organic ginger, seal it in a small freezer bag and store it in the freezer for up to 6 months. Use a sharp grater to grate it straight from the freezer (there's no need to peel it).

BAKING DAY SECRETS

Instant-dissolving sugar has the smallest granules of all of Redpath's sugar. Because it dissolves so easily into the softened butter, it makes the finest-textured shortbread.

Buttery Shortbread

Shortbread has been around since the 12th century. Nine hundred years later, we're still loving its rich flavour. Originating in Scotland, it was a luxury saved for holidays such as Christmas, Hogmanay (Scottish New Year's Eve) and weddings. In the Shetland Islands, it's a tradition to break a decorated shortbread cake over the bride's head when she enters her new house.

Makes about 16 cookies
Prep time: 20 minutes
Chilling time: at least 1 hour
Cooking time: 25 to 30 minutes
Cooling time: at least 20 minutes

5 Tbsp white rice flour

2 cups cake-and-pastry flour

1 cup unsalted butter, softened

¾ cup instant-dissolving sugar (see sidebar)

½ tsp fine sea salt

Granulated sugar for sprinkling (optional)

1. Preheat the oven to 350°F. Line the base and sides of an 8- or 9-inch square baking pan with parchment paper, leaving an overhang of paper on two facing sides. (This will help you remove the shortbread from the pan.) Set aside.

2. If you wish, spread the rice flour out on a small baking sheet. Bake until fragrant, about 12 minutes. Let cool completely. (Baking the rice flour deepens its flavour but you can omit this step, if you prefer.)

3. Sift both flours into a medium bowl. Set aside.

4. In a large bowl and using an electric mixer, beat together the butter, sugar and salt until pale and fluffy.

5. Add the flour mixture to the butter mixture, stirring just until combined. (The dough will be crumbly.) Form the dough into a disc. Wrap it tightly in plastic wrap and refrigerate for at least 1 hour.

6. When ready to bake, preheat the oven to 350°F.

7. Unwrap the chilled dough, then roll it out on a lightly floured work surface to a square the same size as the prepared pan. Carefully transfer the dough to the pan, pressing it into the corners.

8. Using a sharp knife, score the dough into squares, bars or diamonds (aim for about 16 of your chosen shape). Prick the dough all over with a fork. Sprinkle with granulated sugar (if using). Bake until golden, about 25 minutes.

9. Let the shortbread cool in the pan for at least 20 minutes. Cut into pieces, following the scored lines you made before baking. (The shortbread can be stored in an airtight container at room temperature for up to 5 days, or frozen, with parchment paper between the layers, for up to 2 months.)

CHANGE IT UP

Lemon Shortbread: Add the finely grated zest of 1 lemon in Step 4.

Orange-Chocolate Shortbread: Add the finely grated zest of 1 orange in Step 4 and stir ½ cup dark chocolate chips into the dough before chilling.

Chocolate-Hazelnut Shortbread: Stir ½ cup milk chocolate chips and ½ cup finely chopped toasted hazelnuts into the dough before chilling.

Anise-Almond Shortbread: Sift ¼ teaspoonful of ground anise with the flour mixture and stir ½ cup finely chopped toasted almonds into the dough before chilling.

Currant Shortbread: Stir ½ cup currants into the dough before chilling. For a grown-up currant shortbread, soak the currants in 2 tablespoonfuls of dark rum for 1 hour, then drain them well before adding to the dough.

Nut-Crusted Shortbread Cookies

Rich and buttery with a crunchy nut coating, these cookies don't get any better!

Makes about 34 cookies
Prep time: 30 minutes
Chilling time: 45 minutes to 1 hour
Cooking time: 15 to 18 minutes

2 ¾ cups all-purpose flour

¼ cup cornstarch

½ tsp fine sea salt

1 ⅔ cups unsalted butter, softened

1 cup icing sugar, sifted

2 tsp vanilla extract

¼ cup toasted pecans, finely chopped

¼ cup shelled, toasted unsalted pistachios, finely chopped

¼ cup firmly packed demerara-style sugar

CHANGE IT UP

For shortbread with a citrus zip, add the finely grated zest of 1 lemon, orange or lime in Step 5.

1. In a medium bowl, whisk together the flour, cornstarch and salt until well combined. Set aside.

2. In a large bowl and using an electric mixer, beat the butter until pale and fluffy, about 3 minutes.

3. Sift half of the icing sugar over the butter. With the mixer running on low speed, beat the butter and icing sugar just until blended.

4. Sift the remaining icing sugar over the butter mixture. Mix on low speed again until the butter and sugar are well combined.

5. Add the vanilla extract. Increase the speed to medium-high, then beat the butter mixture until very pale in colour, about 5 minutes, scraping down the sides of the bowl once or twice.

6. Add one-third of the flour mixture to the butter mixture. Stir just until combined. Add the remaining flour mixture in two additions, mixing until well blended after each addition.

7. Cover the bowl tightly with plastic wrap. Refrigerate for 30 to 45 minutes. Line two large baking sheets with parchment paper, then set aside.

8. In a small bowl, stir together the pecans, pistachios and demerara-style sugar until well combined.

9. Using a small ice cream scoop or spoon, scoop tablespoonfuls of the chilled dough and form it into balls. Roll each ball in the nut mixture to coat completely. (If the nut mixture doesn't adhere to the dough, roll the ball of dough between slightly damp-ened palms before rolling in the nut mixture.)

10. Place the balls of dough, about 2 inches apart, on the prepared baking sheets. Using the bottom of a heavy drinking glass, gently press down on each ball to make a 2-inch cookie. Refrigerate for 15 minutes.

11. When ready to bake, preheat the oven to 325°F.

12. Bake until the cookies are pale golden brown, 15 to 18 minutes. Let the cookies cool completely on the baking sheets. (The cookies can be stored in an airtight container at room temperature for up to 4 days, or frozen, with parchment paper between the layers, for up to 2 months.)

GET A HEAD START

You can enjoy fresh-baked shortbread any time by freezing the dough:

1. Prep the dough and roll the balls in the nut mixture.

2. Freeze the unbaked balls of dough on the baking sheets until hard, then pack the balls in freezer bags and freeze for up to 2 months.

3. When ready to bake, place the frozen dough balls on parchment-paper-lined baking sheets and let stand at room temperature for 15 minutes.

4. Flatten, then bake as directed.

Coconut Macaroons

When you pair the sweetness of coconut with rich bittersweet chocolate, what's not to like? These macaroons are a no-bake update on a classic. They're egg- and gluten-free and so easy to prepare, they'll become regulars in your cookie jar.

Makes about 24 macaroons
Prep time: 10 minutes
Chilling time: about 1 ½ hours

¼ cup unsalted butter, melted

¼ cup evaporated milk

½ tsp vanilla extract

2 cups icing sugar, sifted

2 cups unsweetened shredded coconut

¾ cup semi-sweet chocolate chips

CHANGE IT UP

For a bigger punch of coconut flavour, replace the vanilla extract with good-quality coconut extract.

1. Line a large baking sheet with parchment paper, then set aside.

2. In a medium bowl, stir together the butter, evaporated milk and vanilla extract.

3. Gradually stir in the icing sugar until the mixture is smooth and free of lumps.

4. Stir in the coconut until completely coated with the sugar mixture.

5. Using a small ice cream scoop or a spoon, drop tablespoonfuls of the coconut mixture onto the prepared baking sheet, doing your best to mound the mixture into little pyramid shapes. Refrigerate the macaroons until cool and firm, about 30 minutes.

6. In a small microwave-safe bowl, melt the chocolate chips in the microwave for 20 seconds on medium power. Stir the chocolate chips. Continue to microwave for 10-second increments, stirring each time, until the chocolate is smooth and melted.

7. Working with one macaroon at a time, dip the flat bottom in the melted chocolate, then return it to the baking sheet.

8. Once all the macaroons have been dipped, return them to the fridge until the chocolate has set, about 1 hour. (The macaroons can be refrigerated in an airtight container for up to 4 days.)

Amaretti

Serve these easy Italian cookies with your favourite gelato—they're particularly good with chocolate or *torrone* (aka Italian nougat) flavours—or enjoy with a shot of espresso.

Makes about 48 amaretti
Prep time: 20 minutes
Cooking time: 12 to 18 minutes

3 cups almond meal or almond flour

⅔ cup turbinado sugar

3 large egg whites

Pinch of fine sea salt

½ cup granulated sugar

1 Tbsp amaretto liqueur or almond extract

1 tsp vanilla extract

48 whole almonds (approx.)

3 Tbsp icing sugar

1. Preheat the oven to 350°F. Line two large baking sheets with parchment paper, then set aside.

2. In a food processor fitted with the steel blade, pulse the almond meal and turbinado sugar about 10 times, or until the mixture is very finely ground and thoroughly combined. Tip the almond mixture into a large bowl and set aside.

3. In a large bowl and using an electric mixer, beat the egg whites and salt on medium-high speed until foamy and white.

4. With the mixer still running on medium-high, gradually add the granulated sugar. Continue beating until the whites just hold medium peaks. The whites should look smooth and glossy. Do not overmix.

5. Add the egg whites to the almond mixture, then gently fold in until well combined. Fold in the liqueur and vanilla extract.

6. Using a very small ice cream scoop or spoon, scoop 2 teaspoonfuls of dough for each cookie and form it into balls. (Dampen your hands with water if the dough sticks to them.) Place the balls, 2 inches apart, on the prepared baking sheets.

7. Gently press an almond into the top of each cookie. Dust the cookies generously with icing sugar. Bake on two separate racks of the oven until golden brown, 12 minutes for softer cookies, 18 minutes for crisper cookies. Rotate the pans halfway through baking time.

8. Let the cookies cool on the baking sheets for 5 minutes, then remove to a wire rack to cool completely. (The amaretti can be stored in an airtight container at room temperature for up to 1 week, or frozen, with parchment paper between the layers, for up to 2 months.)

Crispy Oatmeal Cookies
(recipe opposite)

Soft Oatmeal Cookies
(recipe on page 46)

Crispy Oatmeal Cookies

Some like 'em crispy, some like 'em soft. Oatmeal cookies, that is. Either way, we have a scrumptious recipe for you. Here's the crispy version. Soft-cookie lovers, check out page 46.

Makes about 32 cookies
Prep time: 20 minutes
Chilling time: 20 minutes
Cooking time: 10 to 12 minutes

1 ¼ cups all-purpose flour

1 tsp ground cinnamon

1 tsp baking soda

1 tsp fine sea salt

½ tsp freshly grated nutmeg

½ tsp baking powder

1 cup unsalted butter, softened

1 cup granulated sugar

½ cup firmly packed dark brown sugar

1 large egg

2 tsp vanilla extract

2 ½ cups large-flake rolled oats (not instant or quick oats)

1 cup sultana raisins (optional)

CHANGE IT UP

For chocolatey and/or nutty oatmeal cookies, add 1 cup chocolate chips and/or 1 cup chopped walnuts to the dough along with the oats.

1. In a medium bowl, whisk together the flour, cinnamon, baking soda, salt, nutmeg and baking powder. Set aside.

2. In a large bowl and using an electric mixer, beat the butter on low speed until smooth and creamy.

3. Increase the speed to medium and gradually beat in both sugars until the mixture is smooth, about 2 minutes, scraping down the sides of the bowl once or twice.

4. Add the egg and beat for about 30 seconds. Beat in the vanilla extract.

5. Add the flour mixture to the butter mixture, stirring just until combined. Stir in the oats and raisins (if using). Cover the bowl tightly with plastic wrap and refrigerate the dough for 20 minutes.

6. When ready to bake, preheat the oven to 350°F. Line two large baking sheets with parchment paper, then set aside.

7. Using an ice cream scoop or spoon, scoop about 1 ½ table-spoonfuls of dough for each cookie, about 2 inches apart, onto the prepared baking sheets.

8. Bake the cookies on two separate racks in the oven until light gold around the edges and just barely set in the centre, 10 to 12 minutes, rotating the baking sheets halfway through baking time. Let the cookies cool on the baking sheets for 5 minutes, then remove to wire racks and let cool completely. (The cookies can be stored in an airtight container at room temperature for up to 4 days, or frozen, with parchment paper between the layers, for up to 2 months.)

Soft Oatmeal Cookies

Just as spicy and rich as our crispy oatmeal cookie (page 45), here's our soft oatmeal cookie.

Makes about 32 cookies
Prep time: 20 minutes
Chilling time: 20 minutes
Cooking time: 10 to 12 minutes

1 ¼ cups all-purpose flour

1 ½ tsp baking powder

1 tsp ground cinnamon

1 tsp fine sea salt

½ tsp freshly grated nutmeg

¼ tsp baking soda

¾ cup unsalted butter, softened

¾ cup firmly packed dark brown sugar

¼ cup granulated sugar

1 large egg

2 tsp vanilla extract

1 Tbsp fancy molasses

2 ½ cups large-flake rolled oats (not instant or quick oats)

1 cup sultana raisins (optional)

1. In a medium bowl, whisk together the flour, baking powder, cinnamon, salt, nutmeg and baking soda. Set aside.

2. In a large bowl and using an electric mixer, beat the butter on low speed until smooth and creamy.

3. Increase the speed to medium and gradually beat in both sugars until the mixture is smooth, about 2 minutes, scraping down the sides of the bowl once or twice.

4. Add the egg and beat for about 30 seconds. Beat in the molasses and vanilla extract for about 30 seconds.

5. Add the flour mixture to the butter mixture, stirring just until combined. Stir in the oats and raisins (if using). Cover the bowl tightly with plastic wrap and refrigerate the dough for 20 minutes.

6. When ready to bake, preheat the oven to 375°F. Line two large baking sheets with parchment paper, then set aside.

7. Using an ice cream scoop or spoon, scoop about 1 ½ table-spoonfuls of dough for each cookie, about 2 inches apart, onto the prepared baking sheets.

8. Bake the cookies on two separate racks of the oven until light gold around the edges and just barely set in the centre, 10 to 12 minutes, rotating the baking sheets halfway through baking time. Let the cookies cool on the baking sheets for 5 minutes, then remove to wire racks and let cool completely. (The cookies can be stored in an airtight container at room temperature for up to 4 days, or frozen, with parchment paper between the layers, for up to 2 months.)

GET A HEAD START

Whether you opt for crisp or soft oatmeal cookies, the dough freezes well and is handy to have stored away for unexpected guests:

1. Freeze the unbaked dough on the baking sheets until hard, then pack the unbaked cookies in freezer bags and freeze for up to 1 month.

2. When ready to bake, place the frozen cookies on parchment-paper-lined baking sheets and bake as described in the appropriate oatmeal cookie recipe, adding 2 to 3 minutes to the baking time.

Citrus-Almond Pizzelle

Traditional pizzelle are flavoured with anise, but we love our zesty citrus version. If you prefer a more classic flavour, replace the orange and lemon zests with 2 teaspoonfuls of crushed anise seeds, and the almond extract with anise extract.

Makes about 40 pizzelle
Prep time: 20 minutes
Chilling time: 15 minutes
Cooking time: about 40 seconds
   per batch

2 cups plus 1 Tbsp all-purpose flour

2 ½ tsp baking powder

¼ tsp baking soda

1 cup granulated sugar

4 large eggs

1 Tbsp liquid honey

²/₃ cup unsalted butter, melted and cooled

2 tsp finely grated orange zest

2 tsp finely grated lemon zest

1 tsp almond extract

½ tsp vanilla extract

Pinch of fine sea salt

Nonstick baking spray

1. In a medium bowl, whisk together the flour, baking powder and baking soda. Set aside.

2. In a large bowl and using an electric mixer, beat together the sugar, eggs and honey until pale, about 2 minutes.

3. With the mixer running, slowly add the butter, beating until thoroughly combined.

4. Beat in the orange and lemon zests, almond and vanilla extracts and salt.

5. Using a rubber spatula, fold the flour mixture into the egg mixture until well combined and no white streaks remain.

6. Cover the bowl tightly with plastic wrap and refrigerate the batter for 15 minutes.

7. Preheat a pizzelle iron.

8. Once the batter has chilled and the pizzelle iron is hot, spray the cooking surfaces of the iron with baking spray. Place a heaping teaspoonful of the batter into the centre of each cooking surface on the iron. Close the lid, then cook until the pizzelle are crisp and golden, 35 to 40 seconds.

9. Remove the pizzelle to a wire rack and let cool completely. Repeat with the remaining batter. (The pizzelle can be stored, with parchment or wax paper between the layers, in an airtight container at room temperature for up to 1 week.)

TOOL KIT

You'll need a pizzelle iron—similar to a waffle iron—to prepare these traditional Italian waffle cookies. But the cookies are so rich, sweet and delicious that it's a worthwhile investment.

Blossom Cookies

These stunning cookies, decorated with dried edible flowers, would make perfect sweet treats for a baby or bridal shower. You can cut the dough into any fancy shape you wish. Try using cutters in the shape of the guest of honour's initial for a personal touch.

Makes about 36 cookies
Prep time: 40 minutes
Chilling time: 1 hour
Cooking time: 10 to 12 minutes
Drying time: at least 4 hours

Cookies

2 ½ cups all-purpose flour

¼ tsp baking powder

¼ tsp fine sea salt

¾ cup unsalted butter, softened

⅔ cup granulated sugar

1 large egg

2 tsp finely grated lemon zest

2 tsp vanilla or lemon extract

Icing

1 ¾ cups plus 2 Tbsp icing sugar, sifted

Pinch of fine sea salt

2 Tbsp water

1 Tbsp rose water (see page 10)

1 tsp white corn syrup

Dried edible flowers for garnish (see sidebar)

Dried culinary lavender for garnish (optional)

BAKING DAY SECRET

It's easy to dry your own edible flowers:

1. Take the petals from edible flowers (see sidebar). Choose larger petals, as they shrink during drying.

2. Spread them out in a single layer on a paper-towel-lined plate. Cover with a second sheet of paper towel.

3. Microwave on high power for 30-second intervals, checking after each interval, until the petals are dried, about 2 minutes.

1. For the cookies, whisk together the flour, baking powder and salt in a medium bowl. Set aside.

2. In a large bowl and using an electric mixer, beat together the butter and sugar just until combined, about 30 seconds.

3. Beat in the egg until well combined, about 1 minute. Beat in the lemon zest and vanilla extract until well combined.

4. With the mixer running on low speed, add about half of the flour mixture to the butter mixture, beating just until combined. Add the remaining flour mixture, beating just until combined. Do not overmix.

5. Turn out the dough onto a lightly floured work surface and form into a flat rectangle. Wrap the dough tightly in plastic wrap and refrigerate for 1 hour.

6. Bring the dough out of the fridge to stand at room temperature for about 10 minutes. Line a large baking sheet with parchment paper. Set aside.

7. Place the dough between two sheets of parchment paper, then roll it out to ¼-inch thickness. Using a 2 ½-inch cookie cutter, cut out cookies, rerolling the scraps once. (Rerolling the scraps more than once makes the cookies tough.) Place the cookies, 1 ½ inches apart, on the prepared baking sheet. Refrigerate the sheet of cookies again for about 10 minutes.

8. When ready to bake, preheat the oven to 375°F.

9. Bake the cookies until light golden, 10 to 12 minutes. Let the cookies cool on the baking sheets for 5 minutes, then remove to wire racks and let cool completely. (The undecorated cookies can be stored in an airtight container at room temperature for up to 4 days, or frozen, with parchment paper between the layers, for up to 2 months.)

10. For the icing, whisk together the icing sugar and salt in a medium bowl. Whisk in the water, rose water and corn syrup until the icing is smooth. If the icing is too thick, add a little more water, ½ teaspoonful at a time until the icing is spreadable. If it's too runny, add a little icing sugar, 1 teaspoonful at a time until the icing is spreadable.

11. Using a small offset spatula or a clean pastry brush, spread or brush a little icing onto each cookie. While the icing is still wet, garnish each cookie with the dried edible flowers and lavender (if using). Place the cookies on a wire rack to dry completely, at least 4 hours, but preferably overnight.

EDIBLE FLOWER PRIMER

Look for edible flowers in the produce department of specialty grocery stores. Or use pesticide-free blooms from a trusted source (your own or a friend's backyard), checking out our dos and don'ts first.

- DO make sure the flowers you use are edible (some common ones are violets, pansies, Johnny-jump-ups, nasturtiums, most herb flowers, rose petals and tulip petals). Remember that not all flowers are edible.

- DO wash flowers and petals well before using them in a recipe.

- DO eat only the petals from edible flowers.

- DON'T eat flowers from florists or garden centres (most will have been sprayed with pesticides).

- DON'T pick flowers for eating from the roadside.

- DON'T eat any flower you're not totally sure is edible.

Chocolate Brandy Snaps

These dainty cylindrical cookies make a stunning garnish for a special occasion cake. Alternatively, pipe whipped cream into each end and serve on their own for dessert or, minus the whipped cream, as a crisp accompaniment for ice cream.

Makes about 15 brandy snaps
Prep time: 30 minutes
Cooking time: about 10 minutes

½ cup all-purpose flour

1 Tbsp finely grated orange zest (about 1 orange)

2 tsp unsweetened cocoa powder

½ tsp ground ginger

¼ tsp fine sea salt

⅓ cup lightly packed golden yellow sugar

5 Tbsp unsalted butter, softened

3 Tbsp golden corn syrup

1 tsp vanilla extract

CHANGE IT UP

For a more classic brandy snap flavour, replace the unsweetened cocoa powder with more all-purpose flour.

1. Preheat the oven to 350°F. Line two large baking sheets with parchment paper. Set aside.

2. In a medium bowl, whisk together the flour, orange zest, cocoa powder, ground ginger and salt. Set aside.

3. In a small saucepan, combine the sugar, butter and corn syrup. Cook, stirring, over medium-low heat until the sugar has dissolved and the butter has melted, about 2 minutes.

4. Remove from the heat. Stir in the vanilla extract.

5. Pour the sugar mixture over the flour mixture, stirring until well combined.

6. Drop four heaping teaspoonfuls of the batter, well apart (the brandy snaps spread a lot), onto one prepared baking sheet, reserving the second baking sheet.

7. Bake until the batter is bubbling, 5 to 8 minutes. Remove from the oven and let cool for 30 seconds.

8. Working quickly, use a small offset spatula to gently lift one brandy snap off the parchment. With the lacy side facing outward, quickly wrap the brandy snap around a handle of a clean wooden spoon or a wooden dowel.

9. Let the brandy snap cool on the wooden spoon or dowel for 1 minute. Carefully slip it off and let cool completely on a wire rack. (If the brandy snaps become too brittle to shape, return the baking sheet to the oven for a few seconds to soften the brandy snaps.)

10. Repeat the process with the remaining batter, using the second baking sheet. Alternate the baking sheets when baking the brandy snaps—a baking sheet that's too hot will make the batter spread too much. (The brandy snaps can be stored in an airtight container at room temperature for up to 4 days.)

BRANDY SNAP BOWLS

1. Follow the recipe for Brandy Snaps, dropping the batter by tablespoonfuls (instead of teaspoonfuls) and baking three per baking sheet.

2. Working quickly, use a small offset spatula to gently lift one brandy snap off the parchment. With the lacy side facing outward, quickly drape the brandy snap over an overturned cup or small bowl, gently forming the brandy snap to the shape of the cup or bowl.

3. Let the brandy snap cool for 1 minute. Carefully remove from the cup or bowl and let cool completely on a wire rack. Repeat with the remaining batter.

4. Fill the brandy snap bowls with fresh fruit and scoops of your favourite ice cream.

Lemon-Thyme Poppy Seed Cookies

The crunch of poppy seeds combines with zesty lemon and a hint of thyme in these easy icebox cookies. With the dough tucked away in your freezer, you're ready for company any time.

Makes about 40 cookies
Prep time: 20 minutes
Chilling time: 50 minutes
Freezing time: at least 2 hours
Cooking time: 8 to 10 minutes

2 ¼ cups all-purpose flour

1 tsp baking powder

½ tsp fine sea salt

½ cup granulated sugar

¼ cup lightly packed golden yellow sugar

2 Tbsp finely grated lemon zest (about 3 lemons)

1 Tbsp coarsely chopped fresh thyme leaves

1 cup unsalted butter, softened

6 Tbsp poppy seeds

1 large egg

½ tsp lemon extract

¼ tsp vanilla extract

1. In a medium bowl, whisk together the flour, baking powder and salt. Set aside.

2. In a large bowl, stir together both sugars, the lemon zest and thyme. Using your fingers, rub the ingredients together to infuse the sugar with the flavourings.

3. Using an electric mixer, beat the butter into the sugar mixture until pale and fluffy, about 1 minute.

4. Beat in 3 tablespoonfuls of the poppy seeds, the egg and the lemon and vanilla extracts until well combined.

5. Add half of the flour mixture to the butter mixture. With the mixer running on low speed, mix in the flour just until combined. Add the remaining flour mixture and mix until combined.

6. Divide the dough in half. Wrap each piece tightly in plastic wrap and refrigerate until it's firm enough to form into logs, about 30 minutes.

7. Form the chilled dough into logs, about 2 inches in diameter, and square them off. Refrigerate, unwrapped, until they have hardened slightly, about 20 minutes.

8. Spread the remaining 3 tablespoonfuls of poppy seeds out on a large flat plate. Roll the logs in the poppy seeds to coat completely. Wrap the logs tightly in plastic wrap and freeze for at least 2 hours. (The dough can be frozen for up to 2 months.)

9. When ready to bake, preheat the oven to 375°F. Line a large baking sheet with parchment paper.

10. Remove one log of dough from the freezer. Unwrap the log and, with a sharp knife, cut it crosswise into ¼-inch slices. Place the slices, about ½ inch apart, on the prepared baking sheet. Bake until the edges are firm and lightly browned, 8 to 10 minutes.

11. Remove the cookies to wire racks to cool completely. Repeat with the remaining cookie dough, if liked (or freeze until needed). (The cookies can be stored in an airtight container at room temperature for up to 4 days, or frozen, with parchment paper between the layers, for up to 2 months.)

BAKING DAY SECRETS

- When making any icebox cookie, freeze the cookie dough logs standing on their ends to prevent the finished cookies being slightly flattened on one side.

- For longer storage, pack the wrapped logs in a freezer bag.

- If the cookie dough log becomes too soft while you're slicing it, return it to the freezer for a few minutes before continuing.

Lime & Coconut Sugar
Cookies (recipe on page 54)

Springtime Sugar Cookies
(recipe opposite)

Gluten-Free Vegan Sugar Cookies
(recipe on page 55)

Springtime Sugar Cookies

Here's the perfect cookie to bake—and decorate—when the arrival of spring brings a burst of colour back into our world. A basket of these colourful sweet treats would make a lovely Easter hostess gift. We use springtime-themed cookie cutters, choosing shapes like butterflies, flowers and bunnies. And, of course, the cookies taste just as good at any time of year.

Makes about 36 cookies

Prep time: 30 minutes

Chilling time: at least 1 hour, 10 minutes

Cooking time: 10 to 12 minutes

5 cups all-purpose flour

2 tsp baking powder

1 tsp fine sea salt

1 ½ cups unsalted butter, softened

2 cups granulated sugar

4 large eggs

1 tsp vanilla extract

Easy Royal Icing (page 162)

Gel food colouring of your choice

BAKING DAY SECRETS

To fill a piping bag, twist the tip on firmly to prevent the icing from leaking out. Place the bag, tip down, in a tall glass or jar, folding down the sides of the piping bag over the glass. Spoon in the icing, then lift up the sides of the bag, twisting them together tightly.

1. In a medium bowl, whisk together the flour, baking powder and salt. Set aside.

2. In a large bowl and using an electric mixer, beat the butter with the sugar until pale and fluffy. Beat in the eggs one at a time, beating well after each addition. Beat in the vanilla extract until well combined.

3. Add the flour mixture to the sugar mixture, stirring just until combined.

4. Divide the dough into four even-sized pieces and form each piece into a disc. Wrap each disc tightly in plastic wrap, then refrigerate for at least 1 hour, or overnight.

5. Line two large baking sheets with parchment paper, then set aside.

6. On a lightly floured work surface, roll out one disc of dough to ¼-inch thickness. Using large (about 3-inch) springtime-themed cookie cutters, cut out cookies, rerolling the scraps once. (Rerolling the dough more than once makes the cookies tough.) Place the cookies, 1 inch apart, on the prepared baking sheets. Refrigerate the sheets of cookies for about 10 minutes. Preheat the oven to 350°F.

7. Bake the cookies on two separate racks of the oven until just golden, 10 to 12 minutes, rotating the pans halfway through baking time. Remove the cookies to wire racks to cool completely. Repeat with the remaining cookie dough. (The undecorated cookies can be stored in an airtight container at room temperature for up to 4 days, or frozen, with parchment paper between the layers, for up to 2 months.)

8. When you're ready to decorate the cookies, divide the royal icing among as many bowls as you have food colours. Stir enough colour into each bowl of icing to tint it to your taste.

9. Spoon each colour of icing into a separate piping bag (see sidebar). Decorate the cookies with royal icing, following the decorating tips on pages 170–72.

Lime & Coconut Sugar Cookies

The combo of lime and coconut adds a lovely tropical note to these simple sugar cookies.

Makes about 24 cookies
Prep time: 15 minutes
Cooking time: 10 to 12 minutes

Cookies

2 ¾ cups all-purpose flour

1 tsp baking soda

½ tsp baking powder

½ tsp fine sea salt

1 cup unsalted butter, softened

1 ½ cups granulated sugar

1 large egg

Finely grated zest of 1 lime

Juice of 2 limes

½ tsp vanilla extract

½ cup unsweetened shredded coconut

Coating

½ cup granulated sugar

¼ cup unsweetened shredded coconut

1. Preheat the oven to 350°F. Line two large baking sheets with parchment paper, then set aside.

2. For the cookies, whisk together the flour, baking soda, baking powder and salt in a medium bowl. Set aside.

3. In a large bowl and using an electric mixer, beat the butter with the sugar until pale and fluffy. Beat in the egg, lime zest and juice and vanilla extract until well combined.

4. Add the flour mixture to the sugar mixture, stirring just until combined. Stir in the coconut until well combined.

5. For the coating, stir together the sugar and coconut in a small bowl.

6. Using a small ice cream scoop or spoon, scoop tablespoonfuls of the dough and form it into balls. Roll each ball in the sugar mixture to coat completely. Place the balls of dough, 1 inch apart, on the prepared baking sheets.

7. Bake on two separate racks of the oven until the cookies are light golden brown around the edges, 10 to 12 minutes, rotating the baking sheets halfway through baking time. Let the cookies cool completely on the baking sheets. (The cookies can be stored in an airtight container at room temperature for up to 4 days, or frozen, with parchment paper between the layers, for up to 2 months.)

SWEET HISTORY

The first recorded use of sugar as food was in the southwest Pacific island of New Guinea, but it was in India that the techniques of sugar manufacturing were first developed. Around the 7th century, Arab traders spread sugar's use through the Middle East and Mediterranean. But it took another 400 years for sugar to become popular in northern Europe, where it was introduced as a luxury "spice" from the Middle East.

Gluten-Free Vegan Sugar Cookies

Sugar cookies are a perennial favourite, and so we wanted a version that all our friends could enjoy. These cookies are not only totally yummy but also gluten-free and vegan-friendly. Serve them plain or decorate with our Easy Royal Icing (page 162), which is gluten-free but not suitable for vegans, or our Vegan Royal Icing (page 162).

Makes about 24 cookies
Prep time: 20 minutes
Chilling time: 10 to 20 minutes
Cooking time: about 8 minutes

2 cups oat flour (see sidebar)

1 cup brown or white rice flour

1 cup icing sugar, sifted

4 tsp arrowroot flour (see sidebar) or cornstarch

1 tsp fine sea salt

8 Tbsp coconut oil

1 tsp vanilla extract

BAKING DAY SECRETS

Oat flour, brown rice flour and arrowroot flour can all be found in bulk stores or health food stores. If you can't find oat flour, make your own by grinding 2 ½ cups rolled oats in a food processor or blender.

1. Line a large baking sheet with parchment paper, then set aside.

2. In a large bowl, whisk together both flours, the icing sugar, arrowroot flour and salt. Set aside.

3. In a small bowl and using a wooden spoon or spatula, beat together the coconut oil and vanilla extract until well combined.

4. Add the coconut oil mixture to the flour mixture and mix with a wooden spoon or spatula until the mixture is crumbly. Use your hands to bring the mixture together to form a dough. (The dough will seem very dry and crumbly at first, but don't worry; as you continue to work the mixture with your hands, the coconut oil will soften and the flours will eventually absorb it.)

5. When the dough becomes a little sticky and soft, form it into a ball. Place the dough between two sheets of parchment paper. Roll it out to ¼-inch thickness.

6. Gently remove the top layer of parchment paper. Using a 3-inch cookie cutter, cut out cookies, rerolling the scraps until you have used all the dough. Carefully (the dough is delicate) place the cookies, 1 inch apart, on the prepared baking sheet.

7. Refrigerate the sheet of cookies for 20 minutes or freeze for 10 minutes. (This prevents the cookies from spreading too much during baking.)

8. When ready to bake, preheat the oven to 350°F.

9. Bake the cookies until lightly golden around the edges and dry to the touch, about 8 minutes. Let the cookies cool completely on the baking sheet. (The cookies can be stored in an airtight container at room temperature for up to 4 days, or frozen, with parchment paper between the layers, for up to 2 months.)

Gluten-Free Lemon-Coconut Cookies

These crisp, lemon-coconut cookies are made with our own gluten-free flour mix (recipe follows), and everyone will love their crisp texture and rich flavour. Serve with a cup of tea or coffee, or pair them with your favourite ice cream flavour for homemade ice cream sandwiches.

Makes about 24 cookies
Prep time: 20 minutes
Chilling time: at least 1 hour
Cooking time: 8 to 12 minutes (per batch)

2 cups Gluten-Free Flour Mix (recipe follows)

1 cup granulated sugar

1 cup unsweetened shredded coconut

2 tsp baking powder

½ tsp baking soda

½ cup unsalted butter, melted

2 large eggs

1 tsp vanilla extract

Finely grated zest of 1 lemon

1. In a medium bowl, whisk together the flour mix, sugar, coconut, baking powder and baking soda. Set aside.

2. In a large bowl, whisk together the butter, eggs and vanilla extract.

3. Add the flour mixture and lemon zest to the butter mixture, stirring with a spoon just until the ingredients are combined.

4. Cover the bowl tightly with plastic wrap and refrigerate for at least 1 hour (the dough will thicken).

5. When ready to bake, preheat the oven to 375°F. Line two large baking sheets with parchment paper.

6. Using a small ice cream scoop or spoon, scoop tablespoonfuls of the dough and form it into balls, 3 inches apart, onto the prepared baking sheets. The cookies will spread a lot, so allow only about six cookies per baking sheet.

7. Bake the cookies until they're starting to look dry and their edges are golden, 8 to 12 minutes. Remove the cookies to wire racks to cool completely. Repeat with the remaining cookie dough, or store it for another time (see sidebar). (The cookies can be stored in an airtight container at room temperature for up to 4 days, or frozen, with parchment paper between the layers, for up to 2 months.)

GET A HEAD START

The unbaked cookie dough can be refrigerated in an airtight container for up to 4 days, so you can enjoy freshly baked, gluten-free cookies any time.

Gluten-Free Flour Mix

Makes 4 cups
Prep time: 5 minutes

1 cup white rice flour

1 cup corn flour (see sidebar)

1 cup almond meal or almond flour

½ cup quinoa flour

¼ cup cornstarch

¼ cup ground flax seed

In a large bowl, whisk together both flours, the almond meal, quinoa flour, cornstarch and ground flax seed. Continue to whisk until well blended, about 2 minutes. (The flour mix can be stored in an airtight container in the fridge for up to 3 months, or frozen for up to 6 months.)

BAKING DAY SECRETS

Corn flour—not to be confused with the slightly coarser corn meal—is very finely ground corn which, as its name suggests, is the consistency of flour.

Flourless Peanut Butter Cookies

If you're a fan of peanut butter, you'll love these rich and chewy cookies. They're gluten-free, and perhaps the easiest cookies you will ever make.

Makes about 18 cookies
Prep time: 15 minutes
Cooking time: 9 to 10 minutes

1 cup all-natural smooth or crunchy peanut butter

½ cup lightly packed golden yellow sugar

½ cup granulated sugar

½ tsp baking soda

¼ tsp fine sea salt

1 large egg

1. Preheat the oven to 350°F. Line a large baking sheet with parchment paper, then set aside.

2. In a medium bowl, beat together the peanut butter, both sugars, the baking soda and salt until smooth.

3. Beat in the egg until the dough is thick and holds together.

4. Using a small ice cream scoop or spoon, scoop 1 tablespoonful of dough for each cookie and form it into balls. Place the balls, 1 ½ inches apart, on the prepared baking sheet. Use a fork to press down on each cookie to create a cross-hatch pattern.

5. Bake until lightly browned around the edges, 9 to 10 minutes. Let the cookies cool on the baking sheets for 5 minutes, then carefully (the cookies are very fragile) remove to a wire rack and let cool completely. (The cookies can be stored in an airtight container at room temperature for up to 4 days, or frozen, with parchment paper between the layers, for up to 2 months.)

BARS
&
BROWNIES

Grapefruit Brûlée Bars

Classic citrus-spiked bars go from humble to haute with the sweet-tart flavour of caramelized grapefruit. Serve as an elegant dessert, or as a sweet treat with a pot of tea.

Makes 24 bars
Prep time: 25 minutes
Cooking time: about 40 minutes

Crust

1 cup unsalted butter, softened

⅔ cup icing sugar, sifted

2 cups all-purpose flour

Filling

2 cups granulated sugar

4 large eggs

¼ cup all-purpose flour

2 Tbsp finely grated pink grapefruit zest

¼ cup freshly squeezed pink grapefruit juice

¼ cup freshly squeezed lemon juice (about 2 lemons)

1 tsp baking powder

¼ cup turbinado sugar

1. Preheat the oven to 350°F.

2. For the crust, in a medium bowl and using an electric mixer, beat the butter until pale fluffy. Beat in the icing sugar until well combined. Beat in the flour until a soft dough forms.

3. Press the dough over the base of a nonstick 13- x 9-inch baking pan. Bake until the crust is light golden, about 20 minutes. Leave the oven switched on.

4. For the filling, in a medium bowl and using an electric mixer, beat together the granulated sugar and eggs until blended.

5. With the mixer running on low speed, beat in the flour, grapefruit zest and juice, lemon juice and baking powder until well combined.

6. Pour the filling over the hot crust. Bake until the filling is set in the centre and starting to brown on top, about 20 minutes. Let cool completely in the pan on a wire rack.

7. Cut into 24 bars. Remove the bars from the pan and arrange on a baking sheet. Sprinkle the turbinado sugar evenly over the tops of the bars.

8. Light a butane kitchen torch and play the flame evenly over the tops of the bars to caramelize the sugar, moving the torch constantly so the sugar doesn't burn. (Alternatively, caramelize the sugar for a few minutes under a hot broiler.) Allow the caramelized sugar to cool before transferring the bars to a platter. Serve immediately.

Rhubarb-Raspberry Crumble Squares

When rhubarb isn't in season, you can substitute frozen rhubarb: partially thaw it, then pat it dry on paper towels before tossing it with the rest of the filling ingredients.

Makes 9 squares
Prep time: 20 minutes
Cooking time: 35 to 45 minutes

Fruit Filling

1 cup coarsely chopped fresh rhubarb

1 cup fresh raspberries

¼ cup granulated sugar

1 ½ Tbsp freshly squeezed lemon juice

2 tsp cornstarch

Base and Topping

1 ½ cups all-purpose flour

½ tsp baking powder

½ cup granulated sugar

½ cup unsalted butter, softened

1 large egg

1. Preheat the oven to 375°F. Line the base and sides of a 9-inch square baking pan with parchment paper, leaving an overhang of paper on two facing sides. (This will help you remove the bars from the pan.) Set aside.

2. For the fruit filling, gently toss together the rhubarb, raspberries, sugar, lemon juice and cornstarch in a medium bowl. Set aside.

3. For the base and topping, whisk together the flour and baking powder with the sugar in a large bowl. Add the butter and egg. Using an electric mixer on low speed, or with a spatula, blend until the dough is moist but very crumbly.

4. Divide the dough in half. Press one half of the dough over the base of the prepared pan.

5. Spread the rhubarb mixture over the dough. Sprinkle the remaining dough over the rhubarb mixture to create a crumble top. Do not press it down.

6. Bake until the fruit is bubbling and the topping is starting to brown, 35 to 45 minutes. Let cool completely in the pan on a wire rack.

7. Using the parchment paper overhang, lift the squares from the pan to a cutting board. Cut into 9 squares. (The squares can be refrigerated in an airtight container for up to 1 week.)

CHANGE IT UP

Feel free to swap out the raspberries for your favourite seasonal berry—blueberries, blackberries or sliced strawberries all work well.

Magic Bars
with Homemade Condensed Milk

Loaded with pecans, walnuts and chocolate chips, these super-easy bars are the perfect rainy day treat. Homemade condensed milk is simple to make, and we think it gives the bars great flavour, not to mention an extra sprinkling of fairy dust.

Makes 24 bars
Prep time: 10 minutes
Cooking time: about 30 minutes

½ cup unsalted butter, melted

1 ½ cups graham cracker crumbs

1 ⅓ cups unsweetened shredded coconut

1 cup semi-sweet chocolate chips

1 cup mixed unsalted nuts (pecans, walnuts, almonds and/or hazelnuts)

1 ¾ cups Homemade Condensed Milk (recipe follows)

1. Preheat the oven to 350°F. Line the base and sides of a 9-inch square baking pan with parchment paper, leaving an overhang of paper on two facing sides. (This will help you remove the bars from the pan.) Set aside.

2. Pour the melted butter into the lined pan. Sprinkle the graham cracker crumbs evenly over the butter. Sprinkle evenly with the coconut, then the chocolate chips, then the nuts.

3. Drizzle the condensed milk over the top. Bake until the edges of the bars are golden brown, about 30 minutes. Let cool completely in the pan on a wire rack.

4. Using the parchment paper overhang, remove the bars from the pan to a cutting board. Cut into 24 bars. (The bars can be refrigerated in an airtight container for up to 10 days.)

Homemade Condensed Milk

Makes about 1 ¾ cups
Prep time: 5 minutes
Cooking time: 1 to 2 hours
Chilling time: 2 to 4 hours

1 ½ cups whole milk

½ cup granulated sugar

3 Tbsp unsalted butter, softened

1 tsp vanilla extract

1. In a medium, heavy-bottomed saucepan, stir together the milk and sugar. Bring the milk to a simmer over medium heat, stirring until the sugar has dissolved.

2. Turn down the heat to very low. Cook the milk, stirring often, until it has reduced by about half, 1 to 2 hours.

3. Remove the saucepan from the heat. Whisk in the butter and vanilla extract until the butter melts. Let cool to room temperature, then refrigerate until thickened, 2 to 4 hours. (The condensed milk can be refrigerated in an airtight container for up to 2 weeks.)

Peanut Butter–Chocolate Crispy Bars

These no-bake squares are sweet, simple and ridiculously good. The combo of chocolate and peanut butter on a crispy base is hard to resist, so don't be surprised if these bars disappear quickly.

Makes 16 bars
Prep time: 25 minutes
Cooking time: about 10 minutes
Chilling time: 30 to 40 minutes

Base

1 ¾ cups crispy rice cereal

¼ cup water

½ cup granulated sugar

3 Tbsp white corn syrup

3 Tbsp unsalted butter, softened

Peanut Butter–Chocolate Filling

1 cup milk chocolate chips

1 cup smooth peanut butter

Chocolate Topping

4 oz dark chocolate, finely chopped

¼ cup unsalted butter, softened

½ tsp white corn syrup

TOOL KIT

A candy thermometer is a handy tool to have around. It makes preparing caramel and other candies a cinch, but you can also use it for checking the temperature of oil when deep-frying. Candy thermometers are very affordable and can be found at most grocery and kitchen stores.

1. Line the base and sides of an 8-inch square baking pan with parchment paper, leaving an overhang of paper on two facing sides. (This will help you remove the bars from the pan.) Set aside.

2. For the base, measure the cereal into a large bowl and set aside.

3. Pour the water into a medium saucepan. Sprinkle the sugar over the water, making sure none of the sugar sticks to the sides of the saucepan. Add the corn syrup.

4. Hook a candy thermometer over the side of the saucepan. Cook the sugar mixture over medium heat, without stirring, until the candy thermometer registers 235°F, about 10 minutes. (If you don't have a candy thermometer, drop a little of the mixture into a bowl of cold water. If it forms a soft ball, it's ready.)

5. Immediately remove the saucepan from the heat and stir in the butter.

6. Working quickly so the caramel doesn't harden, pour the caramel over the cereal and stir well, making sure all of the cereal is coated.

7. Scrape the cereal mixture into the prepared pan. Spread it evenly in the pan, pressing it into the corners with a spatula or a square of greased parchment paper. Set aside.

8. For the filling, combine the chocolate chips and peanut butter in a medium saucepan. Cook over low heat, stirring occasionally, until melted and smooth.

9. Pour the filling over the base and spread evenly. Chill in the freezer until the filling is firm, 15 to 20 minutes.

10. For the topping, combine the chocolate, butter and corn syrup in a medium saucepan. Cook over low heat, stirring occasionally, until melted and smooth.

11. Pour the melted chocolate over the filling, spreading evenly to cover the filling completely. Chill in the freezer until the topping is firm, 15 to 20 minutes.

12. Using the parchment paper overhang, lift the bars from the pan to a cutting board. Cut into 16 bars. (The bars can be refrigerated in an airtight container for up to 1 week.)

Coconut Chess Bars

This traditional bar from the American South combines a crisp coconut shortbread base with a rich cream cheese topping.

Makes 24 bars
Prep time: 25 minutes
Cooking time: about 45 minutes

Base

2 cups all-purpose flour

1 ¼ cups granulated sugar

2 tsp baking powder

½ tsp fine sea salt

1 cup unsalted butter, melted

1 large egg

1 cup pecan halves, coarsely chopped

1 cup unsweetened shredded coconut

Topping

1 ½ pkgs (each 8 oz/250 g) brick-style cream cheese (12 oz/350 g in total), at room temperature

3 ¾ cups icing sugar, sifted

2 large eggs

1 tsp vanilla extract

¼ cup unsweetened shredded coconut

1. Preheat the oven to 350°F. Grease a 13- x 9-inch baking pan. Line the base and sides of the pan with parchment paper, leaving an overhang of paper on two facing sides. (This will help you remove the bars from the pan.)

2. For the base, sift the flour, sugar, baking powder and salt into a medium bowl. Using an electric mixer, beat in the butter and egg until well combined and the dough is smooth. Stir in the pecan halves.

3. Press the dough evenly into the prepared pan and sprinkle evenly with the coconut. Set aside.

4. For the topping, in a medium bowl and using an electric mixer, beat the cream cheese until smooth. Beat in the sugar, ½ cup at a time, until completely blended.

5. Beat in the eggs one at a time, beating well after each addition and scraping down the sides of the bowl once or twice. Beat in the vanilla extract.

6. Pour the topping over the base. Sprinkle evenly with the coconut. Bake until the top is golden brown, about 45 minutes.

7. Let cool completely in the pan on a wire rack. Using the parchment paper overhang, lift the bars from the pan to a cutting board. Cut into 24 bars. Serve cold or at room temperature. (The bars can be refrigerated in an airtight container for up to 5 days.)

BAKING DAY SECRETS

For the neatest bars, put the pan in the freezer for 10 minutes before removing the bars from the pan and cutting them.

Crumbly Date Squares

Date squares are one of our all-time favourite desserts. This simple treat reminds us of home and comfort. You can find versions of these squares all over Canada, although in the west they're sometimes called Matrimonial Squares.

Makes 24 squares

Prep time: 15 minutes

Soaking time: 30 minutes

Cooking time: about 55 minutes

Date Filling

2 cups cold brewed black coffee

1 pkg (1 lb/500 g) pitted dates

¾ cup lightly packed golden
   yellow sugar

Oat Crumble

2 ½ cups large-flake rolled oats

1 ¼ cups all-purpose flour

1 cup lightly packed golden
   yellow sugar

¼ tsp fine sea salt

1 cup cold unsalted butter,
   cut into small pieces

1. For the date filling, stir together the coffee, dates and sugar in a medium saucepan. Let them soak for 30 minutes to soften the dates.

2. Bring the mixture to a boil over high heat. Turn down the heat to medium and boil gently, stirring often, until thickened, about 10 minutes. Remove from the heat and let cool to room temperature.

3. Preheat the oven to 350°F. Line the base and sides of an 8-inch square baking pan with parchment paper, leaving an overhang of paper on two facing sides. (This will help you remove the squares from the pan.)

4. For the oat crumble, mix together the oats, flour, sugar and salt in a large bowl. Using a pastry blender or two knives, cut in the butter until the mixture is crumbly and the butter is in pea-size pieces.

5. Press half of the oat crumble into the prepared pan. Spread the date filling over the top, then sprinkle the remaining oat crumble over the date filling. Press the topping down gently.

6. Bake the squares until the topping is golden brown, about 45 minutes. Let cool completely in the pan on a wire rack.

7. Using the parchment paper overhang, lift out the squares to a cutting board. Cut into 24 squares. (The squares can be stored in an airtight container at room temperature for up to 5 days, or frozen for up to 2 months.)

GET A HEAD START

Assemble the squares up to the end of Step 5, but don't bake them. Cover the pan tightly with plastic wrap or aluminum foil and refrigerate for up to 3 days. Or seal the covered pan in a freezer bag and freeze for up to 2 weeks. If frozen, bake straight from the freezer, adding about 10 minutes to the baking time.

Cappuccino Nanaimo Bars

Sweet and chocolatey, with a real kick of coffee, this twist on a classic will provide a burst of energy to help you leap through your day.

Makes 24 bars
Prep time: 20 minutes
Cooking time: about 8 minutes
Chilling time: about 1 hour

Base

1 large egg, beaten

⅔ cup unsalted butter, softened

⅓ cup unsweetened cocoa powder

¼ cup granulated sugar

1 Tbsp instant espresso powder

1 ½ cups graham cracker crumbs

¾ cup sweetened flaked coconut

¾ cup finely chopped almonds

Filling

¼ cup unsalted butter, softened

2 cups icing sugar, sifted

2 Tbsp hot water

1 Tbsp instant espresso powder

Topping

4 oz semi-sweet chocolate, finely chopped

2 Tbsp unsalted butter, softened

1 Tbsp instant espresso powder

1. Line the base and sides of an 8-inch square baking pan with parchment paper, leaving an overhang of paper on two facing sides. (This will help you remove the bars from the pan.) Set aside.

2. For the base, combine the egg, butter, cocoa, sugar and espresso powder in a medium saucepan. Cook, whisking often, over low heat until the mixture is smooth and starts to thicken, about 5 minutes. Do not let the mixture boil.

3. Remove the saucepan from the heat. Add the graham cracker crumbs, coconut and almonds. Stir well until all the ingredients are combined.

4. Press the crumb mixture evenly over the base of the prepared pan. Chill in the freezer until the base is firm, about 15 minutes.

5. For the filling, cream the butter with 1 cup of the icing sugar in a medium bowl until well blended.

6. In a small bowl, dissolve the espresso powder in the hot water. Add the espresso mixture to the icing-sugar mixture, stirring until well combined. Add the remaining icing sugar and stir until the mixture is smooth and creamy.

7. Spread the filling evenly over the base. Chill in the freezer until the filling is firm, about 30 minutes.

8. For the topping, combine the chocolate, butter and espresso powder in a small saucepan. Cook over low heat, stirring often, until melted and smooth.

9. Pour the topping over the filling, spreading evenly with an offset spatula or a knife. Chill in the freezer until the topping is firm, about 15 minutes.

10. Using the parchment paper overhang, lift the bars from the pan to a cutting board. Cut into 24 bars with a sharp knife. For cleaner slices, run the knife under hot water after each cut. (The bars can be refrigerated in an airtight container for up to 5 days.)

Caramel Corn-on-the-Cob Cereal Squares

An interesting combo of sweet and spicy makes these easy no-bake squares a big hit. Cayenne will give them a kick of heat, but you can use the chili powder option if you prefer a milder flavour. You can use Homemade Condensed Milk (page 63) or store-bought condensed milk in these.

Makes 16 squares
Prep time: 15 minutes
Cooking time: about 10 minutes
Cooling time: about 40 minutes

2 cups salted toasted corn kernels

10 cups sweet popped corn cereal (one 11 oz/320 g pkg)

¼ cup unsalted butter, softened

⅔ cup golden corn syrup

½ cup sweetened condensed milk

⅓ cup golden yellow sugar

¼ cup granulated sugar

1 tsp fine sea salt

¼ tsp cayenne or chili powder (see sidebar)

2 Tbsp finely grated lime zest (about 4 limes)

2 Tbsp freshly squeezed lime juice (about 1 lime)

2 tsp vanilla extract

Additional finely grated lime zest for garnish

CHANGE IT UP

Replace the cayenne or chili powder with ground cinnamon or freshly grated nutmeg. Or, replace the toasted corn kernels with salted peanuts.

1. Grease an 8-inch square baking pan. Line the base and sides of the pan with parchment paper, leaving an overhang of paper on two facing sides. (This will help you remove the squares from the pan.)

2. In a food processor fitted with the steel blade, pulse the corn kernels several times until they're coarsely chopped and no whole kernels remain.

3. Lightly grease a large bowl. Place the corn kernels and the corn cereal in the bowl. Toss to combine. Set aside.

4. In a medium saucepan, melt the butter over medium heat. Continue to cook, stirring occasionally to scrape the milk solids from the bottom of the saucepan, until the butter is fragrant, nutty and golden brown. Do not let the butter burn.

5. Add the corn syrup, condensed milk, both sugars, the salt and cayenne to the butter. Bring to a boil, stirring constantly, until the mixture thickens and is nutty brown, about 5 minutes.

6. Remove from the heat. Carefully (the mixture may spatter) stir in the lime zest and juice and the vanilla extract.

7. Pour the butter mixture over the cereal mixture and quickly stir to combine. Immediately scrape the cereal mixture into the prepared pan, pressing down gently but evenly with a greased spatula.

8. Sprinkle with additional lime zest. Let cool completely, about 40 minutes.

9. Using the parchment paper overhang, lift the squares from the pan to a cutting board. With a serrated knife, cut it into 16 squares. (The squares can be stored in an airtight container at room temperature for up to 1 week.)

No-Bake Fig and Coconut Bars

Pretty as a picture, these bite-size bars make an ideal dessert for a cocktail party. They require no cooking, can be prepped in advance and will delight all your guests—especially those who prefer to be gluten-free.

Makes 18 bars
Prep time: 20 minutes
Soaking time: overnight
Freezing time: 2 ½ hours

Vanilla-Coconut Cashew Cream

1 cup unsalted cashews

1 cup unsweetened coconut milk

2 Tbsp instant-dissolving sugar

1 tsp vanilla extract or 2 vanilla beans

½ cup unsweetened shredded coconut

Walnut-Fig Base

1 cup granulated sugar

1 cup walnut halves

1 cup dried whole figs

½ cup almonds

¼ cup unsweetened shredded coconut

¼ cup flax seeds

2 Tbsp water

1 tsp ground cinnamon

Sliced fresh figs for garnish

1. For the vanilla-coconut cashew cream, put the cashews in a medium bowl and add enough cold water to cover them. Let soak overnight.

2. Line the base and sides of an 8-inch square baking pan with plastic wrap, leaving an overhang of plastic wrap on two facing sides. (This will help you remove the bars from the pan.) Set aside.

3. For the walnut-fig base, combine the sugar, walnut halves, dried figs, almonds, coconut, flax seeds, water and cinnamon in a food processor fitted with the steel blade. Process until the ingredients are well combined and the mixture sticks together when pressed between your fingertips.

4. Scrape the fig mixture into the prepared pan. Using a spatula, press the mixture into the pan until it's completely flat and even.

5. Put the pan in the freezer for at least 30 minutes while you continue making the cashew cream.

6. Drain the cashews. In the same food processor bowl (no need to wash it first), process the cashews until they form a thick paste.

7. With the food processor running, slowly add the coconut milk, sugar and vanilla extract. (If using vanilla beans, split them in half lengthwise and scrape the seeds out into the food processor. Discard the pods.)

8. Process until the mixture is very smooth and creamy, scraping down the sides of the processor once or twice. Add the shredded coconut and pulse to combine.

9. Pour the cashew cream layer over the fig base. Return the pan to the freezer until the cashew cream is firm, about 2 hours. The bars can be covered tightly with plastic wrap and frozen for up to 1 week.

10. Fifteen minutes before serving, remove the pan from the freezer and let stand at room temperature.

11. Arrange sliced fresh figs over the top of the cashew cream. Using the plastic wrap overhang, remove the bars from the pan to a cutting board. Cut into 18 bars.

BAKING DAY SECRETS

For a clean cut when slicing into bars, dip your knife in hot water and wipe with a clean cloth between each cut.

Chocolate-Chip Cheesecake Brownies

W ith a decadent swirl of cheesecake running through them, these brownies are as beautiful as they are tasty.

Makes 16 brownies
Prep time: 20 minutes
Cooking time: about 40 minutes

Cheesecake

1 pkg (8 oz/250 g) brick-style cream cheese, at room temperature

¼ cup granulated sugar

1 large egg

½ cup semi-sweet chocolate chips

Brownies

¼ cup unsalted butter, softened

1 cup semi-sweet chocolate chips

½ cup granulated sugar

2 large eggs

⅔ cup all-purpose flour

½ tsp baking powder

¼ tsp fine sea salt

1. Preheat the oven to 350°F. Line the base and sides of a 9-inch square baking pan with parchment paper, leaving an overhang of paper on two facing sides. (This will help you remove the brownies from the pan.) Set aside.

2. For the cheesecake, in a large bowl and using an electric mixer, beat the cream cheese on medium speed until smooth. Add the sugar and beat until smooth. Add the egg and beat just until combined. Stir in the chocolate chips. Set aside.

3. For the brownies, melt the butter in a small saucepan over medium heat. Remove the saucepan from the heat and add the chocolate chips. Stir until the chocolate chips are completely melted.

4. Scrape the chocolate mixture into a medium bowl. Whisk in the sugar and eggs until the mixture is smooth and glossy.

5. In a separate bowl, whisk together the flour, baking powder and salt. Stir the flour mixture into the brownie mixture until the batter is smooth and free of lumps.

6. Pour half of the brownie mixture into the prepared pan. Spread the cheesecake mixture evenly over the batter in the pan.

7. Dollop the remaining brownie mixture over the cheesecake mixture. Glide a butter knife through both mixtures to swirl them together.

8. Bake until a toothpick inserted in the centre comes out clean, 35 to 40 minutes. Let cool completely in the pan on a wire rack.

9. Using the parchment paper overhang, lift the brownies from the pan to a cutting board. Cut into 16 pieces. (The brownies can be refrigerated in an airtight container for up to 4 days.)

Double Chocolate Brownies

When a chocolate craving strikes, fight back with these rich brownies. They're easy to whip up, and the addition of espresso powder helps to kick the chocolate flavour up a notch. What's not to love?

Makes 16 brownies
Prep time: 20 minutes
Cooking time: about 35 minutes

¾ cup all-purpose flour

1 Tbsp unsweetened cocoa powder

¼ tsp fine sea salt

½ cup unsalted butter, softened

1 tsp instant espresso powder

5 oz semi-sweet chocolate, finely chopped

¾ cup granulated sugar

¼ cup lightly packed golden yellow sugar

3 large eggs

1 tsp vanilla extract

¾ cup semi-sweet chocolate chips

1. Preheat the oven to 350°F. Line the base and sides of an 8-inch square baking pan with parchment paper, leaving an overhang of paper on two facing sides. (This will help you remove the brownies from the pan.) Set aside.

2. In a medium bowl, whisk together the flour, cocoa powder and salt. Set aside.

3. In a large saucepan, combine the butter and espresso powder. Cook, stirring, over low heat until the butter has melted.

4. Add the chopped chocolate. Cook over low heat, stirring constantly, until the chocolate has melted and the mixture is smooth.

5. Remove the saucepan from the heat and stir in both sugars until well combined. Let cool slightly.

6. In a large bowl, whisk together the eggs and vanilla extract.

Gradually add the chocolate mixture, a little at a time, whisking well after each addition.

7. Once all of the chocolate mixture has been incorporated, stir in the flour mixture just until combined. Fold in the chocolate chips.

8. Scrape the batter into the prepared pan, smoothing the top with a silicone or offset spatula. Bake until a toothpick inserted in the centre comes out with just a few moist crumbs attached, 25 to 30 minutes. Be careful not to overbake. Let the brownies cool completely in the pan on a wire rack.

9. Using the parchment paper overhang, lift the brownies from the pan to a cutting board. Cut into 16 pieces. (The brownies can be stored in an airtight container, at room temperature or in the fridge, for up to 4 days.)

Walnut-Almond Baklava

This baklava is the real deal. Once you find out how easy it is to make, store-bought baklava just won't cut it. Our version features walnuts and almonds in the filling but feel free to substitute pistachios—the traditional nuts for baklava—or change it up with cashews or pecans.

Makes 20 pieces
Prep time: 1 hour
Cooking time: about 1 hour
Chilling time 10 minutes
Setting time: at least 6 hours

Syrup

1 cup granulated sugar

½ cup water

½ cup liquid honey

Finely grated zest and squeezed juice of 1 lemon

Finely grated zest and squeezed juice of 1 orange

6 whole cloves

2 cinnamon sticks (each 3 inches)

¼ tsp fine sea salt

Baklava

2 ½ cups walnut pieces

2 cups slivered almonds

½ cup granulated sugar

1 Tbsp ground cinnamon

½ cup unsalted butter, melted

1 pkg (1 lb/454 g) frozen phyllo pastry, thawed

1. For the syrup, combine the sugar, water, honey, lemon and orange zest and juice, cloves, cinnamon sticks and salt in a medium saucepan. Bring to a boil over medium heat. Simmer, uncovered, for 10 minutes. Remove from the heat and set aside.

2. For the baklava, pulse the walnuts in a food processor fitted with the steel blade until coarsely chopped. Add the almonds, sugar and cinnamon. Pulse about five times—the nuts should be finely chopped but not ground to a powder.

3. Tip the nut mixture (this is the filling) into a medium bowl. Measure ¼ cup of it into a small bowl to use for the topping. Set aside.

4. Brush a 13- x 9-inch baking dish or baking pan with some of the butter. Unroll the phyllo pastry on a large work surface with one short end facing you. Cut the stack of pastry in half parallel to the edge of the work surface.

5. Lay one sheet of phyllo over the base of the prepared dish and brush lightly with some of the melted butter. Repeat with seven more sheets of phyllo pastry, brushing each sheet with butter and keeping the remaining phyllo covered with a clean, lightly dampened cloth.

6. Spread half of the nut filling evenly over the top sheet of phyllo. Top the nut filling with six more sheets of phyllo, brushing each sheet with butter before you add it on top.

7. Sprinkle the top sheet of phyllo with butter and the remaining nut filling. Top the nut filling with eight more sheets of phyllo, brushing each sheet with butter.

8. Press down gently on the top of the baklava to compress the layers. Refrigerate the baklava for 10 minutes.

9. When ready to bake, preheat the oven to 350°F.

10. Remove the baklava from the fridge and, leaving it in its dish and using a sharp knife, cut it into 20 diamond shapes or rectangles.

11. Bake the baklava for 40 minutes. Sprinkle with the reserved ¼ cup of nut mixture. Bake until crispy and golden brown, about 10 minutes.

11. Meanwhile, reheat the syrup over low heat until warm but not hot. Strain the syrup through a fine mesh sieve, discarding the flavourings.

12. Carefully pour the warm syrup over the baked baklava. Let the baklava set at room temperature overnight (or for at least 6 hours) before serving.

13. Serve the baklava at room temperature or warmed in the oven. (The baklava can be stored in an airtight container at room temperature for up to 1 week.)

CANNELÉS 101

- A local beekeeper should be able to supply you with food-grade beeswax, or check out your nearest farmers' market.

- If you can't find beeswax, use a thick coat of softened unsalted butter to grease the moulds. However, the flavour of the finished cannelés won't be as authentic and the outsides won't be as crisp.

- If the cannelés puff up too much while baking at 375°F, remove the moulds from the oven and let stand until the cannelés deflate, then immediately return them to the oven.

- If using silicone cannelé moulds, cut the moulds along the gridlines to separate the moulds, making them easier to coat with beeswax.

- For chocolate cannelés, simply add a couple of chocolate chips to each filled cannelé mould before baking.

Cannelés de Bordeaux

Cannelés are traditional French pastries shaped like miniature Bundt cakes. They're known for their crispy, caramelized outsides and soft, custardy interiors. And did we mention they're also *très délicieux*?

Makes 20 cannelés
Prep time: 1 hour
Chilling time: 48 hours
Cooking time: 1 hour

Cannelés

2 cups whole milk

3 ½ Tbsp unsalted butter, softened

1 vanilla bean

¾ cup all-purpose flour

2 cups icing sugar, sifted

1 tsp fine sea salt

2 large eggs

2 large egg yolks

¼ cup dark rum

For Greasing

1 ½ oz food-grade beeswax (see sidebar)

3 Tbsp unsalted butter, softened

1. In a medium saucepan, combine the milk and butter. Using a sharp knife, split the vanilla bean in half lengthwise. Scrape the seeds out into the milk, then drop in the pod.

2. Heat the milk over medium heat until it reaches 180°F to 185°F on a candy thermometer, about 5 minutes.

3. Remove the saucepan from the heat. Place the vanilla bean pod in a large bowl and set aside.

4. Let the milk cool until it reaches 120°F on the thermometer (cool enough that you can leave your finger in the milk for a few seconds).

5. Meanwhile, sift the flour, sugar and salt into a medium bowl.

6. In a small bowl and using a fork, gently combine the eggs and egg yolks. Do not use a whisk. For best results, the batter must contain no air pockets.

7. Pour the eggs into the flour mixture and mix gently to combine until a lumpy batter forms.

8. Pour the cooled milk into the flour mixture and stir gently to combine.

9. Pour the batter through a fine mesh sieve into the bowl with the vanilla bean pod. Stir in the rum. Cover the bowl tightly and refrigerate for 48 hours.

10. For greasing the cannelé moulds, melt the beeswax and butter in a small saucepan over low heat just until the mixture melts and is transparent. Do not boil. Strain through a fine mesh sieve into a small bowl. (This will remove the milk solids and any imperfections in the wax which may burn during baking.)

11. Let the melted wax mixture cool slightly. Ensuring the moulds are clean and dry, brush the insides of 20 cannelé moulds thoroughly with the wax mixture. Place the coated moulds in the freezer until needed.

12. When ready to bake, preheat the oven to 500°F. Set a wire rack in a large shallow roasting pan.

13. Discard the vanilla bean pod. The batter will have separated a little, so stir it gently just before baking.

14. Remove the moulds from the freezer and fill each one with batter to within ½ inch of the top. Place the moulds, 2 inches apart, on the wire rack in the roasting pan.

15. Turn down the oven temperature to 450°F. Put the roasting pan in the oven and bake for 15 minutes.

16. Rotate the roasting pan through 180 degrees and turn down the oven temperature to 375°F. Bake for 45 minutes, rotating the roasting pan through 180 degrees every 15 minutes.

17. Remove the cannelés from the oven. Gently tap all around each mould with tongs or a wooden spoon to loosen the cannelés. Unmould the hot cannelés onto a wire rack to cool. Eat within 2 hours of baking.

TOOL KIT

To prepare cannelés, you'll need special moulds—traditional copper moulds and nonstick silicone versions are both available online—as well as food-grade beeswax (see sidebar for more information).

Vegan Black Bean Brownies

N o one will ever guess that these rich-tasting, gooey brownies are made with beans. And they're vegan and gluten-free, so you can share them with all your friends no matter what their dietary needs are.

Makes 16 brownies
Prep time: 15 minutes
Cooking time: 20 to 25 minutes

½ cup quick or large-flake rolled oats (see sidebar)

1 ¾ cups drained and rinsed canned black beans

½ cup golden yellow sugar

¼ cup vegetable or coconut oil

3 Tbsp unsweetened cocoa powder

2 Tbsp strong black coffee

2 tsp vanilla extract

½ tsp baking powder

½ tsp fine sea salt

2/3 cup vegan chocolate chips (see sidebar)

1. Preheat the oven to 350°F. Line the base and sides of an 8-inch square baking pan with parchment paper, leaving an overhang of paper on two facing sides. (This will help you remove the brownies from the pan.) Brush the parchment paper with a little oil. Set aside.

2. In a food processor fitted with the steel blade, process the oats until finely ground. Tip the oats into a medium bowl and set aside.

3. Place the beans in the food processor (there's no need to clean the bowl). Process until smooth, scraping down the sides of the processor once or twice. Add the sugar and oil. Process until well blended.

4. Scrape the bean mixture into the bowl containing the processed oats. Add the cocoa, coffee, vanilla extract, baking powder and salt. Stir until well combined. Stir in the chocolate chips.

5. Scrape the batter into the prepared pan and smooth the surface with a spatula.

6. Bake until the centre of the brownies is set, 20 to 25 minutes. Let cool completely in the pan on a wire rack.

7. Using the parchment paper overhang, remove the brownies from the pan to a cutting board. Cut into 16 pieces. (The brownies can be refrigerated in an airtight container for up to 1 week.)

BAKING DAY SECRETS

- For gluten-free brownies, be sure the oats you use are labelled gluten-free.
- For vegan brownies, check that the chocolate chips don't contain any dairy products.

MUFFINS & BREAKFAST TREATS

Apple Streusel Muffins

These muffins, packed with apple chunks and finished with a crunchy cinnamon streusel topping, are the perfect way to start a crisp fall day. Use your favourite apple for these—any variety will work.

Makes 12 muffins
Prep time: 15 minutes
Cooking time: about 20 minutes

Muffins

2 cups all-purpose flour

2 tsp pumpkin pie spice

1 tsp baking powder

½ tsp baking soda

½ tsp fine sea salt

½ cup unsalted butter, softened

1 cup granulated sugar

2 large eggs

1 tsp vanilla extract

2 large apples, peeled, cored and chopped

Streusel Topping

⅓ cup firmly packed dark brown sugar

1 Tbsp all-purpose flour

¼ tsp ground cinnamon

1 Tbsp unsalted butter, cut into small pieces

1. Preheat the oven to 375°F. Line a muffin pan with 12 large paper liners, then set aside.

2. For the muffins, whisk together the flour, pumpkin pie spice, baking powder, baking soda and salt in a medium bowl. Set aside.

3. In a large bowl and using an electric mixer, beat the butter with the sugar, eggs and vanilla extract until smooth. Stir in the apples until well combined.

4. Add the flour mixture to the sugar mixture, stirring just until combined and the dry ingredients are moistened. Do not overmix.

5. Fill the paper liners about three-quarters full with batter.

6. For the streusel topping, stir together the dark brown sugar, flour and cinnamon in a small bowl.

7. Add the butter and, using your fingers, rub it into the sugar mixture until the mixture resembles coarse crumbs.

8. Sprinkle the streusel topping evenly over the muffins. Bake until a wooden skewer inserted in the centre of a muffin comes out clean, about 20 minutes.

9. Let the muffins cool in the pan for 5 minutes, then remove to a wire rack and let cool to room temperature. (The muffins are best served the day they're baked, but can be stored in an airtight container at room temperature for up to 4 days, or frozen for up to 2 months. Thaw and reheat frozen muffins before serving.)

BAKING DAY SECRETS

The streusel topping can be sprinkled on just about any muffin. Or, spread it out on a small baking sheet and bake in a 350°F oven, stirring once or twice, until golden and fragrant, 10 to 15 minutes, then sprinkle it over ice cream or yogurt to add a touch of crunch.

Chocolate Chip–Banana Muffins

Chocolate and bananas are a classic pairing that we absolutely love. Watch as these muffins get gobbled up!

Makes 12 muffins
Prep time: 15 minutes
Cooking time: 25 to 30 minutes

1 ½ cups all-purpose flour

1 ½ tsp baking powder

¼ tsp fine sea salt

⅔ cup granulated sugar

½ cup unsalted butter, melted

2 large or 3 small ripe bananas,
    peeled and mashed

¼ cup whole milk

1 large egg

1 tsp vanilla extract

1 cup semi-sweet chocolate chips

Additional semi-sweet chocolate
    chips for sprinkling

1. Preheat the oven to 350°F. Line a muffin pan with 12 large paper liners, then set aside.

2. In a medium bowl, whisk together the flour, baking powder and salt. Set aside.

3. In a large bowl and using an electric mixer, beat together the sugar and butter until well combined.

4. Beat in the mashed bananas, milk, egg and vanilla extract.

5. Add the flour mixture to the banana mixture, stirring just until combined and the dry ingredients are moistened. Stir in the 1 cup of chocolate chips. Do not overmix.

6. Fill the paper liners at least three-quarters full with batter. Sprinkle additional chocolate chips over top.

7. Bake until a wooden skewer inserted in the centre of a muffin comes out clean, 25 to 30 minutes.

8. Let the muffins cool in the pans for 5 minutes, then remove to a wire rack and let cool to room temperature. (The muffins are best served the day they're baked, but can be stored in an airtight container at room temperature for up to 4 days, or frozen for up to 2 months. Thaw and reheat frozen muffins before serving.)

Our Favourite Bran Muffins

Everybody needs a good bran muffin recipe—this is our favourite. It's easy to prepare, and you can switch up the recipe to suit your tastes. Not a fan of raisins? Add fresh blueberries or dried cranberries instead.

Makes 12 muffins
Prep time: 15 minutes
Soaking time: 10 minutes
Cooking time: about 20 minutes

1 ½ cups wheat bran

1 cup buttermilk (see page 11)

²⁄₃ cup firmly packed dark brown sugar

¹⁄₃ cup vegetable oil

1 large egg

½ tsp vanilla extract

1 cup whole wheat flour

1 tsp baking powder

1 tsp baking soda

½ tsp fine sea salt

½ cup raisins

1. Preheat the oven to 375°F. Line a muffin pan with 12 large paper liners, then set aside.

2. In a large bowl, stir together the wheat bran and buttermilk. Let them soak at room temperature for 10 minutes.

3. In a medium bowl, whisk together the sugar, oil, egg and vanilla extract until well combined.

4. Add the sugar mixture to the bran mixture, stirring until well combined.

5. In a separate medium bowl, whisk together the whole wheat flour, baking powder, baking soda and salt.

6. Add the flour mixture to the bran mixture, stirring just until combined and the dry ingredients are moistened. Stir in the raisins until evenly distributed. Do not overmix.

7. Fill the paper liners at least three-quarters full with batter. Bake until a wooden skewer inserted in the centre of a muffin comes out clean, about 20 minutes.

8. Let the muffins cool in the pans for 5 minutes, then remove to a wire rack and let cool to room temperature. (The muffins are best served the day they're baked, but can be stored in an airtight container at room temperature for up to 4 days, or frozen for up to 2 months. Thaw and reheat frozen muffins before serving.)

BAKING DAY SECRETS

If your raisins seem too dry, soften and plump them by soaking them in hot water for 10 minutes. Drain well before adding to the muffin batter.

CHANGE IT UP

- Add ½ cup chopped, toasted walnuts or almonds to the muffin batter along with the raisins.

- Replace the raisins with ½ cup fresh blueberries or raspberries, tossing the fresh fruit with a little of the flour mixture to coat them before adding to the batter.

- Replace the wheat bran with oat bran.

- Bump up the omega-3s by adding 2 tablespoonfuls of flax or chia seeds along with the raisins.

- Replace the whole wheat flour with whole-grain spelt flour.

Lemon-Blueberry Poppy Seed Muffins

Classic lemon–poppy seed muffins get a punch of flavour from sweet, juicy blueberries. Use fresh blueberries in season, or frozen ones during the rest of the year to bring a taste of summer sunshine to your breakfast table.

Makes 12 muffins
Prep time: 15 minutes
Cooking time: 25 to 30 minutes

2 cups all-purpose flour

½ tsp baking soda

½ tsp fine sea salt

½ cup unsalted butter, softened

1 cup lightly packed golden yellow sugar

2 large eggs

Finely grated zest of 1 lemon

²/₃ cup sour cream (14%)

1 ½ cups fresh or frozen blueberries

¼ cup poppy seeds

1. Preheat the oven to 350°F. Line a muffin pan with 12 large paper liners, then set aside.

2. In a medium bowl, whisk together the flour, baking soda and salt. Set aside.

3. In a large bowl and using an electric mixer, beat the butter with the sugar until pale and fluffy.

4. Beat in the eggs one at a time, beating well after each addition. Beat in the lemon zest until well combined.

5. Add the sour cream, then beat briefly just until combined.

6. If using frozen blueberries, add them to the flour mixture and toss gently. If using fresh blueberries, add them to the flour mixture and fold in until evenly distributed. Add the flour mixture to the sugar mixture, stirring just until combined. Do not overmix.

7. Fill the paper liners at least three-quarters full with batter. Sprinkle the muffins evenly with poppy seeds.

8. Bake until a wooden skewer inserted in the centre of a muffin comes out clean, 25 to 30 minutes.

9. Let the muffins cool in the pans for 5 minutes, then remove to a wire rack and let cool to room temperature. (The muffins are best served the day they're baked, but can be stored in an airtight container at room temperature for up to 4 days, or frozen for up to 2 months. Thaw and reheat frozen muffins before serving.)

Morning Glory Muffins

We love these spiced muffins because they're packed with fresh and dried fruit. Change them up as you wish. You can substitute toasted chopped pecans, walnuts, hazelnuts or almonds for the coconut, and your favourite dried fruit in place of the apricots and/or cherries, and even omit the crystallized ginger if you're not a fan.

Makes 15 muffins
Prep time: 15 minutes
Cooking time: 25 to 30 minutes

1 cup all-purpose flour

¾ cup whole wheat flour

½ cup firmly packed dark brown sugar

⅓ cup granulated sugar

2 tsp baking powder

1 ½ tsp ground cinnamon

1 tsp ground ginger

½ tsp fine sea salt

¼ tsp baking soda

¼ tsp freshly grated nutmeg

½ cup dried apricots, finely chopped

⅓ cup dried cherries, finely chopped

⅓ cup sweetened flaked or unsweetened shredded coconut

¼ cup crystallized ginger, finely chopped

1 ½ cups grated carrots (about 2 medium)

1 firm Bosc or Bartlett pear, peeled, cored and grated

⅔ cup unsweetened applesauce

⅓ cup vegetable oil

2 large eggs

1 Tbsp finely grated orange zest

3 Tbsp freshly squeezed orange juice (about 1 medium orange)

1 Tbsp liquid honey

2 ½ tsp vanilla extract

1. Preheat the oven to 375°F. Line two muffin pans with 15 large paper liners, then set aside. Add some water to the empty wells to avoid burning.

2. In a large bowl, whisk together both flours, both sugars, the baking powder, cinnamon, ground ginger, salt, baking soda and nutmeg.

3. Add the apricots, cherries, coconut and crystallized ginger to the flour mixture and toss well.

4. Add the grated carrots and pear to the flour mixture and toss well. Set aside.

5. In a medium bowl, whisk together the applesauce, oil, eggs, orange zest and juice, honey and vanilla extract.

6. Make a well in the flour mixture. Pour the applesauce mixture into the well. Stir just until the dry ingredients are moistened. Do not overmix.

7. Fill the paper liners at least three-quarters full with batter. Bake until a wooden skewer inserted in the centre of a muffin comes out clean, 25 to 30 minutes.

8. Let the muffins cool in the pans for 5 minutes, then remove to a wire rack and let cool to room temperature. (The muffins are best served the day they're baked but can be stored in an airtight container at room temperature for up to 4 days, or frozen for up to 2 months. Thaw and reheat frozen muffins before serving.)

CHANGE IT UP

No vegetable oil in the cupboard? Substitute a mild-flavoured olive oil or melted coconut oil.

Brownie Belgian Waffles

Belgian waffles first became popular at the 1964 New York World's Fair. But they were called "Bel-Gem Waffles" at the fair because Americans were unfamiliar with where the waffles originated. Now, of course, they're a North American breakfast staple. This brownie-inspired version is a decadent twist on the classic recipe.

Makes 4 servings

Prep time: 15 minutes

Cooking time: about 3 minutes per batch

1 ¾ cups all-purpose flour

3 Tbsp granulated sugar

3 Tbsp unsweetened cocoa powder

2 tsp baking powder

1 tsp baking soda

1 tsp fine sea salt

1 ¾ cups buttermilk (see page 11)

2 large eggs

¼ cup unsalted butter, melted

2 tsp vanilla extract

Icing sugar for dusting

1. Preheat the oven to 170°F. Preheat an 8-inch waffle iron according to the manufacturer's instructions.

2. In a medium bowl, whisk together the flour, sugar, cocoa powder, baking powder, baking soda and salt. Set aside.

3. In a second medium bowl, whisk together the buttermilk, eggs, butter and vanilla extract.

4. Add the flour mixture to the buttermilk mixture, then stir together just until combined. Do not overmix.

5. Using about ⅓ cup of the batter for each waffle and following the manufacturer's instructions, cook the waffles in the waffle iron. Cook until the waffle iron stops steaming, about 3 minutes.

6. Transfer the waffles to a large plate as each batch cooks. Keep the waffles warm in the oven while you cook the remaining batter. Dust with icing sugar before serving. Or try them with fresh berries or strawberry jam and dollops of whipped cream.

SWEET HISTORY

Throughout the Middle Ages and the Renaissance, sugar was so expensive that only the very wealthy could buy and consume it.

German Pancake with Spiced Apple Compote

This German-style pancake, also known as a Dutch baby pancake, resembles a thick crêpe but is much easier to prep than its lacy cousin. We like it topped with a spiced apple compote, but it's equally yummy with fresh berries scattered on top.

Makes 4 servings
Prep time: 20 minutes
Cooking time: 30 to 40 minutes

Spiced Apple Compote

¼ cup unsalted butter, softened

4 Golden Delicious apples, peeled, cored and each cut into 8 wedges

¼ cup granulated sugar

1 tsp ground cinnamon

Pinch of freshly grated nutmeg

Pancake

¾ cup all-purpose flour

¼ cup granulated sugar

Pinch of fine sea salt

¾ cup whole milk

3 large eggs

1 tsp vanilla extract

1 Tbsp unsalted butter, softened

¼ cup icing sugar or cinnamon sugar

1. For the spiced apple compote, melt the butter in a large skillet over medium heat.

2. Stir in the apples, sugar, cinnamon and nutmeg. Cook, stirring occasionally, until the apples are tender, about 10 minutes. (The spiced apple compote can be refrigerated in an airtight container for up to 4 days. Serve at room temperature or warm it slightly before eating.)

3. Preheat the oven to 425°F.

4. For the pancake, whisk together the flour, sugar and salt in a medium bowl.

5. Whisk in the milk until smooth. Whisk in the eggs one at a time, whisking well after each addition. Whisk in the vanilla extract.

6. Put the butter in a 12-inch ovenproof skillet (cast iron works well). Put the skillet in the oven until the butter melts, about 3 minutes.

7. Remove the skillet from the oven and use a pastry brush to brush the butter around the base and up the sides of the skillet.

8. Pour the batter into the skillet. Return the skillet to the oven and bake until golden brown and puffy, 15 to 20 minutes.

9. Top the pancake with the spiced apple compote, then dust with icing sugar. Cut into wedges and serve immediately.

CHANGE IT UP

If you prefer, you can make individual pancakes by baking the batter in four 6-inch skillets. Divide the butter among the skillets, then melt in the oven for 1 to 2 minutes. Divide the batter among the skillets, then bake for 10 to 12 minutes.

BAKING DAY SECRETS

To speed up prep time, put all the pancake ingredients in a food processor fitted with the steel blade or a blender, then pulse just until well combined and smooth. Do not overmix.

Lemon-Cranberry Scones

The crunch of pecans adds texture to these classic scones. A fantastic breakfast treat, they're also ideal for afternoon tea. Serve the scones warm with plenty of butter and your favourite jams, preserves or curds.

Makes 12 scones
Prep time: 15 minutes
Cooking time: 20 minutes

Lemon Topping

2 Tbsp icing sugar

1 Tbsp freshly squeezed lemon juice

Scones

3 cups all-purpose flour

1 cup granulated sugar

1 Tbsp baking powder

1 Tbsp finely grated lemon zest (1 to 2 lemons)

1 tsp fine sea salt

¾ cup cold unsalted butter, cut into small pieces

1 cup dried cranberries

½ cup coarsely chopped pecans (optional)

½ cup cold half-and-half cream (10%), plus a little more if necessary

¼ cup turbinado sugar, for sprinkling

1. Preheat the oven to 375°F. Line a large baking sheet with parchment paper. Set aside.

2. For the lemon topping, whisk together the icing sugar and lemon juice in a small bowl until smooth. Set aside.

3. For the scones, whisk together the flour, sugar, baking powder, lemon zest and salt in a large bowl.

4. Add the butter to the flour mixture. Using a pastry cutter or your hands, work it in just until pea-size lumps of butter are still visible. Stir in the cranberries and pecans (if using).

5. Add ½ cup of the cream and toss the ingredients together with a fork until the dough comes together in moist clumps. Add a little more cream if the dough is dry.

6. Gather the dough into a ball and cut it in half. On a lightly floured work surface, gently pat out each piece to a 6-inch disc. Cut each disc into six wedges.

7. Transfer the scones to the prepared baking sheet. Brush the top of each scone with the lemon topping. Sprinkle the scones evenly with turbinado sugar.

8. Bake until golden brown and a wooden skewer inserted in the centre of a scone comes out clean, about 20 minutes. Remove the scones to a wire rack and let cool slightly. Serve warm. (The scones are best served the day they're made, but can be stored in an airtight container at room temperature for up to 3 days.)

BAKING DAY SECRETS

For the lightest, fluffiest scones, make sure all your ingredients and utensils are as cold as possible.

White Chocolate, Raspberry & Macadamia Scones

We used a round cutter for these decadent scones, but try cutting them with a heart-shaped cutter for a Valentine's Day or wedding anniversary breakfast.

Makes 12 scones
Prep time: 20 minutes
Cooking time: 25 to 30 minutes

2 cups all-purpose flour

2 Tbsp granulated sugar

1 Tbsp baking powder

½ tsp fine sea salt

6 Tbsp unsalted butter, cut into small pieces and softened

⅓ cup whipping cream (35%)

1 large egg

1 tsp vanilla extract

½ cup coarsely chopped macadamia nuts

½ cup white chocolate chips

½ cup fresh raspberries

Additional granulated sugar for sprinkling

1. Preheat the oven to 350°F. Line a large baking sheet with parchment paper. Set aside.

2. In a large bowl, whisk together the flour, sugar, baking powder and salt.

3. Add the butter to the flour mixture. Using a pastry cutter or your hands, work it in until the mixture resembles coarse meal.

4. In a small bowl, whisk together the cream, egg and vanilla extract.

5. Add the cream mixture to the flour mixture and toss the ingredients together with a fork until the dough comes together in moist clumps. Stir in the nuts, chocolate chips and raspberries.

6. On a lightly floured work surface, knead the dough gently just until it comes together. Gently pat out the dough to a disc about 1 inch thick.

7. Using a 2 ½-inch round cookie cutter, cut out scones, gently rerolling the trimmings once. Put the scones on the prepared baking sheet, then sprinkle with additional sugar.

8. Bake until the scones are a light golden brown, 25 to 30 minutes. Remove the scones to a wire rack and let cool slightly. Serve warm. (The scones are best served the day they're made, but can be stored in an airtight container at room temperature for up to 3 days.)

Maple Bacon Scones

Two classic Canadian flavours combine in these sweet-savoury scones. Serve them warm for brunch, or with an afternoon cup of tea or coffee.

Makes 12 scones
Prep time: 20 minutes
Cooking time: 12 to 14 minutes

Scones

3 ¼ cups all-purpose flour

⅓ cup firmly packed golden yellow sugar

2 ½ tsp baking powder

½ tsp ground cinnamon

½ tsp baking soda

½ tsp fine sea salt

¼ tsp freshly grated nutmeg

¾ cup cold, unsalted butter, cut into small pieces

1 cup buttermilk (see page 11)

1 tsp vanilla extract

5 slices Cinnamon Candied Bacon, crumbled (recipe follows)

1 Tbsp unsalted butter, melted

Maple Glaze

1 cup icing sugar, sifted

1 ½ Tbsp maple syrup

¼ tsp vanilla extract

1 Tbsp milk

Additional crumbled Cinnamon Candied Bacon

1. Preheat the oven to 425°F. Line a large baking sheet with parchment paper. Set aside.

2. For the scones, whisk together the flour, sugar, baking powder, cinnamon, baking soda, salt and nutmeg in a large bowl.

3. Add the cold butter to the flour mixture. Using a pastry cutter or your hands, work it in until the mixture resembles coarse meal.

4. In a small bowl, stir together the buttermilk and vanilla extract.

5. Add the buttermilk mixture to the flour mixture and toss the ingredients together with a fork until the dough comes together in moist clumps. Stir in the crumbled bacon.

6. On a lightly floured work surface, knead the dough gently just until it comes together. Gently pat out the dough to a disc about 1 ½ inches thick.

7. Using a 3-inch round cookie cutter, cut out scones, gently rerolling the trimmings once.

Put the scones on the prepared baking sheet. Brush the top of each scone with melted butter.

8. Bake until the scones are cracked on top and a light golden brown, 12 to 14 minutes. Remove the scones to a wire rack and let cool completely.

9. For the maple glaze, whisk together the icing sugar, maple syrup and vanilla extract in a medium bowl.

10. Whisk in the milk, a little at a time, until the glaze is a pourable consistency but not so thin that it rolls right off the scones.

11. Pour the glaze over the cooled scones. Sprinkle each scone with a little additional crumbled bacon. (The scones are best served the day they're made, but can be stored in an airtight container at room temperature for up to 3 days.)

Cinnamon Candied Bacon

Makes 8 slices
Prep time: 5 minutes
Cooking time: 30 to 45 minutes

3 Tbsp lightly packed golden yellow sugar

½ tsp ground cinnamon

8 slices bacon

1. Preheat the oven to 375°F. Line a rimmed baking tray with foil, then set a wire rack over it. Set aside.

2. On a large plate, stir together the sugar and cinnamon. Coat the bacon slices evenly and thoroughly with the sugar mixture.

3. Lay the bacon slices, in a single layer, on the wire rack. Bake until the bacon slices are browned and crisp, 30 to 45 minutes, flipping them halfway through cooking time.

4. Remove the bacon slices to a paper-towel-lined plate to drain. (The cinnamon candied bacon can be refrigerated in an airtight container for up to 5 days.)

Pancake Mix-in-a-Jar

This easy mix is the perfect gift for the pancake-lover in your life. It's also great to have on hand for when you want to whip up a quick batch of pancakes.

Makes about 3 cups pancake mix; enough for about twenty-four 4-inch pancakes
Prep time: 5 minutes
Cooking time: about 4 minutes per batch

2 ½ cups all-purpose flour

⅓ cup icing sugar, sifted

3 Tbsp baking powder

2 tsp baking soda

1 tsp fine sea salt

1. In a 4-cup Mason jar, layer all the ingredients in the order listed.

2. Seal the jar, then write the following instructions on a label and tie it around the jar:

- Pour this mix in a large mixing bowl. Whisk in 1 ¼ cups of milk, 3 eggs and 5 table-spoonfuls of melted butter.

- Heat a griddle or large skillet over medium heat.

- Drop the batter onto the griddle, using ¼ cup of the batter per pancake. Cook until bubbles appear on the surface of the pancakes, 1 to 2 minutes.

- Flip the pancakes, then cook for 1 to 2 minutes. Enjoy.

Peanut Butter–Banana Pancakes

These fluffy pancakes are bursting with the flavours of bananas and peanut butter. A stack of these drizzled in syrup is just what we crave on a lazy Saturday morning. We like these topped with extra bananas and peanut butter chips, but serve with your favourite pancakes fixings, if you prefer.

Makes about sixteen 4-inch pancakes
Prep time: 15 minutes
Cooking time: 4 to 5 minutes per batch

2 cups all-purpose flour

½ cup granulated sugar

1 Tbsp baking powder

1 tsp ground cinnamon

1 tsp fine sea salt

2 large eggs

1 ¼ cups whole milk

½ cup unsalted butter, melted then cooled slightly

1 tsp vanilla extract

2 bananas, peeled and sliced

2 Tbsp unsalted butter, softened, or vegetable oil for frying

⅓ cup peanut butter chips

Additional peeled, sliced bananas and peanut butter chips for garnish

Icing sugar for dusting

Maple syrup for serving

1. In a large bowl, whisk together the flour, sugar, baking powder, cinnamon and salt. Set aside.

2. In a medium bowl, beat the eggs. Whisk in the milk, melted butter and vanilla extract.

3. Add the milk mixture to the flour mixture, whisking until the batter is smooth. Stir in the banana slices.

4. Heat a griddle or large skillet over medium heat, then grease with a little of the butter or oil.

5. Drop the batter onto the griddle, using about ¼ cup of the batter for each pancake. Sprinkle a few peanut butter chips over each pancake. Cook until bubbles appear on the surface, 2 to 3 minutes.

6. Flip the pancakes, then cook until golden brown on the bottom, about 2 minutes.

7. Place the cooked pancakes on a baking sheet or plate lined with foil and cover with more foil to keep them warm while you cook the rest.

8. Top the pancakes with additional banana slices and peanut butter chips and a dusting of icing sugar. Serve drizzled with maple syrup.

CHANGE IT UP

Here are a few suggestions to make these pancakes your own:

- Instead of sliced bananas, add 1 cup fresh blueberries, raspberries or sliced strawberries to the batter.
- Use 1 cup whole wheat or whole-grain spelt flour in place of 1 cup of the all-purpose flour.
- Replace the peanut butter chips with semi-sweet chocolate chips or toasted, chopped walnuts.
- Replace half of the melted butter with applesauce.

Peach & Pecan French Toast

Could French toast get any more decadent? If you find cutting the pockets in the bread slices difficult, pop the bread slices in the freezer for 20 minutes first. The slightly frozen bread will slice more cleanly.

Makes 4 servings
Prep time: 30 minutes
Cooking time: about 6 minutes per batch

1 pkg (8 oz/250 g) brick-style cream cheese, at room temperature

¾ cup icing sugar, sifted

1 tsp freshly squeezed lemon juice

1 tsp vanilla extract

¼ tsp ground cinnamon

Pinch of fine sea salt

4 thick (1 ½-inch) slices cut from a large loaf of white bread

¼ cup chopped pecans

2 large fresh peaches, pitted and cut into ½-inch slices

4 large eggs

½ cup whole milk

2 Tbsp unsalted butter, softened, for frying

Icing sugar for dusting

1. In a medium bowl and using an electric mixer, beat together the cream cheese, icing sugar, lemon juice, vanilla extract, cinnamon and salt until smooth. Set aside.

2. Using a sharp, serrated knife, cut into one side of one slice of bread to create a pocket, being careful not to cut through the crust on the other three sides. Repeat with the remaining slices of bread.

3. Spread one-quarter of the cream cheese mixture in the pocket of each slice of bread. Divide the pecans among the pockets, distributing them evenly over the cream cheese mixture.

4. Divide the peach slices among the pockets. Press the bread slices gently to seal the pockets and prevent the filling from falling out.

5. Preheat the oven to 250°F. Put a rimmed baking sheet in the oven to warm.

6. In a large shallow dish, whisk together the eggs and milk.

7. Dip the stuffed bread slices into the egg mixture, letting each slice soak for about 30 seconds on each side.

8. In a large skillet, melt the butter over medium heat. Fry the French toast, in batches if necessary, until each slice is deep golden brown on both sides, about 3 minutes per side.

9. As each batch browns, transfer it to the oven to keep warm while you cook the remaining French toast. Dust with icing sugar and serve warm.

Tropical Granola

You can substitute any of your favourite dried fruit in this easy granola, but we love the tropical flavours of pineapple and banana. Serve this with Greek yogurt or milk.

Makes about 8 ½ cups
Prep time: 15 minutes
Cooking time: 35 to 40 minutes

2 ½ cups rolled oats

1 ½ cups whole almonds

1 cup unsweetened shredded coconut

1 cup whole unsalted cashews or macadamias

⅓ cup raw pumpkin seeds

½ cup firmly packed golden yellow sugar

⅓ cup coconut oil, melted

⅓ cup maple syrup

¼ cup pineapple juice or freshly squeezed orange juice

1 ½ tsp coconut extract

¾ tsp fine sea salt

½ tsp ground ginger

¾ cup dried pineapple, chopped

½ cup dried cranberries

½ cup dried banana chips, broken into pieces

¼ cup golden raisins

CHANGE IT UP

This granola recipe is very forgiving. No maple syrup in the fridge? Substitute liquid honey. Can't find coconut extract? Use vanilla extract.

1. Preheat the oven to 325°F. Line two large rimmed baking sheets with parchment paper. Set aside.

2. In a large bowl, combine the rolled oats, almonds, coconut, cashews and pumpkin seeds. Set aside.

3. In a medium bowl, whisk together the sugar, coconut oil, maple syrup, pineapple juice, coconut extract, salt and ginger.

4. Add the sugar mixture to the rolled oats mixture and toss well until thoroughly combined and the dry ingredients are moistened.

5. Divide the granola between the prepared baking sheets and spread it out evenly. Bake on two separate racks of the oven, stirring every 10 minutes (see sidebar) and rotating the baking sheets halfway through cooking time, until the granola is completely dry and golden brown, 35 to 40 minutes.

6. Let the granola cool to room temperature on the baking sheets.

7. In a large bowl, combine the pineapple, cranberries, banana chips and raisins. Add the warm granola, then toss well to combine. Let cool completely in the bowl. (The granola can be stored in an airtight container at room temperature for up to 1 month, or frozen for up to 6 months.)

BAKING DAY SECRETS

Before baking the granola, spread it out thinly on the baking sheet, then use a spatula to draw an X through it. Every time you stir the granola during baking, redraw the X. This will speed up the browning and drying process.

DIY Granola Bars

These are our favourite granola bars. They're easy to make and keep well. Best of all, you can dress them up with whatever add-ins you fancy (see sidebar).

Makes 16 bars
Prep time: 15 minutes
Cooking time: 30 to 40 minutes
Setting time: 30 to 45 minutes

1 ⅔ cups quick rolled oats

½ cup granulated sugar

⅓ cup oat flour (see sidebar)

½ tsp ground cinnamon (optional)

½ tsp fine sea salt

2 to 3 cups add-ins (see sidebar)

½ cup smooth peanut butter or almond butter

6 Tbsp unsalted butter, melted

¼ cup liquid honey

1 tsp vanilla extract

BAKING DAY SECRETS

Look for oat flour in your local bulk store. If you can't find it, pulse an equivalent amount of quick rolled oats in a food processor or blender until finely ground.

1. Preheat the oven to 350°F. Line the base and sides of an 8-inch square baking pan with parchment paper, leaving an overhang of paper on two facing sides. (This will help you remove the bars from the pan.) Set aside.

2. In a large bowl, whisk together the rolled oats, sugar, oat flour, cinnamon (if using) and salt. Stir in your choice of add-ins (we used raisins, pumpkin seeds, wheat bran, chocolate chips, almonds and pecans). Set aside.

3. In a medium bowl, whisk together the peanut butter, melted butter, honey and vanilla extract until smooth.

4. Add the peanut butter mixture to the rolled oat mixture, stirring until well combined.

5. Spoon the granola mixture into the prepared pan. Using the back of a spoon or a piece of plastic wrap, flatten the mixture and smooth the surface level.

6. Bake until brown around the edges, 30 to 40 minutes. The granola mixture will appear soft and not quite baked in the centre, but it will set once it has cooled.

7. Let the granola bars cool completely in the pan on a wire rack. Using the parchment paper overhang, lift the bars from the pan to a cutting board. Cut into 16 bars or squares. If the granola mixture is too crumbly to cut neatly, return the bars (with the parchment) to the pan and refrigerate for 30 minutes. (The granola bars can be stored in an airtight container, either with wax paper between the layers or individually wrapped in plastic wrap, at room temperature for up to 1 month, or frozen for up to 2 months.)

GRANOLA BAR ADD-INS

- Raisins, apricots, cranberries, cherries, blueberries and/or dates
- Chopped or whole almonds, walnuts, pecans, peanuts, macadamias and/or hazelnuts
- Sunflower, sesame, pumpkin, flax and/or chia seeds
- Unsweetened shredded or sweetened flaked coconut
- Wheat germ
- Wheat or oat bran
- Chocolate chips

Breakfast Fruit Pastries

Flaky, buttery and bursting with jam, these little hand-held pies taste way better than any you'll find in your grocery store. The pastries freeze well, so they're ideal to make ahead to reheat for a quick breakfast on the go.

Makes 9 pastries
Prep time: 30 minutes
Chilling time: at least 1 hour, 15 minutes
Cooking time: 20 to 25 minutes

Pastries

2 cups all-purpose flour

1 Tbsp granulated sugar

1 tsp fine sea salt

1 cup cold unsalted butter, cut into small pieces

2 large eggs

2 Tbsp milk

¾ cup jam (any flavour)

Glaze

¼ cup icing sugar, sifted

2 to 3 Tbsp whipping cream (35%)

Sprinkles (optional)

1. For the pastries, whisk together the flour, sugar and salt in a large bowl.

2. Add the butter to the flour mixture. Using a pastry cutter or your hands, work it in just until pea-size lumps of butter are still visible and the mixture holds together when you squeeze it in your hand.

3. In a small bowl, whisk together one of the eggs and the milk.

4. Add the egg mixture to the flour mixture, stirring just until combined. Use your hands to knead the dough just until it holds together.

5. Divide the dough in half. Shape each piece into a rectangle, then wrap each rectangle tightly in plastic wrap. Refrigerate for at least 1 hour, or up to 2 days. Remove the dough from the fridge 15 to 30 minutes before you roll it out.

6. Line a large baking sheet with parchment paper. Set aside.

7. On a lightly floured work surface, roll out one piece of dough to a rectangle about ⅛ inch thick. Trim the edges neatly. Cut the dough into nine even-sized rectangles. Place the rectangles on the prepared baking sheet. Set aside.

8. Repeat with the other piece of dough. Set aside.

9. In a small bowl, beat the remaining egg. Brush the pastry rectangles on the baking sheet all over with egg, reserving the remaining beaten egg.

10. Spoon a heaping tablespoonful of jam onto each egg-brushed rectangle. Top each with one of the reserved pastry rectangles. Use a fork to seal the edges, then make a pattern around the edge of each pastry with the tines of the fork.

11. Prick the top of each pastry with the fork so the steam can escape during baking. Chill, uncovered, in the fridge or freezer for about 15 minutes. While they chill, preheat the oven to 350°F.

12. Just before baking, brush the pastries with the remaining beaten egg. Bake until the pastries are light golden brown, 20 to 25 minutes. Remove from the baking sheet and let cool completely on wire racks.

13. For the glaze, whisk together the icing sugar and 1 tablespoonful of the cream, adding a little more cream until the glaze is a pourable consistency but not too thin.

14. Pour the glaze evenly over the cooled pastries. Scatter the tops with sprinkles (if using). (The pastries can be stored in an airtight container at room temperature for up to 3 days. Reheat in a 350°F oven for 8 to 10 minutes before serving. Or, freeze, without the glaze and sprinkles, for up to 2 months. Reheat the pastries, straight from the freezer, in a 375°F oven for 18 to 20 minutes. Let cool, then glaze and decorate as described above.)

CAKES
&
SHORTCAKES

Simple Chocolate Cake

This is the easiest chocolate cake ever. If you're looking for a simple yet tasty dessert, it's the recipe to turn to. And if you use coconut oil and vegan chocolate chips in the ganache, you can make the cake vegan-friendly too.

Makes one 13- x 9-inch cake; 18 to 24 servings
Prep time: 25 minutes
Cooking time: 35 to 40 minutes
Setting time: about 15 minutes

Cake

2 cups cold water

2/3 cup vegetable oil

2 Tbsp white vinegar or apple cider vinegar

1 Tbsp vanilla extract

3 cups all-purpose flour

2 cups granulated sugar

1/3 cup unsweetened cocoa powder

2 tsp baking soda

1 tsp fine sea salt

Quick Chocolate Ganache

1 cup semi-sweet chocolate chips or finely chopped dark chocolate

2 Tbsp coconut oil or unsalted butter, softened

½ cup white chocolate chips, melted (optional)

1. Preheat the oven to 350°F. Grease a 13- x 9-inch baking pan, then dust with cocoa powder. Set aside.

2. For the cake, stir together the water, oil, vinegar and vanilla extract in a medium bowl. Set aside.

3. In a large bowl, whisk together the flour, sugar, cocoa powder, baking soda and salt.

4. Make a well in the flour mixture. Pour the water mixture into the well. Stir until the batter is smooth and no lumps of flour remain. Scrape the batter into the prepared pan. Tap the pan lightly on the counter a couple of times to remove any air bubbles.

5. Bake until a wooden skewer inserted in the centre of the cake comes out clean, 35 to 40 minutes.

6. Let the cake cool in the pan on a wire rack for 5 to 10 minutes. Run a knife around the edge of the pan to loosen the cake. Turn the cake out onto the wire rack and let cool completely.

7. For the quick chocolate ganache, melt the chocolate and coconut oil in a small bowl set over a saucepan of hot, but not boiling, water. Stir often until smooth.

8. Set the wire rack holding the cake over a rimmed baking tray. Using a wooden skewer or lollipop stick, poke holes in the top of the cake. Pour the ganache over the cake. Using a spatula, spread the ganache evenly and let it soak into the cake.

9. Drizzle the cake with melted white chocolate (if using), then let set before serving, about 15 minutes.

Portuguese Honey Cake (*Bolo de Mel*)

For the best flavour, choose a floral-tasting honey for this traditional cake from the island of Madeira.

Makes one 8-inch Bundt cake or
8- x 4-inch loaf; 10 servings
Prep time: 20 minutes
Cooking time: 30 to 35 minutes

1 ¼ cups all-purpose flour

1 tsp ground cinnamon

1 tsp baking powder

¼ tsp fine sea salt

¾ cup granulated sugar

4 large egg yolks

⅓ cup liquid honey

Finely grated zest of 1 lemon

1 Tbsp freshly squeezed lemon juice

⅓ cup extra virgin olive oil

3 large egg whites

⅓ cup flaked almonds

1. Preheat the oven to 350°F. Butter an 8-inch Bundt pan or 8- x 4-inch loaf pan, then dust the pan with flour. Set aside.

2. In a medium bowl, whisk together the flour, cinnamon, baking powder and salt. Set aside.

3. In a large bowl and using an electric mixer, beat together the sugar and egg yolks for 3 minutes.

4. Add the honey and the lemon zest and juice. Beat for 1 minute.

5. Add the flour mixture to the sugar mixture alternately with the oil, making three additions of flour and two of oil, and beginning and ending with the flour. Beat until just a few wisps of flour remain.

6. In a large bowl and using clean beaters, beat the egg whites until stiff peaks form. Fold half of the beaten egg whites into the batter. Fold in the remaining egg whites just until combined. Do not overmix.

7. Scrape the batter into the prepared pan. Tap the pan lightly on the counter a couple of times to remove any air bubbles. Sprinkle the almonds evenly over the batter.

8. Bake until the cake is golden and a wooden skewer inserted in the centre of the cake comes out clean, 30 to 35 minutes. Cover the pan loosely with foil if the top starts to brown too much.

9. Let the cake cool in the pan on a wire rack for 5 to 10 minutes. Run a knife around the edge of the pan to loosen the cake. Turn the cake out onto the wire rack and let cool completely before slicing. (The cake can be stored in an airtight container at room temperature for up to 4 days.)

Lovely Vanilla Layer Cake

This rich, moist vanilla cake is our favourite for any celebration. Fill and frost it with your choice of buttercream.
We used Quick Buttercream (page 154) between the layers and
Swiss Buttercream (page 156) on top. For an easier presentation, omit the simple syrup and fill with your choice of jam or
preserves, then dust the top of the cake lightly with icing sugar.

Makes one 9-inch or 8-inch cake;
8 to 12 servings
Prep time: 40 minutes
Cooking time: 35 to 40 minutes
Chilling time: 15 to 20 minutes

4 cups cake-and-pastry flour OR
  3 ½ cups all-purpose flour plus
  ½ cup cornstarch

2 tsp baking powder

1 ½ tsp baking soda

1 tsp fine sea salt

1 cup unsalted butter, softened

2 cups granulated sugar

4 large eggs

2 cups buttermilk (see page 11)

2 tsp vanilla extract

Buttercream of your choice

Simple Syrup (recipe follows)

Frosting of your choice

1. Preheat the oven to 350°F.
Butter two 9-inch or three 8-inch
round baking pans, then dust the
pans lightly with flour. Set aside.

2. In a medium bowl, whisk
together the flour (or the flour
and cornstarch), baking powder,
baking soda and salt. Set aside.

3. In a large bowl and using an
electric mixer, beat the butter
with the sugar until pale and
fluffy.

4. Beat in the eggs one at a time,
beating well and scraping down
the sides of the bowl after each
addition. Beat in the buttermilk
and vanilla extract until well
combined.

5. Add the flour mixture to the
sugar mixture, stirring just until
the flour is incorporated. Do not
overmix.

6. Divide the batter evenly
between the prepared pans. Tap
the pans lightly on the counter a
couple of times to remove any air
bubbles.

7. Bake until the cakes are golden
brown and a wooden skewer
inserted in the centre of the
cakes comes out clean, 35 to
40 minutes.

8. Let the cakes cool in the pans
on a wire rack for 5 to 10 minutes.
Run a knife around the edges of
the pans to loosen the cakes.
Turn the cakes out onto the wire
rack and let cool completely.

9. To fill and frost the cakes, use
a serrated knife to gently slice off
the tops of the cakes to create a
smooth surface. If you wish, slice
each cake in half horizontally to
create extra layers.

10. Spread a small dollop of your
chosen buttercream in the centre
of a cake stand or serving plate.
(This will help prevent the cake
from moving around as you
assemble it.) Centre one cake
layer on the cake stand.

11. Using a pastry brush, gently
brush a generous amount of
simple syrup over the cake. (This
will help keep the cake moist.)

12. Place a large dollop of your
chosen buttercream on the cake,
then spread it evenly to cover the
top of the cake.

13. Continue stacking the cake
layers, brushing each one with
simple syrup before spreading
with the buttercream, until
all the cake layers have been
stacked.

14. Using about one-third of your chosen frosting, spread a thin layer over the top and sides of the cake to seal in the crumbs and prevent them from getting mixed in with the rest of the frosting as you frost the cake. (This is called a crumb coat.) Place the cake in the fridge for 15 to 20 minutes to set the crumb coat.

15. Once the crumb coat has set, spoon a large dollop of frosting on top of the cake. Using an offset spatula or a knife, spread the frosting over the top and right to the sides of the cake so it hangs over the edge.

16. Spread the overflowing frosting down and evenly over the sides of the cake. As you spread it around the sides of the cake, keep turning the cake stand to help create a smooth surface. To create an extra-smooth and glossy look, dampen the spatula or knife in hot water once or twice while spreading the frosting. (The cake can be stored in an airtight container at room temperature for up to 3 days.)

Simple Syrup

Makes about 1 ¼ cups
Prep time: 5 minutes
Cooking time: about 5 minutes
Cooling time: at least 30 minutes

1 cup granulated or turbinado sugar

1 cup water

1. Stir together the sugar and water in a small saucepan. Cook over medium heat, stirring occasionally, until the sugar dissolves.

2. Remove from the heat and let cool for at least 30 minutes. (The syrup can be refrigerated in an airtight container for up to 1 week.)

Pineapple Upside-Down Cake

Pineapple upside-down cake is a classic everyone loves. The sweet, buttery mixture spread in the bottom of the pan before baking creates a rich, caramelized topping that tastes as good as it looks.

Makes one 9- or 10-inch cake; 10 to 12 servings
Prep time: 25 minutes
Cooking time: 45 to 55 minutes

Topping

¼ cup unsalted butter, melted

¾ cup lightly packed dark brown sugar

6 to 8 pineapple rings (peeled, cored fresh pineapple or drained canned pineapple)

16 to 18 drained maraschino cherries (optional)

Cake

1 ¾ cups all-purpose flour

2 tsp ground ginger

1 ½ tsp baking powder

½ tsp ground cinnamon

½ tsp fine sea salt

¼ tsp freshly grated nutmeg

½ cup unsalted butter, softened

¾ cup granulated sugar

2 large eggs

1 ½ tsp vanilla extract

½ cup whole milk

Whipped cream for serving (optional)

1. For the topping, pour the melted butter into a 9-inch square or 10-inch round baking pan, or a 10-inch ovenproof skillet. (Don't use a cast iron skillet as the acid in the pineapple can react with the metal.) Stir in the sugar. Spread the mixture evenly to coat the base of the pan or skillet.

2. Arrange the pineapple rings in an attractive pattern over the butter mixture. Place a maraschino cherry (if using) in the centre of each pineapple ring, then scatter the rest in between the rings. Set aside.

4. Preheat the oven to 350°F.

5. For the cake, whisk together the flour, ginger, baking powder, cinnamon, salt and nutmeg in a medium bowl. Set aside.

6. In a large bowl and using an electric mixer, beat the butter with the sugar until pale and fluffy.

7. Beat in the eggs one at a time, beating well and scraping down the sides of the bowl after each addition. Beat in the vanilla extract.

8. Add the flour mixture to the sugar mixture alternately with the milk, making three additions of flour and two of milk, and beginning and ending with the flour. Stir just until combined and the batter is smooth.

9. Scrape the batter over the pineapple topping. Use an offset spatula to spread it evenly in the pan.

10. Bake until a wooden skewer inserted in the centre of the cake comes out clean and the cake springs back when lightly pressed, 45 to 55 minutes.

11. Let the cake cool in the pan on a wire rack for 10 minutes. Run a knife around the edge of the pan to loosen the cake. Invert the pan onto a serving plate or cake stand, then carefully remove the pan.

12. Serve the cake warm or at room temperature, with whipped cream (if using). (The cake can be stored in an airtight container at room temperature for up to 2 days.)

Cinnamon-Chocolate Swirl Coffee Cake

Here's our go-to coffee cake when company's coming. As the cake bakes, the cinnamon-chocolate layer forms a swirl, while the crunchy pecan topping makes it a surefire winner.

Makes one 13- x 9-inch cake;
18 to 24 servings
Prep time: 25 minutes
Cooking time: 45 to 50 minutes

Cake

3 ½ cups all-purpose flour

1 ½ tsp baking soda

1 tsp baking powder

½ tsp fine sea salt

1 cup unsalted butter, softened

2 cups granulated sugar

4 large eggs

2 cups sour cream (14%)

1 ½ tsp vanilla extract

Cinnamon-Chocolate Swirl

½ cup granulated sugar

1 ½ tsp ground cinnamon

1 tsp unsweetened cocoa powder

Pecan Topping

¾ cup all-purpose flour

¾ cup lightly packed dark brown sugar

½ cup cold unsalted butter, cut into small pieces

½ tsp fine sea salt

¾ cup chopped pecans

1. Preheat the oven to 350°F. Grease a 13- x 9-inch baking pan. Set aside.

2. For the cake, whisk together the flour, baking soda, baking powder and salt in a medium bowl. Set aside.

3. In a large bowl and using an electric mixer, beat the butter with the sugar until pale and fluffy.

4. Beat in the eggs one at a time, beating well and scraping down the sides of the bowl after each addition. Add the sour cream and vanilla extract, then beat just until incorporated.

5. Add the flour mixture to the sugar mixture. Stir until well combined.

6. For the cinnamon-chocolate swirl, whisk together the sugar, cinnamon and cocoa in a medium bowl. Set aside.

7. For the pecan topping, stir together the flour, sugar, butter and salt in a medium bowl. Using a pastry cutter, mix the ingredients until the butter is in pea-size pieces. Stir in the pecans.

8. Scrape half of the cake batter into the prepared pan, using an offset spatula to spread it evenly.

9. Sprinkle the cinnamon-chocolate swirl evenly over the batter. Top with the remaining batter, spreading it evenly in the pan again. Sprinkle the pecan topping evenly over top.

10. Bake until the cake is a deep golden brown and a wooden skewer inserted in the centre of the cake comes out clean, 45 to 50 minutes.

11. Let the cake cool completely in the pan on a wire rack. Invert it onto a serving plate before slicing. (The cake can be stored in an airtight container at room temperature for up to 3 days.)

Carrot Cake

Here's the perfect cake for a crowd. Moist cake topped with creamy frosting: what's not to like?

Makes one 8-inch cake; 8 to 10 servings

Prep time: 40 minutes

Cooking time: 20 to 25 minutes

Cake

2 ½ cups all-purpose flour

1 ½ cups lightly packed golden yellow sugar

1 Tbsp ground cinnamon

1 tsp freshly grated nutmeg

1 tsp baking powder

1 tsp baking soda

1 tsp fine sea salt

¼ tsp ground allspice

Pinch of ground cloves

1 cup unsalted butter, melted and cooled

4 large eggs

1 tsp vanilla extract

3 cups grated carrots (3 large carrots)

½ cup raisins

Cream Cheese Frosting

2 pkgs (each 8 oz/250 g) brick-style cream cheese, at room temperature

1 cup unsalted butter, softened

1 Tbsp vanilla extract

2 cups icing sugar, sifted

½ cup chopped pecans or walnuts, toasted (optional)

1. Preheat the oven to 350°F. Grease three 8-inch round baking pans. Line the base of each pan with parchment paper, then dust the parchment and sides of the pans with flour. Set aside.

2. For the cake, whisk together the flour, sugar, cinnamon, nutmeg, baking powder, baking soda, salt, allspice and cloves in a large bowl. Set aside

3. In a medium bowl, whisk together the butter, eggs and vanilla extract.

4. Add the butter mixture to the flour mixture. Stir just until combined. Stir in the carrots and raisins.

5. Divide the batter evenly between the prepared pans. Bake until golden and a wooden skewer inserted in the centre of the cakes comes out clean, 20 to 25 minutes.

6. Let the cakes cool in the pans on a wire rack for 5 to 10 minutes. Run a knife around the edges of the pans to loosen the cakes. Turn the cakes out onto the wire rack and let cool completely.

7. For the cream cheese frosting, in a large bowl and using an electric mixer, beat together the cream cheese, butter and vanilla extract. Add the sugar and beat until the frosting is smooth and creamy.

8. To fill and frost the cakes, use a serrated knife to gently slice off the tops of the cakes to create a smooth surface.

9. Spread a small dollop of cream cheese frosting in the centre of a cake stand or serving plate. (This will help prevent the cake from moving around as you assemble it.) Centre one cake layer on the cake stand.

10. Spoon one-third of the remaining frosting onto the cake layer, then spread it evenly to cover the cake. Sprinkle with half of the pecans (if using).

11. Top with another cake layer. Spread with half of the remaining frosting and sprinkle with the remaining pecans (if using).

12. Top with the third cake layer. Frost the top of the cake with the remaining frosting. (The cake can be refrigerated in an airtight container for up to 3 days.)

Rosemary-Lemon Olive Oil Cake

This cake is the perfect ending to an Italian-themed dinner—especially if you serve it with small glasses of limoncello or shots of espresso.

Makes one 9-inch cake; 10 to 12 servings
Prep time: 25 minutes
Cooking time: 40 to 50 minutes

1 ¾ cups cake-and-pastry flour

2 tsp baking powder

Pinch of fine sea salt

1 cup granulated sugar

Finely grated zest of 4 lemons

3 sprigs rosemary, leaves removed and finely chopped

3 large eggs

1 cup plain yogurt (3%)

¼ cup freshly squeezed lemon juice (about 2 lemons)

⅔ cup extra virgin olive oil

¼ cup icing sugar, sifted

Finely grated lemon zest and additional rosemary sprigs for garnish

1. Preheat the oven to 375°F. Grease a 9-inch round baking pan with olive oil, then dust the pan with flour. Set aside.

2. In a medium bowl, whisk together the flour, baking powder and salt. Set aside.

3. In a large bowl, stir together the sugar, lemon zest and rosemary. Using your fingers, rub the ingredients together to infuse the sugar with the flavourings.

4. Add the eggs to the bowl. Using an electric mixer, beat the sugar mixture on medium-high speed until the mixture is pale and has doubled in volume, 2 to 3 minutes.

5. Turn down the speed to low. Gradually add the yogurt and lemon juice.

6. With the mixer still running on low speed, gradually add the olive oil in a slow, thin stream. Beat until the ingredients are well combined.

7. With the mixer still running on low speed, add the flour mixture, mixing just until combined.

8. Scrape the batter into the prepared pan. Tap the pan lightly on the counter a couple of times to remove any air bubbles. Bake until a wooden skewer inserted in the centre of the cake comes out clean, 40 to 50 minutes.

9. Let the cake cool in the pan on a wire rack for 20 minutes. Run a knife around the edge of the pan to loosen the cake. Turn the cake out onto the wire rack and let cool completely.

10. Sift the icing sugar evenly over the top of the cake and garnish with more lemon zest and sprigs of rosemary.

Linzer Torte

This lattice-topped torte is a Christmas tradition in its native Austria, but we love it any time of year. Although you can serve it immediately after baking, the flavour develops nicely if the cake is stored in an airtight container at room temperature overnight.

Makes one 9- or 10-inch torte;
10 to 12 servings
Prep time: 1 hour
Cooking time: 70 to 80 minutes
Chilling time: about 1 hour

Raspberry Preserves

5 ½ cups fresh raspberries

¾ cup granulated sugar, or to taste

1 tsp finely grated lemon zest

2 Tbsp freshly squeezed lemon juice

1 tsp finely grated orange zest

Linzer Torte

¾ cup almonds

¾ cup hazelnuts

1 ½ cups all-purpose flour

2/3 cup granulated sugar

1 Tbsp finely grated lemon zest (1 to 2 lemons)

1 tsp ground cinnamon

½ tsp baking powder

¼ tsp freshly grated nutmeg

¼ tsp fine sea salt

Pinch of ground cloves

¾ cup plus 2 Tbsp cold unsalted butter, cut into small pieces

2 large egg yolks

1 ½ tsp almond extract

Icing sugar for dusting (optional)

Whipped cream for serving

1. For the raspberry preserves, stir together the raspberries and sugar in a medium saucepan. Bring to a boil over medium heat. Turn down the heat to low and simmer, stirring occasionally, until most of the liquid has evaporated, 15 to 20 minutes. Watch carefully toward the end of cooking time. Turn down the heat as far as possible if the mixture looks like it might burn.

2. Remove from the heat and pour the raspberry mixture into a heatproof bowl. Stir in the lemon zest and juice and the orange zest. Cover and refrigerate while you make the crust. (The raspberry preserves can be refrigerated in an airtight container for up to 1 week.)

3. With the oven rack in the middle position, preheat the oven to 350°F.

4. For the linzer torte, spread the almonds out on a rimmed baking sheet. Bake until fragrant and lightly browned, 8 to 10 minutes. Put the almonds in a small bowl. Set aside to cool.

5. Spread the hazelnuts out on the same baking sheet. Bake until fragrant and the outer skins begin to flake and crack, 10 to 15 minutes. Remove from the oven and place the baking sheet on a wire rack until the hazelnuts are cool. Enclose the hazelnuts in a clean towel, then rub them vigorously through the towel to remove most of their papery skins.

6. In a food processor fitted with the steel blade, combine the almonds, hazelnuts and ½ cup of the flour. Process until the nuts are finely ground.

7. Add the remaining flour to the food processor, along with the sugar, lemon zest, cinnamon, baking powder, nutmeg, salt and cloves. Process until well combined.

8. Add the butter to the food processor. Pulse until the mixture resembles fine crumbs. Add the egg yolks and almond extract. Pulse until the mixture forms a dough that just begins to come together.

9. Tip the dough onto a work surface and gather it into a ball. Divide it into two balls, one slightly larger than the other. Wrap the smaller ball of dough in plastic wrap and refrigerate until firm enough to roll out, about 1 hour.

10. Meanwhile, butter a 9- or 10-inch tart pan with a removable base, or a 9- or 10-inch spring-form pan. Press the larger ball of dough over the base and up the sides of the prepared pan.

(If using a springform pan, press the dough about 1 inch up the sides of the pan.)

11. Spread the cooled raspberry preserves over the crust. Cover with plastic wrap and refrigerate.

12. Line a baking sheet with parchment paper.

13. Once the smaller ball of dough is firm, roll it out to a 12-inch disc between two sheets of parchment paper. Using a pastry wheel or pizza cutter, cut the pastry into 1-inch strips.

14. Place the strips of pastry on the prepared baking sheet, cover with plastic wrap and refrigerate until firm, about 10 minutes.

15. Preheat the oven to 350°F.

16. Using an offset spatula, gently transfer half of the strips of dough to the torte, spacing them evenly across the top. Arrange the remaining strips at right angles to the first strips. If desired, weave the top strips over and under the bottom strips. (Don't worry if the pastry tears; just press it back together as best as you can.) Trim the edges of the strips to fit the pan.

17. If you have any leftover scraps of dough, roll them into a long rope. (Don't worry if the rope breaks.) Lay the rope around the outer edge of the tart where the ends of the lattice strips meet

the bottom crust. Using a fork or your fingers, press the rope into the edges of the bottom crust to seal them.

18. Bake the torte until the pastry is golden brown and set, 30 to 35 minutes. Let the torte cool slightly in the pan on a wire rack before removing. Remove or release the sides of the pan and slide the torte onto a serving plate. Sift icing sugar evenly over top (if using). Serve warm or at room temperature with whipped cream. (The torte can be stored in an airtight container at room temperature for 3 days, refrigerated for 1 week or frozen for up to 1 month.)

Vanilla-Chocolate Marble Slab Cake

To make this easy slab cake into a rather more decadent affair, frost it with chocolate-flavoured whipped cream or Quick Chocolate Buttercream (page 154). If you prefer a plain vanilla cake, omit the cocoa powder mixture and simply scrape all of the batter into the prepared pan, then bake as directed.

Makes one 13- x 9-inch cake;
18 to 24 servings
Prep time: 20 minutes
Cooking time: 45 to 50 minutes

5 ¼ cups all-purpose flour

5 tsp baking powder

1 ½ tsp fine sea salt

1 ½ cups unsalted butter, softened

3 cups granulated sugar

9 large eggs

2 Tbsp vanilla extract

2 cups buttermilk (see page 11)

²/₃ cup unsweetened cocoa powder

¹/₃ cup plus 1 Tbsp hot water

1. Preheat the oven to 350°F. Butter a 13- x 9-inch baking pan, then line the base of the pan with parchment paper. Grease the parchment paper, then dust the parchment and the sides of the pan with flour. Set aside.

2. In a medium bowl, whisk together the flour, baking powder and salt. Set aside.

3. In a large bowl and using an electric mixer, beat the butter with the sugar until pale and fluffy, about 5 minutes. Scrape down the sides of the bowl once or twice with a spatula.

4. Beat in the eggs one at a time, beating well after each addition and scraping down the sides of the bowl as needed. Beat in the vanilla extract.

5. With the mixer running on low speed, add the flour mixture to the sugar mixture alternately with the buttermilk, making three additions of flour and two of buttermilk, and beginning and ending with the flour. Beat until well combined. Scrape half of the batter into a separate bowl.

6. In a small bowl, whisk the cocoa powder with half of the hot water until a smooth paste forms. Whisk in the remaining water until smooth. Add the cocoa mixture to one of the bowls of batter. Beat until well combined.

7. Spoon 4 large spoonfuls of the vanilla batter into the prepared pan, spacing them far enough apart that you can create a checkerboard pattern when you add the chocolate batter. Spoon the chocolate batter into the empty spaces to cover the bottom of the pan completely.

8. Repeat with a second layer, spooning the remaining vanilla batter over the chocolate and vice versa. Using the handle of a wooden spoon, swirl the batter to create a marbled effect. Tap the pan lightly on the counter a couple of times to remove any air bubbles.

9. Bake until the cake is lightly browned and a wooden skewer inserted in the centre of the cake comes out clean, 45 to 50 minutes, rotating the pan 180 degrees halfway through baking time.

10. Let the cake cool in the pan on a wire rack for 5 to 10 minutes. Run a knife around the edge of the pan to loosen the cake. Turn the cake out onto the wire rack and let cool completely. (The cake can be stored in an airtight container at room temperature for up to 3 days, or frozen for 2 months.)

Lemon–White Chocolate Cheesecake Mousse Cake

If it's too hard to choose between cake and cheesecake, make this and have both! This special occasion cake combines a light, airy lemon sponge with a rich white chocolate cheesecake mousse filling. For best results, use pure white chocolate for the filling.

Makes one 8-inch cake; 8 to 12 servings

Prep time: 1 hour

Cooking time: about 30 minutes

Chilling time: at least 4 hours, 10 minutes

Lemon Cake

3 ¼ cups cake-and-pastry flour, sifted

1 Tbsp baking powder

1 Tbsp finely grated lemon zest (1 to 2 lemons)

1 ½ tsp fine sea salt

7 large eggs

1 ¾ cups granulated sugar

3 Tbsp freshly squeezed lemon juice (1 to 2 lemons)

2 tsp vanilla extract

1 cup unsalted butter, melted and cooled

White Chocolate Cheesecake Mousse

¼ cup freshly squeezed lemon juice, chilled (about 2 lemons)

2 ½ tsp unflavoured powdered gelatin

1 cup whipping cream (35%)

⅓ cup plus 1 Tbsp white chocolate chips or finely chopped white chocolate

1 pkg (8 oz/250 g) brick-style cream cheese, at room temperature

1 ½ tsp vanilla extract

1 large egg white

Pinch of fine sea salt

½ cup granulated sugar

To Assemble

Simple Syrup (made with granulated sugar and still warm) (page 107)

½ tsp lemon extract

1 cup whipping cream (35%), chilled

2 Tbsp instant-dissolving sugar

Finely grated lemon zest and thinly sliced lemon for garnish

1. Preheat the oven to 350°F. Grease the base of two 8-inch round baking pans, then line the base of each pan with parchment paper.

2. For the lemon cake, whisk together the flour, baking powder, lemon zest and salt in a medium bowl until well combined.

3. In a large heatproof bowl and using a hand whisk, whisk together the eggs, sugar, lemon juice and vanilla extract.

4. Set the bowl over a saucepan of gently simmering water. Whisk until the mixture reaches 110°F on an instant-read thermometer.

5. Using an electric mixer, beat the egg mixture on high speed until it becomes pale and thick, and falls in ribbons when the beaters are lifted, about 8 minutes.

6. Using a spatula, gently fold the flour mixture into the egg mixture, one-third at a time, folding just until combined after each addition.

7. Slowly pour the butter down the sides of the bowl. Fold it into the batter.

8. Immediately divide the batter evenly between the prepared pans. Bake until the cakes spring back when gently pressed and a wooden skewer inserted in the centre of the cakes comes out clean, 25 to 30 minutes.

9. Let the cakes cool in the pans on a wire rack for 5 to 10 minutes. Run a knife around the edges of the pans to loosen the cakes. Turn the cakes out onto the wire rack and let cool completely.

10. For the white chocolate cheesecake mousse, pour the lemon juice into a small bowl. Sprinkle the gelatin over the surface. Set aside until puffy, at least 5 minutes.

11. In a large bowl and using an electric mixer, beat ¾ cup of the cream until medium peaks form. Scrape the whipped cream into a medium bowl, cover and refrigerate until needed.

12. Put the white chocolate in a medium heatproof bowl. In a small saucepan, heat the remaining ¼ cup of cream over medium heat until it just comes to a simmer (do not boil). Pour half of the hot cream over the chocolate. Let stand for 30 seconds. Stir until combined. Add the remaining hot cream and stir until smooth.

13. Add the lemon juice–gelatin mixture to the chocolate. Stir until the gelatin is completely dissolved and the ingredients are well combined. Set aside.

14. In a separate large bowl and using an electric mixer, beat the cream cheese until smooth. Scrape down the sides of the bowl. Beat in the vanilla extract.

15. Add the white chocolate mixture to the cream cheese. Beat until well combined.

16. In a medium bowl and using an electric mixer with clean beaters, beat the egg white and salt until very frothy. Gradually add the sugar, beating until stiff peaks form and the mixture is glossy.

17. Using a spatula, fold the egg white into the cheese mixture until well combined. Fold in the whipped cream until well combined.

18. Stir the lemon extract into the simple syrup and let cool completely.

19. Grease an 8-inch round baking pan. Line the base with parchment paper. Cut a strip of parchment paper slightly longer than the pan's circumference and 2 inches wider than its depth. Line the sides of the pan with the strip of paper so the paper extends 2 inches above the top of the pan.

20. Using a serrated knife, trim the tops of the cakes so they're level. Place one cake, cut side up, in the prepared pan. Using a pastry brush, generously brush the cake with lemon simple syrup. Pour the mousse over the cake and smooth it level with an offset spatula. Refrigerate for 10 minutes.

21. Generously brush the top of the second cake with lemon simple syrup. Place the cake, syrup side down, over the chilled mousse, pressing down gently. Refrigerate for at least 4 hours, or overnight. (At this stage, the cake can be covered and refrigerated for up to 3 days.)

22. When ready to serve, whip the cream with the sugar in a medium bowl until soft peaks form. Carefully invert the cake onto a cake stand or serving plate. Peel off the paper. Pile the whipped cream on top of the cake. Garnish with lemon zest and lemon slices. Serve immediately.

Blueberry Cake

A layer of fresh blueberries baked right into this easy cake makes it super moist and fruity. When blueberries aren't in season, substitute frozen berries instead. See Baking Day Secrets below for instructions.

Makes one 9-inch cake; 10 to 12 servings
Prep time: 20 minutes
Cooking time: 45 to 60 minutes

Cake

2 ½ cups all-purpose flour

1 Tbsp baking powder

½ tsp fine sea salt

½ cup unsalted butter, softened

1 ¼ cups granulated sugar

2 large eggs

1 tsp vanilla extract

¾ cup whole milk

Blueberry Layer

3 cups fresh blueberries

2 Tbsp granulated sugar

Topping

¾ cup whipping cream (35%)

¼ cup fresh blueberries

1. Preheat the oven to 350°F. Grease a 9-inch round baking pan.

2. For the cake, whisk together the flour, baking powder and salt in a medium bowl. Set aside.

3. In a large bowl and using an electric mixer, beat the butter with the sugar until pale and fluffy. Add the eggs and vanilla extract and beat well.

4. Add the flour mixture to the sugar mixture alternately with the milk, making three additions of flour and two of milk, and beginning and ending with the flour. Stir until well combined. Scrape half of the batter into the prepared pan.

5. For the blueberry layer, scatter the blueberries over the batter in the pan. Sprinkle evenly with the sugar.

6. Gently spread the remaining cake batter over the blueberries, being carefully not to disturb

them. Bake until the cake is well risen and golden brown and a wooden skewer inserted in the centre of the cake comes out clean, 45 to 60 minutes.

7. Let the cake cool completely in the pan on a wire rack. Remove the cake from the pan and place on a serving plate.

8. For the topping, in a small bowl, whip the cream until it holds soft peaks. Spread the whipped cream over the top of the cake. Scatter blueberries over the cream.

BAKING DAY SECRETS

To use frozen blueberries in this cake, reserve 2 tablespoonfuls of the flour and toss with the blueberries before spreading them over the batter. Increase the baking time by 10 to 15 minutes. Scatter toasted nuts over the whipped cream topping instead of more blueberries.

Chocolate Genoise Cake

A genoise is an airy cake with a delicate texture that, unlike other sponge cakes, stays wonderfully moist for several days. This chocolate version has a rich flavour but retains its lightness, making it an ideal dessert to follow a rich meal.

Makes one 8-inch cake; 8 to 10 servings

Prep time: 30 minutes

Cooking time: about 20 minutes

Cake

4 large eggs

⅔ cup granulated sugar

½ cup cake-and-pastry flour

⅓ cup unsweetened cocoa powder

¼ teaspoon fine sea salt

3 Tbsp unsalted butter, melted and cooled

1 tsp vanilla extract

Frosting

2 ½ Tbsp unsalted butter, softened

2 Tbsp whole milk

1 ¼ cups icing sugar, sifted

2 Tbsp unsweetened cocoa powder

1. Preheat the oven to 350°F. Grease an 8-inch round baking pan. Dust the pan with a little cocoa powder.

2. For the cake, bring the eggs to room temperature by placing them in a bowl and adding enough warm water to cover them. Let stand for about 5 minutes.

3. In a large bowl and using an electric mixer on high speed, beat the eggs and sugar until the mixture becomes pale and thick, and falls in ribbons when the beaters are lifted, about 8 minutes.

4. Sift the flour, cocoa powder and salt into the egg mixture, then gently fold in the flour mixture until well combined. Fold in the butter and vanilla extract.

5. Scrape the batter into the prepared pan. Bake until the cake springs back when lightly pressed, about 20 minutes.

6. Let the cake cool in the pan on a wire rack for 5 to 10 minutes. Run a knife around the edge of the pan to loosen the cake. Turn the cake out onto the wire rack and let cool completely.

7. For the frosting, combine the butter and milk in a microwave-able bowl. Microwave on medium until the butter has melted, about 30 seconds.

8. In a medium bowl, whisk together the icing sugar and cocoa powder. Stir in the warm milk mixture. Whisk until smooth.

9. Pour the icing onto the cake. Spread it evenly over the top and (if you wish) let it dribble down the sides. Let stand until the frosting is set before serving, 10 to 15 minutes. (The cake can be refrigerated in an airtight container for up to 3 days.)

Flourless Chocolate-Hazelnut Cake

This super-simple flourless cake might be gluten-free, but it doesn't stint on flavour. Use the best chocolate you can find to ensure it wows the most discerning chocoholic.

Makes one 8-inch cake; 8 to 10 servings
Prep time: 30 minutes
Cooking time: 25 to 30 minutes

¾ cup chopped dark chocolate

½ cup unsalted butter, softened

3 large eggs, separated

¾ cup granulated sugar

1 tsp vanilla extract

½ tsp fine sea salt

½ cup unsweetened cocoa powder

½ cup hazelnuts, toasted (see sidebar on page 22) and chopped

Chopped toasted hazelnuts and/ or unsweetened cocoa powder for garnish

Whipped cream for serving (optional)

1. Preheat the oven to 350°F. Grease an 8-inch springform pan, then line the base with parchment paper.

2. In a medium saucepan, melt the chocolate and butter over low heat, stirring until smooth. Remove from the heat and set aside.

3. In a large bowl and using an electric mixer, beat the egg whites on high speed until soft peaks form. Add half of the sugar. Continue to beat on high speed until stiff, glossy peaks form. Set aside.

4. In a separate large bowl, whisk together the egg yolks, the remaining sugar, vanilla extract and salt. Whisk in the melted chocolate until well combined.

5. Sift the cocoa powder into the egg yolk mixture and stir to combine. Stir in the hazelnuts.

6. Gently fold the egg whites into the chocolate batter, just until incorporated and no white streaks remain.

7. Scrape the batter into the prepared pan. Bake until puffed and set, 25 to 30 minutes. Do not overbake.

8. Let the cake cool in the pan on a wire rack for 10 minutes. Release the sides of the pan and slide the cake onto a serving plate. (The cake can be stored in an airtight container at room temperature for up to 3 days.)

9. Garnish with hazelnuts and/or a light dusting of cocoa powder, then serve warm or at room temperature with dollops of whipped cream (if using).

SWEET HISTORY

During the Middle Ages, sugar gained a reputation as a "wonder drug" and was used to treat conditions as diverse as stomach ulcers and childbirth pain. It was such a ubiquitous medicine that the expression "Like an apothecary without sugar," meaning being unable to function properly, became popular.

Queen Elizabeth Cake

The origins of this cake are shrouded in mystery, although some sources claim the cake was first made for Queen Elizabeth II's coronation in 1953. The event required a cake that took little sugar and butter and few eggs—all still rationed in the UK in the early 1950s. Whatever its history, the cake has become a Canadian classic, and you'll understand why when you taste it.

Makes one 8-inch cake; 8 to 10 servings
Prep time: 30 minutes
Cooking time: about 1 hour

Cake

1 cup pitted dates, cut in half

1 cup water

1 ½ cups all-purpose flour

1 tsp baking powder

½ tsp baking soda

¼ tsp fine sea salt

¼ cup unsalted butter, softened

1 cup granulated sugar

1 tsp vanilla extract

1 large egg

½ cup chopped walnuts

Topping

¾ cup unsweetened shredded coconut

½ cup lightly packed golden yellow sugar

⅓ cup unsalted butter, softened

2 Tbsp whipping cream (35%)

Sauce

1 cup lightly packed golden yellow sugar

1 cup granulated sugar

1 cup whipping cream (35%)

1. Preheat the oven to 350°F. Grease an 8-inch springform pan, then line the base with parchment paper.

2. For the cake, combine the dates and water in a medium saucepan. Bring to a boil over medium-high heat. Turn down the heat to medium and simmer, stirring often, until the dates have absorbed the water and turn into a pulpy mixture, about 5 minutes. Remove from the heat and set aside.

3. In a medium bowl, whisk together the flour, baking powder, baking soda and salt. Set aside.

4. In a large bowl and using an electric mixer, beat the butter with the sugar and vanilla extract until pale and fluffy. Beat in the egg until well combined.

5. Add the flour mixture to the sugar mixture alternately with the dates, making three additions of flour and two of dates, and beginning and ending with the flour. Stir until well combined. Stir in the walnuts.

6. Scrape the batter into the prepared pan. Bake until a wooden skewer inserted in the centre of the cake comes out clean, 40 to 50 minutes.

7. For the topping, just before the cake is ready, combine the coconut, sugar, butter and cream in a medium saucepan. Bring to a boil over medium-high heat, stirring constantly. Turn down the heat to medium and simmer for 2 minutes, stirring often.

8. As soon as the cake comes out of the oven, preheat the broiler to high. Spread the hot topping over the top of the cake. Broil the cake until the topping is dark golden brown, 2 to 3 minutes. Watch it carefully, as the topping burns easily. Let the cake cool in the pan on a wire rack for 10 minutes.

9. For the sauce, combine both sugars and the cream in a medium saucepan. Bring to a boil over medium-high heat. Turn down the heat to medium and simmer, stirring constantly, until thickened and smooth. (The sauce can be cooled, then refrigerated in an airtight container for up to 5 days. Reheat gently before serving.)

10. Release the sides of the pan and slide the cake onto a serving plate. Serve the cake warm or at room temperature with the warm sauce. (The cake can be stored in an airtight container at room temperature for up to 3 days.)

Pink Champagne Cake

An elegant, indulgent cake like this is perfect for any celebration, but the pink frosting would make it especially appropriate for a bridal shower. You can, of course, tint it any colour you wish.

Makes one 8-inch cake; 8 to 12 servings
Prep time: 45 minutes
Cooking time: about 35 minutes
Chilling time: 45 to 50 minutes

Cake

- 3 cups cake-and-pastry flour
- 1 ½ tsp baking powder
- ¾ tsp baking soda
- ¾ tsp fine sea salt
- ¾ cup unsalted butter, softened
- 2 cups granulated sugar
- 6 large egg whites
- 1 tsp vanilla extract
- 2 cups Champagne or sparkling wine, at room temperature

Frosting & Filling

- 1 ½ cups plus 2 Tbsp unsalted butter, softened
- 3 to 5 cups icing sugar, sifted
- 1 tsp vanilla extract
- Pinch of fine sea salt
- 2 to 4 Tbsp Champagne or sparkling wine
- Red gel food colouring
- ⅓ cup raspberry jam or strawberry jam

1. Preheat the oven to 350°F. Grease two 8-inch round baking pans, then dust with flour.

2. For the cake, whisk together the flour, baking powder, baking soda and salt in a medium bowl. Set aside.

3. In a large bowl and using an electric mixer, beat the butter with the sugar until pale and fluffy.

4. Gradually beat in the egg whites until well combined. Beat in the vanilla extract.

5. Add the flour mixture to the sugar mixture alternately with the Champagne, making three additions of flour and two of Champagne, and beginning and ending with the flour. Stir until well combined.

6. Divide the batter evenly between the prepared pans. Bake on two separate racks of the oven, rotating their position halfway through baking, until a wooden skewer inserted in the centre of the cakes comes out clean and the tops of the cakes spring back when touched gently, about 35 minutes.

7. Let the cakes cool in the pans on a wire rack for 10 minutes. Remove the cakes from the pans and let cool completely on the wire rack.

8. For the frosting and filling, in a large bowl and using an electric mixer, beat the butter until pale and creamy.

9. Beat in the icing sugar, 1 cup at a time, until the frosting is spreadable (you may not need all of the icing sugar). Beat in the vanilla extract and salt.

10. Add the Champagne, 1 tablespoonful at a time, according to your taste: for a milder flavour, add 2 tablespoonfuls; for a more pronounced flavour, add 4 tablespoonfuls. Add the food colouring, one drop at a time, until the frosting is tinted pale pink. If the frosting is too runny to spread after you add the Champagne and food colouring, beat in a little more icing sugar.

11. To fill and frost the cake, use a serrated knife to gently slice off the tops of the cakes to create a smooth surface. Spread a small dollop of frosting in the centre of a cake stand or serving plate. (This will help prevent the cake from moving around as you assemble it.) Centre one cake, upside down, on the cake stand.

12. Spread the jam evenly over the cake, spreading it right to the edges. Carefully centre the second cake, right side up, on top of the jam.

13. Using about one-third of the frosting, spread a thin layer over the top and sides of the cake to seal in the crumbs and prevent them from getting mixed in with the rest of the frosting as you frost the cake. (This is called a crumb coat.) Place the cake in the fridge for 15 to 20 minutes to set the crumb coat.

14. Once the crumb coat has set, spoon a large dollop of frosting on top of the cake. Using an offset spatula or a knife, spread the frosting over the top and right to the sides of the cake so it hangs over the edge.

15. Spread the overflowing frosting down and evenly over the sides of the cake. As you spread it around the sides of the cake, keep turning the cake stand to help create a smooth surface. To create an extra-smooth and glossy look, dampen the spatula or knife in hot water once or twice while spreading the frosting.

16. If liked, spoon any remaining frosting into a piping bag fitted with a ⅜-inch closed star tip, then pipe the frosting around the top and bottom edges of the cake. Chill the cake for at least 30 minutes before serving.

Strawberry Shortcakes

This classic warm-weather favourite features fluffy biscuits, juicy strawberries and oodles of whipped cream, which all add up to the perfect way to celebrate summer's arrival.

Makes 12 shortcakes
Prep time: 20 minutes
Cooking time: 10 to 12 minutes

Shortcakes

½ cup whipping cream (35%)

½ cup plain Greek yogurt (2%)

1 large egg

1 tsp vanilla extract

2 ½ cups all-purpose flour

½ cup granulated sugar

1 tsp baking powder

¼ tsp fine sea salt

½ cup cold unsalted butter, cut into small pieces

Filling

2 lb medium strawberries, hulled and halved

½ cup granulated sugar

1 cup whipping cream (35%)

Mint sprigs for garnish (optional)

Ice cream for garnish (optional)

1. Preheat the oven to 400°F. Line a large baking sheet with parchment paper.

2. For the shortcakes, whisk together the cream, yogurt, egg and vanilla extract in a small bowl. Set aside.

3. In a large bowl, whisk together the flour, sugar, baking powder and salt.

4. Using a pastry cutter or two knives, cut the butter into the flour mixture until the mixture resembles coarse crumbs.

5. Add the cream mixture to the flour mixture and mix just until the dough comes together. Do not overmix.

6. Tip the dough onto a lightly floured work surface and knead just until it holds together. Roll or pat out the dough to 1-inch thickness. Using a 3-inch round cookie cutter, cut out 12 rounds, rerolling the dough scraps once. (Rerolling the scraps more than once makes the shortcakes tough.)

7. Arrange the rounds of dough, a little apart, on the prepared baking sheet. Bake until risen and lightly browned, 10 to 12 minutes. Remove to a wire rack and let cool slightly before serving.

8. For the filling, toss the strawberries with ¼ cup of the sugar in a large bowl. Set aside.

9. In a medium bowl, whip the cream with the remaining ¼ cup of sugar until it holds soft peaks.

10. Slice each shortcake in half horizontally. Spoon the strawberries on the bottom half of each shortcake. Top each with whipped cream or ice cream. Replace the top of each shortcake, garnish with mint (if using) and serve immediately.

CUPCAKES
& OTHER SMALL CAKES

Orange Chiffon Cupcakes

These light, moist chiffon cupcakes have a zesty hit of citrus. To bump up the orange flavour even more, add 2 teaspoonfuls of orange liqueur to the cream before whipping it for the garnish.

Makes 12 cupcakes
Prep time: 30 minutes
Cooking time: about 20 minutes

Cupcakes

1 cup plus 2 Tbsp all-purpose flour

2 Tbsp finely grated orange zest

1 ½ tsp baking powder

¼ tsp ground cardamom

¼ tsp fine sea salt

2 ½ cups granulated sugar

4 large eggs

¼ cup freshly squeezed orange juice

¼ cup unsalted butter, melted

Topping

1 cup whipping cream (35%)

1 Tbsp icing sugar

1. Preheat the oven to 350°F. Grease the wells of a muffin pan, then set aside.

2. For the cupcakes, whisk together the flour, orange zest, baking powder, cardamom and salt in a large bowl.

3. In a medium bowl, whisk together the sugar, eggs, orange juice and melted butter. Add the egg mixture to the flour mixture and whisk just until smooth.

4. Fill the wells of the muffin pan about two-thirds full with batter. Bake until the cupcakes spring back when lightly touched and a wooden skewer inserted in the centre of a cupcake comes out clean, about 20 minutes.

5. Let the cupcakes cool completely in the pan on a wire rack. Run a knife gently around the edge of each cupcake, then remove them from the pan to the rack to cool completely. (The undecorated cupcakes can be refrigerated in an airtight container for up to 4 days.)

6. For the topping, whip the cream and icing sugar in a medium bowl until the cream holds stiff peaks.

7. Using an offset spatula or a piping bag, swirl the whipped cream on top of the cupcakes. Serve immediately.

BAKING DAY SECRETS

For classy ways to frost your favourite cupcakes, check out the Frostings, Icings & Decorating Basics chapter (pages 154 to 172).

Molten Chocolate Cakes for Two

Nothing says romance like chocolate, so if you're having a dinner à deux, these delectable cakes, with their molten centres, are the perfect dessert. Best of all, you can prepare the batter ahead of time (see sidebar).

Makes 2 cakes
Prep time: 30 minutes
Cooking time: 10 to 13 minutes

Unsweetened cocoa powder for dusting

2 oz chopped semi-sweet chocolate or ⅓ cup semi-sweet chocolate chips

2 Tbsp unsalted butter, softened

¼ tsp vanilla extract

1 large egg

2 Tbsp granulated sugar

¼ tsp fine sea salt

1 Tbsp all-purpose flour

Icing sugar for dusting (optional)

Whipped cream and fresh berries for serving

1. Preheat the oven to 400°F. Generously butter two ¾-cup ramekins, then dust the base and sides of each with cocoa powder. Set aside.

2. In a medium saucepan over low heat, melt the chocolate and butter together, stirring occasionally until completely smooth. Remove from the heat and stir in the vanilla extract. Set aside.

3. In a medium bowl and using an electric mixer, beat the egg on medium speed until foamy.

4. Add the sugar and salt. Beat on high speed until the mixture is pale yellow and very thick, 5 to 10 minutes.

5. Add the egg mixture to the melted chocolate mixture. Sift the flour into the chocolate mixture, then, using a spatula, gently fold the ingredients just until combined.

6. Divide the batter between the prepared ramekins, smoothing the tops as best you can. Place the ramekins on a small rimmed baking sheet and bake until the cakes have puffed up slightly but still jiggle a little in the centre when the ramekins are shaken gently, 10 to 13 minutes.

7. Immediately run a knife around the edge of each cake. Invert the ramekins onto serving plates and let them sit for about 1 minute to allow the cakes to release, then lift the ramekins off the cakes. Dust the cakes with icing sugar (if using) and serve immediately with whipped cream and fresh berries.

GET A HEAD START

You can prep the batter for these dainty cakes up to 2 days ahead. Divide the batter between the ramekins. Cover them tightly with plastic wrap, then refrigerate for up to 2 days. Bring them to room temperature before baking.

Raspberry Lemonade Cupcakes

H ere's the perfect summer cupcake—chock full of fresh raspberries and slathered with a zesty lemonade frosting.

Makes 16 cupcakes
Prep time: 40 minutes
Cooking time: about 30 minutes

Raspberries

2 cups raspberries, cut in half

¼ cup all-purpose flour

Cupcakes

¾ cup all-purpose flour

¾ cup cake-and-pastry flour

1 tsp baking powder

½ tsp baking soda

¼ tsp fine sea salt

½ cup buttermilk (see page 11)

2 large eggs

2 Tbsp finely grated lemon zest (about 3 lemons)

1 Tbsp freshly squeezed lemon juice

2 tsp lemon extract

½ tsp vanilla extract

½ cup plus 2 Tbsp unsalted butter, softened

1 cup granulated sugar

Lemonade Frosting

3 large egg whites

¾ cup plus 1 Tbsp granulated sugar

⅓ cup frozen pink or regular lemonade concentrate, thawed

1 Tbsp white corn syrup

16 additional fresh raspberries for garnish (optional)

Curls of lemon zest for garnish (optional)

1. Preheat the oven to 350°F. Line two muffin pans with 16 large paper liners, then set aside. Pour water into any empty wells to prevent burning.

2. For the raspberries, toss the halved berries with the flour in a medium bowl. Set aside.

3. For the cupcakes, whisk together both flours, the baking powder, baking soda and salt in a large bowl. Set aside.

4. In a small bowl, whisk together ¼ cup of the buttermilk, the eggs, lemon zest and juice, and lemon and vanilla extracts. Set aside.

5. In a large bowl and using an electric mixer, beat the butter until pale and fluffy.

6. Add the sugar and beat until pale and fluffy, about 2 minutes, scraping down the sides of the bowl once or twice.

7. With the mixer running on low speed, add the flour mixture and the remaining ¼ cup buttermilk. Mix just until combined.

8. Increase the mixer speed to medium and beat until everything is well combined, about 2 more minutes, scraping down the sides of the bowl three or four times.

9. Turn down the mixer speed to low and add one-third of the egg mixture. Increase the speed to medium and beat until the egg mixture is fully incorporated.

Add the remaining egg mixture in two additions, beating just until combined after each addition.

10. Gently fold in the raspberry-flour mixture until well combined.

11. Fill the paper liners about two-thirds full with batter. Bake until the cupcakes spring back when lightly touched and a wooden skewer inserted in the centre of a cupcake comes out clean, about 20 minutes.

12. Let the cupcakes cool in the pans for 10 minutes, then remove to a wire rack and let cool completely. (The undecorated cupcakes can be refrigerated in an airtight container for up to 4 days.)

13. For the lemonade frosting, put the egg whites in a large bowl and have an electric mixer ready.

14. In a medium, heavy-bottomed saucepan, stir together ¾ cup of the sugar, the lemonade concentrate and corn syrup. Bring to a boil over medium heat.

15. Hook a candy thermometer over the side of the saucepan. Cook the sugar mixture, without stirring, until the candy thermometer registers 240°F, about 10 minutes. (If you don't have a candy thermometer, drop a little of the mixture into a bowl of cold water. If it forms a soft ball, it's ready.)

16. When the syrup reaches 220°F, start beating the egg whites on medium-high speed until soft peaks form. Beat in the remaining 1 tablespoonful of sugar. The temperature of the syrup will continue to increase.

17. Once the boiling sugar mixture has reached 240°F, immediately pour the syrup down the side of the bowl while you beat the egg white mixture on medium speed, being careful of splashes.

18. When all the syrup has been added, increase the mixer speed to medium-high. Beat until the frosting is completely cool and stiff peaks form, 3 to 5 minutes.

19. Spoon the frosting into a piping bag fitted with a plain, round tip. Pipe a swirl of lemonade frosting on top of each cupcake. Decorate each cupcake with a raspberry and/or curls of lemon zest (if using). (The decorated cupcakes can be refrigerated in an airtight container for up to 3 days. Bring them to room temperature before serving.)

Frosty Orange Cupcakes

These cupcakes taste just like a popular creamy orange iced treat. Bake up a batch for a birthday party and watch them disappear.

Makes 18 cupcakes
Prep time: 40 minutes
Cooking time: about 20 minutes

Cupcakes

2 ¼ cups all-purpose flour

1 cup granulated sugar

1 ½ tsp baking powder

½ tsp baking soda

½ tsp fine sea salt

¾ cup unsalted butter, cut into 1-inch pieces and softened

2 large eggs, lightly beaten

2 Tbsp finely grated orange zest

½ cup whipping cream (35%)

½ cup carbonated orange soft drink

Creamy Orange Frosting

1 ½ cups unsalted butter, softened

6 cups icing sugar, sifted

1 tsp vanilla extract

1 tsp fine sea salt

1 cup whipping cream (35%), chilled

2 Tbsp finely grated orange zest

2 tsp freshly squeezed lemon juice

1 tsp orange extract

Orange gel food colouring (see sidebar)

1. Preheat the oven to 350°F. Line two muffins pans with 18 large paper liners, then set aside. Pour water into any empty wells to prevent burning.

2. For the cupcakes, whisk together the flour, sugar, baking powder, baking soda and salt in a large bowl.

3. Using an electric mixer on low speed, add the butter one piece at a time, mixing until the butter is evenly distributed and the mixture resembles coarse crumbs.

4. With the mixer still running on low speed, add the eggs, a few tablespoonfuls at a time, incorporating fully after each addition. Add the orange zest and beat just until combined.

5. Slowly pour in the cream, beating until well combined. Gradually beat in the orange soft drink, then beat for about 30 seconds.

6. Fill the paper liners about two-thirds full with batter. Bake until the cupcakes spring back when lightly touched and a wooden skewer inserted in the centre of a cupcake comes out clean, about 20 minutes.

7. Let the cupcakes cool in the pans for 10 minutes, then remove to a wire rack and let cool completely. (The undecorated cupcakes can be refrigerated in an airtight container for up to 4 days.)

8. For the creamy orange frosting, in a large bowl and using an electric mixer, beat the butter until smooth.

9. Beat in the icing sugar, ½ cup at a time, then beat for about 3 minutes. Beat in the vanilla extract and salt. Add the cream and beat until fluffy, about 1 minute.

10. Spoon half of the frosting into a medium bowl. Beat the orange zest, lemon juice and orange extract into the medium bowl of frosting. Beat in enough orange food colouring to tint it bright orange.

11. Fit a large piping bag with a ½-inch plain tip. Spoon the white and orange frostings into two separate medium disposable piping bags. Snip off the end of each bag to make a ½-inch aperture.

12. Place the filled piping bags, side by side, in the large bag (the cut ends of the smaller bags should be about ½ inch above the opening of the tip). Twist the large bag to close it. Squeeze it until the two frostings emerge evenly.

13. Swirl the frosting on top of the cupcakes, using about 3 tablespoonfuls of frosting per cupcake. (The decorated cupcakes can be refrigerated in an airtight container for up to 3 days. Bring them to room temperature before serving.)

BAKING DAY SECRETS

To give the orange frosting the most vivid colour, use gel food colouring rather than the liquid kind. You need to use less gel to achieve a bright-coloured frosting. If you use liquid food colouring, add an additional 2 to 3 tablespoons of sifted icing sugar to the frosting so its consistency is similar to that of the white frosting.

Pumpkin Spice Cupcakes
with Cinnamon–Cream Cheese Frosting

F ull of spice and everything nice, these pumpkin cupcakes are the perfect fall treat.

Makes 18 cupcakes
Prep time: 40 minutes
Cooking time: about 20 minutes

Cupcakes

1 ²/₃ cups all-purpose flour

1 ¼ tsp ground cinnamon

1 ¼ tsp baking powder

¾ tsp fine sea salt

½ tsp baking soda

¼ tsp ground cloves

Pinch of freshly grated nutmeg

²/₃ cup unsalted butter, softened

½ cup firmly packed dark brown sugar

½ cup granulated sugar

¾ cup fresh or canned pumpkin purée (not pie filling)

2 large eggs

¹/₃ cup whole milk

Cinnamon–Cream Cheese Frosting

1 pkg (8 oz/250 g) brick-style cream cheese, at room temperature

½ cup unsalted butter, softened

3 cups icing sugar, sifted

2 tsp ground cinnamon

Cinnamon sugar for garnish

1. Preheat the oven to 350°F. Line two muffin pans with 18 large paper liners, then set aside. Pour water into any empty wells to prevent burning.

2. For the cupcakes, whisk together the flour, cinnamon, baking powder, salt, baking soda, cloves and nutmeg in a medium bowl. Set aside.

3. In a large bowl and using an electric mixer, beat together the butter and both sugars until light and fluffy.

4. Beat in the pumpkin purée until well combined. Beat in the eggs one at a time, beating well after each addition.

5. Add the flour mixture to the butter mixture alternately with the milk, making three additions of flour and two of milk, and beginning and ending with the flour. Stir until well combined.

6. Fill the paper liners about two-thirds full with batter. Bake until the cupcakes spring back when lightly touched and a wooden skewer inserted in the centre of a cupcake comes out clean, about 20 minutes.

7. Let the cupcakes cool in the pans for 10 minutes, then remove to a wire rack and let cool completely. (The undecorated cupcakes can be refrigerated in an airtight container for up to 4 days.)

8. For the frosting, in a medium bowl and using an electric mixer, beat together the cream cheese and butter until pale and fluffy.

9. Beat in the icing sugar, ½ cup at a time, until the frosting is a spreadable consistency. Beat in the cinnamon.

10. Using an offset spatula or a piping bag, swirl the frosting on top of the cupcakes. Sprinkle with cinnamon sugar. (The decorated cupcakes can be refrigerated in an airtight container for up to 3 days. Bring them to room temperature before serving.)

Butterscotch–Peanut Butter Cupcakes

I f you love peanut butter cookies, just wait until you try these cupcakes! Smooth peanut butter is best for the buttercream. Don't be tempted to use old-fashioned or natural peanut butter, because it may separate.

Makes 18 cupcakes
Prep time: 40 minutes
Cooking time: about 20 minutes

Cupcakes

1 ½ cups all-purpose flour

½ cup cake-and-pastry flour

1 ½ tsp baking powder

½ tsp baking soda

½ tsp fine sea salt

1 cup butterscotch chips

½ cup unsalted butter, softened

1 cup firmly packed dark brown sugar

3 large eggs

1 Tbsp vanilla extract

1 cup buttermilk (see page 11)

Peanut Butter Buttercream

½ cup unsalted butter, softened

1 cup smooth peanut butter (see note above)

1 tsp vanilla extract

½ tsp fine sea salt

3 to 4 cups icing sugar, sifted

2 Tbsp whipping cream (35%)

½ cup roasted salted peanuts, chopped

1. Preheat the oven to 350°F. Line two muffin pans with 18 large paper liners, then set aside. Pour water into any empty wells to prevent burning.

2. For the cupcakes, whisk together both flours, the baking powder, baking soda and salt in a medium bowl. Stir in the butterscotch chips. Set aside.

3. In a large bowl and using an electric mixer, beat the butter with the sugar until light and fluffy.

4. Beat in the eggs one at a time, beating well after each addition and scraping down the sides of the bowl once or twice. Beat in the vanilla extract.

5. Add the flour mixture to the sugar mixture alternately with the buttermilk, making three additions of flour and two of buttermilk, and beginning and ending with the flour. Stir until well combined.

6. Fill the paper liners about two-thirds full with batter. Bake until the cupcakes spring back when lightly touched and a wooden skewer inserted in the centre of a cupcake comes out clean, about 20 minutes.

7. Let the cupcakes cool in the pans for 10 minutes, then remove to a wire rack and let cool completely. (The undecorated cupcakes can be refrigerated in an airtight container for up to 4 days.)

8. For the peanut butter buttercream, in a large bowl and using an electric mixer, beat the butter until pale and fluffy. Beat in the peanut butter, vanilla extract and salt.

9. Add about 1 ½ cups of the icing sugar and beat on low speed. Beat in the cream and enough of the remaining icing sugar to make a smooth, fluffy, spreadable buttercream.

10. Using an offset spatula or a piping bag, swirl the buttercream on top of the cupcakes. Sprinkle with the peanuts. (The decorated cupcakes can be refrigerated in an airtight container for up to 3 days. Bring them to room temperature before serving.)

Carrot Cupcakes with Maple Frosting
(recipe opposite)

Mojito Cupcakes
(recipe page 138)

Carrot Cupcakes
with Maple Frosting

C rowd-pleasing carrot cake gets an update here, trans-
formed into tasty cupcakes slathered with maple-spiked
cream cheese frosting.

Makes 12 cupcakes
Prep time: 40 minutes
Cooking time: about 20 minutes

Cupcakes

2 large carrots

1 cup all-purpose flour

1 ¼ tsp ground cinnamon

½ tsp baking powder

½ tsp freshly grated nutmeg

½ tsp fine sea salt

¼ tsp baking soda

½ cup unsalted butter, softened

½ cup granulated sugar

½ cup lightly packed golden
    yellow sugar

2 large eggs

½ tsp vanilla extract

Maple Frosting

1 cup brick-style cream cheese,
    at room temperature

¼ cup unsalted butter, softened

2 to 4 cups icing sugar, sifted

1 Tbsp maple syrup

Additional ground cinnamon
    for garnish

1. Preheat the oven to 350°F. Line a muffin pan with 12 large paper liners, then set aside.

2. For the cupcakes, grate the carrots on the largest holes of a box grater into a medium bowl. You'll need 1 ½ cups grated carrots. Add 1 tablespoonful of the flour to the carrots and toss well. Set aside.

3. In a medium bowl, whisk together the remaining flour, the cinnamon, baking powder, nutmeg, salt, and baking soda. Set aside.

4. In a large bowl and using an electric mixer, beat the butter with both sugars until pale and fluffy.

5. Beat in the eggs one at a time, beating well after each addition. Beat in the vanilla extract.

6. Using a wooden spoon or spatula, add the flour mixture to the sugar mixture in three separate additions, stirring well after each addition, until well combined. Stir in the grated carrots.

7. Fill the paper liners about two-thirds full with batter. Bake until the cupcakes spring back when lightly touched and a wooden skewer inserted in the centre of a cupcake comes out clean, about 20 minutes.

8. Let the cupcakes cool in the pans for 10 minutes, then remove to a wire rack and let cool completely. (The undecorated cupcakes can be refrigerated in an airtight container for up to 4 days.)

9. For the frosting, in a medium bowl and using an electric mixer, beat together the cream cheese and butter until pale and fluffy.

10. Beat in the icing sugar, 1 cup at a time, until the frosting is smooth and fluffy. Beat in the maple syrup.

11. Using an offset spatula or a piping bag, swirl the frosting on top of the cupcakes, then sprinkle with cinnamon. (The decorated cupcakes can be refrigerated in an airtight container for up to 3 days. Bring them to room temperature before serving.)

Mojito Cupcakes

We love the vibrant mint-lime flavours in a classic mojito cocktail, and found that the same combo works really well in a cupcake. Brushing the baked cupcakes with a mint-flavoured syrup before adding the frosting makes them super moist.

Makes 12 cupcakes
Prep time: 40 minutes
Cooking time: about 20 minutes

Cupcakes

1 ½ cups all-purpose flour

1 ½ tsp baking powder

¼ tsp fine sea salt

½ cup unsalted butter, softened

1 cup granulated sugar

2 large eggs

Finely grated zest and squeezed juice of 2 limes

1 Tbsp very finely chopped mint leaves

¼ tsp vanilla extract

½ cup buttermilk (see page 11)

Mint Simple Syrup

½ cup water

½ cup granulated sugar

¼ cup firmly packed mint leaves

Frosting

Finely grated zest and squeezed juice of 1 lime

1 Tbsp very finely chopped mint leaves

½ cup unsalted butter, softened

2 to 3 cups icing sugar, sifted

1 Tbsp whipping cream (35%)

CHANGE IT UP

To mimic the rum flavour of a mojito cocktail, replace the granulated sugar in the Mint Simple Syrup with lightly packed golden yellow sugar.

1. Preheat the oven to 350°F. Line a muffin pan with 12 large paper liners, then set aside.

2. For the cupcakes, whisk together the flour, baking powder and salt in a medium bowl. Set aside.

3. In a large bowl and using an electric mixer, beat the butter with the sugar until pale and fluffy.

4. Beat in the eggs one at a time, beating well after each addition and scraping down the sides of the bowl once or twice. Beat in the lime zest and juice, mint and vanilla extract.

5. Add the flour mixture to the sugar mixture alternately with the buttermilk, making three additions of flour and two of buttermilk, and beginning and ending with the flour. Stir until well combined.

6. Fill the paper liners about two-thirds full with batter. Bake until the cupcakes spring back when lightly touched and a wooden skewer inserted in the centre of a cupcake comes out clean, about 20 minutes.

7. While the cupcakes are baking, prepare the mint simple syrup.

In a small saucepan, stir together the water, sugar and mint leaves. Bring to a boil over medium-high heat, stirring to dissolve the sugar. Strain through a fine-mesh sieve, making sure all the mint leaves are strained out of the syrup. Let the syrup cool completely.

8. Let the cupcakes cool in the pans for 10 minutes, then remove to a wire rack set over parchment paper to catch any drips. Brush the top of each warm cupcake generously with the syrup. Let the cupcakes absorb the syrup, then brush generously with any remaining syrup. Let the cupcakes cool completely. (The undecorated cupcakes can be refrigerated in an airtight container for up to 4 days.)

9. For the frosting, stir together the lime zest and juice and mint in a small bowl.

10. In a large bowl and using an electric mixer, beat the butter until pale and fluffy. Beat in the lime zest mixture until well combined.

11. Beat in the icing sugar, 1 cup at a time, until the frosting is smooth and fluffy. Beat in the cream.

12. Using an offset spatula or a piping bag, swirl the frosting on top of the cupcakes. (The decorated cupcakes can be refrigerated in an airtight container for up to 3 days. Bring them to room temperature before serving.)

Lemon–White Chocolate Cupcakes
with Blackberry Buttercream

T hese luscious cupcakes team juicy berries with rich white chocolate to make a special summer treat.

Makes 18 cupcakes
Prep time: 40 minutes
Cooking time: about 30 minutes

Chocolate Chips

¾ cup white chocolate chips

1 Tbsp all-purpose flour

Cupcakes

1 ¾ cups all-purpose flour

1 ½ tsp baking powder

½ tsp fine sea salt

¼ tsp baking soda

⅔ cup unsalted butter, softened

1 cup granulated sugar

2 large eggs

1 Tbsp finely grated lemon zest (1 to 2 lemons)

1 Tbsp freshly squeezed lemon juice

1 tsp vanilla extract

½ cup whole milk

Blackberry Buttercream

1 ½ cups fresh or frozen black-berries

2 Tbsp freshly squeezed lemon juice

1 Tbsp water

1 ½ cups granulated sugar

4 large egg whites

½ tsp fine sea salt

1 ¼ cups unsalted butter, cut into 1-inch pieces and softened

Additional fresh blackberries and finely grated lemon zest for garnish (optional)

1. Preheat the oven to 350°F. Line two muffins pans with 18 large paper liners, then set aside. Pour water into any empty wells to prevent burning.

2. For the chocolate chips, toss them with the flour in a small bowl. Set aside.

3. For the cupcakes, whisk together the flour, baking powder, salt and baking soda in a medium bowl. Set aside.

4. In a large bowl and using an electric mixer, beat the butter on medium-low speed until creamy. Gradually beat in the sugar, increasing the speed to medium. Beat until pale and fluffy.

5. Turn down the speed to low and beat in the eggs one at a time. Beat in the lemon zest and juice and vanilla extract.

6. Add the flour mixture to the butter mixture alternately with the milk, making three additions of flour and two of milk, and beginning and ending with the flour. Stir until well combined. Fold in the chocolate chips.

7. Fill the paper liners about two-thirds full with batter. Bake until the cupcakes spring back when lightly touched and a wooden skewer inserted in the centre of a cupcake comes out clean, about 20 minutes.

8. Let the cupcakes cool in the pans for 10 minutes, then remove to a wire rack and let cool completely. (The undecorated

cupcakes can be refrigerated in an airtight container for up to 4 days.)

9. For the buttercream, stir together the blackberries, lemon juice and water in a small saucepan. Mash the berries well with a fork. Bring to a simmer over low heat, then cook, stirring occasionally, until the mixture has reduced to about ½ cup.

10. Strain the blackberry mixture through a fine-mesh sieve, pressing on the solids to extract as much blackberry purée as pos-sible. Cool and discard the seeds.

11. In a large heatproof bowl, stir together the sugar, egg whites and salt. Set the bowl over a saucepan of simmering water. Whisk constantly until the mixture registers 140°F on an instant-read thermometer, 6 to 8 minutes.

12. Remove the bowl from the heat and, using an electric mixer, beat the mixture on medium-high until it has cooled, about 10 minutes. Turn down the mixer speed to low and beat in the butter, one piece at a time, beating to incorporate after each addition. Beat in the blackberry purée until well combined.

13. Using an offset spatula or a piping bag, swirl the buttercream on top of the cupcakes. Garnish with blackberries and lemon zest. (The frosted cupcakes—without the garnish—can be refrigerated in an airtight container for up to 3 days. Bring them to room temperature before serving.)

Chocolate-Coconut Panda Cupcakes

W hip up these fun cupcakes in no time, and get ready for kids young and old to have fun creating panda faces on them.

Makes 16 cupcakes
Prep time: 50 minutes
Cooking time: about 20 minutes

Cupcakes

1 cup all-purpose flour

¾ cup unsweetened cocoa powder

¾ tsp baking soda

½ tsp baking powder

½ tsp fine sea salt

1 cup granulated sugar

⅔ cup sour cream (14%)

½ cup vegetable oil

2 large eggs

2 tsp vanilla extract

Decoration

½ batch of Seven-Minute Frosting (page 158)

1 tsp coconut extract

2 cups sweetened flaked coconut

40 dark chocolate wafers (see sidebar)

32 chocolate-covered almonds

32 mini chocolate chips

Chocolate sprinkles

1. Preheat the oven to 350°F. Line two muffins pans with 16 large paper liners, then set aside. Pour water into any empty wells to prevent burning.

2. For the cupcakes, whisk together the flour, cocoa powder, baking soda, baking powder and salt in a large bowl. Set aside.

3. In a separate large bowl, whisk together the sugar, sour cream, oil, eggs and vanilla extract until well combined.

4. Add the sugar mixture to the flour mixture, stirring until no white streaks remain.

5. Fill the paper liners about two-thirds full with batter. Bake until the cupcakes spring back when lightly touched and a wooden skewer inserted in the centre of a cupcake comes out clean, about 20 minutes.

6. Let the cupcakes cool in the pans for 10 minutes, then remove to a wire rack and let cool completely. (The undecorated cupcakes can be refrigerated in an airtight container for up to 4 days.)

7. For the decoration, stir together the frosting and coconut extract in a medium bowl. Place the coconut in a separate medium bowl.

8. Using an offset spatula, spread the frosting on top of the cupcakes, using about 2 tablespoonfuls per cupcake. Dip each cupcake in the coconut to coat the frosting.

9. To decorate the tops of the cupcakes to resemble panda faces, stick two chocolate wafers into the frosting on either side for ears. Cut the remaining wafers in half, then place one half in the centre of the top of each cupcake for a nose.

10. Place a chocolate-covered almond on either side of the nose for eyes. Spoon a little frosting on each one and top with a chocolate chip for the pupils.

11. Place three chocolate sprinkles on each cupcake, under the nose, for the mouth. (The decorated cupcakes can be refrigerated in an airtight container for up to 3 days. Bring them to room temperature before serving.)

BAKING DAY SECRETS

The dark chocolate wafers you need for this recipe are made from solid chocolate and about the size of a nickel. Don't confuse them with chocolate wafer cookies. Look for dark chocolate wafers at your local bulk or baking supply store.

Vanilla Vegan Cupcakes
(recipe page 145)

Blueberry-Filled
Cupcakes
(recipe opposite)

Dulce de Leche Cupcakes
(recipe page 144)

Blueberry-Filled Cupcakes
with Lime Frosting

T here's a lovely surprise in these cupcakes: a sweet blueberry filling hides under a rich, citrusy cream cheese frosting.

Makes 18 cupcakes
Prep time: 50 minutes
Cooking time: about 30 minutes

Cupcakes

1 cup cake-and-pastry flour

1 cup all-purpose flour

2 tsp baking powder

½ tsp fine sea salt

½ cup whole milk

2 large eggs

2 tsp vanilla extract

1 vanilla bean

¾ cup unsalted butter, softened

1 cup granulated sugar

Blueberry Filling

⅓ cup granulated sugar

1 tsp cornstarch

1 cup fresh or frozen blueberries

⅓ cup water

1 Tbsp freshly squeezed lime juice (1 lime)

Lime Frosting

1 pkg (8 oz/250 g) brick-style cream cheese, at room temperature

¼ cup unsalted butter, softened

4 cups icing sugar, sifted

1 Tbsp finely grated lime zest (2 to 3 limes)

1 Tbsp freshly squeezed lime juice (1 lime)

1 tsp vanilla extract

½ tsp fine sea salt

Additional fresh blueberries and lime slices for garnish (optional)

1. Preheat the oven to 350°F. Line two muffin pans with 18 large paper liners, then set aside. Pour water into any empty wells to prevent burning.

2. For the cupcakes, whisk both flours, the baking powder and salt in a medium bowl. Set aside.

3. In a small bowl, whisk ¼ cup of milk, the eggs and vanilla extract.

4. Using a sharp knife, split the vanilla bean in half lengthwise. Scrape out the seeds into the milk mixture. Whisk well, then set aside. Discard the vanilla bean.

5. In a large bowl and using an electric mixer, beat the butter with the sugar until pale and fluffy, about 3 minutes. With the mixer running on low speed, beat in the flour mixture and the remaining ¼ cup of milk just until combined. Increase the speed to medium-high. Beat for 2 minutes, scraping down the sides of the bowl once or twice.

6. With the mixer running on low speed, beat one-third of the egg mixture into the sugar mixture. Increase the speed to medium and beat until the egg mixture is fully incorporated before adding half of the remaining egg mixture. Repeat with the remaining egg.

7. Fill the paper liners about two-thirds full with batter. Bake until the cupcakes spring back when lightly touched and a wooden skewer inserted in the centre of a cupcake comes out clean, about 20 minutes.

8. Let the cupcakes cool in the pans for 10 minutes, then remove to a wire rack and cool completely. (The undecorated cupcakes can be refrigerated in an airtight container for up to 4 days.)

9. For the blueberry filling, whisk the sugar and cornstarch in a small saucepan. Stir in the blueberries, water and lime juice. Cook over medium-low heat, stirring occasionally, until the blueberries have burst and the mixture coats the back of a spoon, 8 to 10 minutes. Let cool completely.

10. For the frosting, in a large bowl and using an electric mixer on medium speed, beat the cream cheese and butter until smooth. Beat in the icing sugar, 1 cup at a time, until the frosting is smooth and fluffy. Beat in the lime zest and juice, vanilla extract and salt until well combined.

11. To assemble the cupcakes, use a small, sharp knife to cut a cone-shaped piece, about 1 inch deep and ¾ inch wide, from the top of each cupcake. Slice off and discard the pointy underside of each cone-shaped piece. Fill the cavity in each cupcake with the blueberry filling. Replace the tops.

12. Using an offset spatula or a piping bag, swirl the frosting on top of the cupcakes. Garnish with blueberries and lime slices. (The frosted cupcakes—without the garnish—can be refrigerated in an airtight container for up to 3 days. Bring them to room temperature before serving.)

Dulce de Leche Cupcakes

Dulce de leche adds a luscious, caramel filling to these cupcakes, and the dark chocolate topping is the perfect finishing touch.

Makes 18 cupcakes
Prep time: 50 minutes
Cooking time: about 20 minutes
Cooling time: 15 to 20 minutes
Setting time: 5 to 20 minutes

Cupcakes

Dulce de Leche (page 21)

1 cup cake-and-pastry flour

1 cup all-purpose flour

2 ¼ tsp baking powder

½ tsp fine sea salt

¾ cup whole milk

2 large eggs

1 large egg white

2 tsp vanilla extract

¾ cup unsalted butter, softened

1 cup firmly packed dark brown sugar

Dark Chocolate Ganache

1 cup dark chocolate chips

¾ cup whipping cream (35%)

Sea salt flakes for garnish

1. Preheat the oven to 350°F. Line two muffin pans with 18 large paper liners, then set aside. Pour water into any empty wells to prevent burning.

2. For the cupcakes, spoon the dulce de leche into a piping bag fitted with a small, round, plain tip. Refrigerate until ready to use.

3. In a medium bowl, whisk together both flours, the baking powder and salt. Set aside.

4. In a separate medium bowl, whisk together ¼ cup of the milk, the eggs, egg white and vanilla extract. Set aside.

5. In a large bowl and using an electric mixer, beat the butter until pale and fluffy.

6. Beat in the sugar until pale and fluffy, scraping down the sides of the bowl once or twice.

7. With the mixer running on low speed, beat in the flour mixture and the remaining ½ cup of milk, just until combined.

8. Increase the speed to medium and beat for 2 minutes, scraping down the sides of the bowl once or twice.

9. Turn down the mixer speed to low, then beat one-third of the egg mixture into the sugar mixture. Increase the speed to medium and beat until the egg mixture is fully incorporated before adding half of the remaining egg mixture. Repeat with the remaining egg mixture.

10. Fill the paper liners about two-thirds full with batter. Bake until the cupcakes spring back when lightly touched and a wooden skewer inserted in the centre of a cupcake comes out clean, about 20 minutes.

11. Let the cupcakes cool in the pans for 10 minutes, then remove to a wire rack and let cool completely. (The undecorated cupcakes can be refrigerated in an airtight container for up to 4 days.)

12. Using a small, sharp knife, cut a cone-shaped piece, about 1 inch deep and ¾ inch wide, from the top of each cupcake. Slice off and discard the pointy underside of each cone-shaped piece.

13. Pipe the dulce de leche into the cavity in each cupcake, filling each about three-quarters full. Replace the tops of the cupcakes.

14. For the ganache, place the chocolate chips in a medium heatproof bowl. In a small saucepan, heat the cream over medium-low heat just until it begins to simmer.

15. Pour one-third of the hot cream over the chocolate chips. Let stand about 30 seconds, then stir until well combined. Add half of the remaining hot cream and stir again. Repeat with the remaining cream, stirring until the mixture is smooth and shiny.

16. Let cool until the ganache has thickened and is at room temperature, 15 to 20 minutes.

17. Spoon about 1 tablespoonful of ganache over each cupcake, spreading with an offset spatula or the back of a spoon to cover the top of each cupcake. Sprinkle each cupcake with a pinch of sea salt flakes.

18. Let the ganache set before serving, 15 to 20 minutes at room temperature or 5 to 10 minutes in the fridge. (The decorated cupcakes can be refrigerated in an airtight container for up to 3 days. Bring them to room temperature before serving.)

Vanilla Vegan Cupcakes

These cupcakes are so moist and full of flavour, it's hard to believe they're dairy- and egg-free. We like them iced with vanilla frosting, but they pair well with just about any flavour, so feel free to customize.

Makes 12 large or 24 mini cupcakes
Prep time: 30 minutes
Cooking time: 15 to 18 minutes (large cupcakes), 8 to 10 minutes (mini cupcakes)

Cupcakes

1 ¾ cups all-purpose flour

1 cup granulated sugar

1 tsp baking powder

1 tsp baking soda

½ tsp fine sea salt

1 cup unsweetened plain soy milk or almond milk

½ cup vegetable oil

2 Tbsp vanilla extract

1 Tbsp white vinegar or apple cider vinegar

Vanilla Frosting

1 cup coconut oil, at room temperature

2 cups icing sugar, sifted

½ tsp vanilla extract

Coloured sprinkles (optional)

1. Preheat the oven to 350°F. Line a regular muffin pan with 12 large paper liners, or a mini muffin pan with 24 mini paper liners, then set aside.

2. For the cupcakes, whisk together the flour, sugar, baking powder, baking soda and salt in a large bowl.

3. In a medium bowl, whisk together the soy milk, oil, vanilla extract and vinegar.

4. Make a well in the centre of the flour mixture. Pour the soy milk mixture into the well. Whisk just until combined and no white streaks remain. Do not overmix.

5. Fill the paper liners about two-thirds full with the batter. Bake until the cupcakes spring back when lightly touched and a wooden skewer inserted in the centre of a cupcake comes out clean, 15 to 18 minutes for the large cupcakes, 8 to 10 minutes for the minis.

6. Let the cupcakes cool in the pans for 10 minutes, then remove to a wire rack and let cool completely. (The undecorated cupcakes can be refrigerated in an airtight container for up to 4 days.)

7. For the frosting, in a bowl and using an electric mixer, beat the coconut oil until smooth and creamy.

8. Beat in the icing sugar, ½ cup at a time, and beat well after each addition. Beat in the vanilla extract until smooth and fluffy.

9. Using an offset spatula or a piping bag, swirl the frosting on top of the cupcakes. Scatter with sprinkles (if using). (The decorated cupcakes can be refrigerated in an airtight container for up to 3 days. Bring them to room temperature before serving.)

Cute Baby Shower Cupcakes

You can use homemade marzipan decorations (pages 164 and 165) to make these darling cupcakes very personal. Or simply frost them with the buttercream then sprinkle with flaked coconut or pastel- or silver-coloured dragées.

Makes 18 cupcakes
Prep time: 1 hour
Cooking time: about 20 minutes

Cupcakes

1 cup cake-and-pastry flour

¾ cup all-purpose flour

1 ½ tsp baking powder

½ tsp baking soda

½ tsp fine sea salt

1 large egg

2 large egg whites

¼ cup plain yogurt (3%)

2 ½ tsp vanilla extract

¾ cup unsalted butter, softened

1 cup granulated sugar

¼ cup whole milk

Decorations

1 ½ cups Marzipan (page 163; about half of the recipe)

Gel food colouring of your choice

Icing sugar for dusting

1 batch of Quick Buttercream (page 154)

1 tsp vanilla extract

¼ tsp fine sea salt

1. Preheat the oven to 350°F. Line two muffin pans with 18 large paper liners, then set aside. Pour water into any empty wells to prevent burning.

2. For the cupcakes, whisk together both flours, the baking powder, baking soda and salt in a medium bowl. Set aside.

3. In a small bowl, whisk the egg and egg whites, yogurt and vanilla until smooth. Set aside.

4. In a large bowl and using an electric mixer, beat the butter until pale and fluffy. Beat in the sugar until well combined, scraping down the sides of the bowl once or twice.

5. With the mixer running on low speed, beat in the flour mixture and milk just until combined. Increase the speed to medium and beat for 2 minutes, scraping down the sides of the bowl.

6. Turn down the mixer speed to low, then beat one-third of the egg mixture into the butter mixture. Increase the speed to medium and beat until the egg mixture is fully incorporated before adding half of the remaining egg mixture. Repeat with the remaining egg mixture.

7. Fill the paper liners about two-thirds full with batter. Bake until the cupcakes spring back when lightly touched and a wooden skewer inserted in the centre of a cupcake comes out clean, about 20 minutes.

8. Let the cupcakes cool in the pans for 10 minutes, then remove to a wire rack and let cool completely. (The undecorated cupcakes can be refrigerated in an airtight container for up to 4 days.)

9. For the decorations, divide the marzipan into three or more even-sized pieces (depending on the number of shades of food colouring you have). Using a toothpick or a wooden skewer, add a small amount of food colouring to each piece of marzipan. Knead the colouring into the marzipan until it's uniformly distributed. Keep the pieces of marzipan wrapped well in plastic wrap until you're ready to roll them.

10. On a surface lightly dusted with icing sugar, roll out each piece of marzipan to ⅛-inch thickness. Cut out 18 scalloped circles or stars, slightly smaller than the tops of the cupcakes.

11. From the remaining marzipan, cut out shapes of your choice. Brush each circle or star lightly with water and top with a marzipan shape.

12. Arrange the marzipan decorations on a parchment-paper-lined baking sheet, cover tightly with plastic wrap and set aside at room temperature (or in the fridge) until ready to use.

13. Prepare the buttercream, adding the 1 teaspoonful of vanilla and the salt as listed.

14. Using an offset spatula or a piping bag, swirl the buttercream on top of the cupcakes. Gently press a marzipan decoration onto the buttercream. (The decorated cupcakes can be refrigerated in an airtight container for up to 3 days. Bring them to room temperature before serving.)

Lavender Cupcakes
with Vanilla Bean Frosting

These lavender cupcakes are light, sweet and buttery, and their floral flavour makes them perfect for spring and summer.

Makes 12 cupcakes
Prep time: 40 minutes
Cooking time: about 20 minutes

Cupcakes

2 Tbsp dried culinary lavender (see sidebar)

1 ½ cups all-purpose flour

½ tsp baking powder

¼ tsp fine sea salt

½ cup unsalted butter, softened

1 cup granulated sugar

2 large eggs

1 tsp vanilla extract

⅔ cup half-and-half cream (10%)

Vanilla Bean Frosting

½ cup unsalted butter, softened

2 cups icing sugar, sifted

1 Tbsp whole milk

1 vanilla bean

1 tsp vanilla extract

Purple (or blue and red) gel food colouring

White pearlized sprinkles (see sidebar)

BAKING DAY SECRETS

When buying lavender for cooking, look for culinary lavender so you know it's safe to eat and has good flavour. Choose dried lavender packaged by a major herb producer or, if buying lavender from a lavender farm or farmers' market, ask if it's edible.

1. Preheat the oven to 350°F. Line a muffin pan with 12 large paper liners.

2. For the cupcakes, pound the lavender in a mortar and pestle until finely ground, or finely chop it by hand. (This helps to release its flavour.)

3. In a medium bowl, whisk together the flour, baking powder, salt, and lavender. Set aside.

4. In a large bowl and using an electric mixer, beat the butter with the sugar until pale and fluffy.

5. Beat in the eggs one at a time, beating well after each addition. Beat in the vanilla extract.

6. Add the flour mixture to the sugar mixture alternately with the cream, making three additions of flour and two of cream, and beginning and ending with the flour. Stir until well combined.

7. Fill the paper liners about two-thirds full with the batter. Bake until the cupcakes spring back when lightly touched and a wooden skewer inserted in the centre of a cupcake comes out clean, about 20 minutes.

8. Let the cupcakes cool in the pans for 10 minutes, then remove to a wire rack and let cool completely. (The undecorated cupcakes can be refrigerated in an airtight container for up to 4 days.)

9. For the frosting, in a medium bowl and using an electric mixer, beat together the butter and ½ cup of the icing sugar until pale and fluffy.

10. Beat in another ½ cup of the icing sugar and the milk. Continue beating in the icing sugar, ½ cup at a time, until the frosting is smooth and fluffy.

11. Using a sharp knife, split the vanilla bean in half lengthwise. Scrape the seeds out into the frosting, discarding the pod. Add the vanilla extract to the frosting, then mix until smooth.

12. Add enough purple food colouring (or a mixture of blue and red) to tint the frosting purple.

13. Fit a piping bag with a leaf tip, then spoon in the frosting. Pipe the frosting on top of the cupcakes, then scatter with sprinkles. (The decorated cupcakes can be refrigerated in an airtight container for up to 3 days. Bring them to room temperature before serving.)

BAKING DAY SECRETS

Look for white pearlized sprinkles in bulk, craft or baking supply stores.

Elegant Petits Fours

No posh afternoon tea would be complete without these little treats. They take some time to prepare, but they would be a fun afternoon project to enjoy with your kids or good friends.

Makes 48 petits fours
Prep time: 1 ½ hours
Cooking time: 20 to 30 minutes
Setting time: at least 5 hours
Freezing time: 30 minutes

Cake

2 ½ cups plus 2 Tbsp cake-and-pastry flour

2 tsp baking powder

¾ tsp fine sea salt

½ tsp baking soda

6 Tbsp unsalted butter, softened

1 ½ cups granulated sugar

2 large eggs

1 ½ tsp vanilla extract

1 ½ tsp finely grated lemon zest

½ cup water

2 Tbsp freshly squeezed lemon juice

¾ cup whole milk

To Assemble

⅔ cup raspberry jam

¾ cup Marzipan (page 163; one-quarter of the recipe)

Icing sugar for dusting

Poured Fondant (recipe follows)

Pearl dragées (optional)

---

1. Preheat the oven to 350°F. Butter a 17- x 11-inch jelly roll pan, then line the base and sides with parchment paper, leaving an overhang of paper on two facing sides. (This will help you remove the cake from the pan.) Set aside.

2. For the cake, whisk together the flour, baking powder, salt and baking soda in a large bowl. Set aside.

3. In a large bowl and using an electric mixer, beat the butter with the sugar until pale and fluffy.

4. Beat in the eggs one at a time, beating well after each addition. Beat in the vanilla extract and lemon zest, scraping down the sides of the bowl once or twice.

5. Stir in the water and lemon juice. Don't worry if the mixture looks slightly curdled. It will come together once you add the flour.

6. Add the flour mixture to the sugar mixture alternately with the milk, making three additions of flour and two of milk, and beginning and ending with the flour. Stir until well combined.

7. Scrape the batter into the prepared pan, using an offset spatula to spread the batter evenly in the pan. Bake until the edges of the cake are golden and the centre springs back when lightly pressed, 20 to 30 minutes.

8. Let the cake cool in the pan on a wire rack until just warm, 15 to 25 minutes. When the cake is cool enough to handle, use the parchment paper overhang to carefully lift the cake from the pan to a cutting board.

9. To assemble the petits fours, use a serrated knife to trim off the edges of the cake (these make great snacks for any hungry helpers). Cut the cake crosswise into four even-sized rectangles, each about 11 x 4 ¼ inches.

10. In a small saucepan over low heat, warm the raspberry jam until it's spreadable. Spread the jam evenly over two of the cake layers. Top each jam-covered cake with one of the remaining cakes to make two rectangular cakes. Trim the edges of each cake to neaten them. Set aside.

11. Divide the marzipan in half. Knead each piece until it softens and becomes workable. On a surface lightly dusted with icing sugar, roll out one piece of marzipan to a rectangle slightly larger than the top of one of the jam-filled cakes.

12. Brush water over the rectangle of marzipan. Carefully flip the marzipan and place it, water side down, on top of one of the cakes. Using scissors or a very sharp knife, trim the edges of the marzipan so it's flush with the edges of the cake. Repeat with the remaining marzipan and cake.

13. Place the cakes, side by side, on a large platter, then cover tightly with plastic wrap. Refrigerate until set, at least 4 hours, or overnight.

14. Using a ruler and a very sharp knife, score the marzipan on each cake into 24 even-sized squares. Following the score marks, cut each cake neatly into squares and transfer to a large baking sheet. Cover the cake squares with plastic wrap and place in the freezer for 30 minutes. (Freezing the cakes briefly makes it easier to dip them in the warm fondant.).

15. Prepare the poured fondant (recipe follows).

16. Set a large wire rack over a large piece of parchment paper. Have ready the bowl of poured fondant and two forks.

17. Pick up one square of cake with the two forks and carefully dip it into the fondant to coat completely. Remove the fondant-covered cake with the forks and carefully transfer it to the wire rack. If the fondant coating looks uneven, use a spoon to pour a little extra over the top of the petit four.

18. Repeat with the remaining cake squares, keeping the undipped cake covered with plastic wrap as you work. If the fondant becomes too thick to coat the petits fours, warm it by microwaving on high power for 30-second intervals until the fondant liquefies. Or, place the bowl of fondant over a saucepan of hot, not boiling, water, then stir until the fondant liquefies.

19. Decorate the petits fours with pearl dragées (if using), then let them stand at room temperature until the fondant has set and hardened, at least 1 hour. You may need to use a sharp knife to remove the petits fours cleanly from the wire rack. (The petits fours can be refrigerated in an airtight container for up to 3 days. Bring them to room temperature before serving.)

BAKING DAY SECRETS

If you find using two forks to dip the cakes in the fondant a little fiddly, try this method: Grasp a cake square with your thumb on the bottom and your middle finger on the top (marzipan side), then quickly dip the four sides of cake in the fondant. Place the cake, marzipan-side up, on the wire rack. Quickly spoon a little fondant on top of the cake to cover it. Gently tap the wire rack to encourage the fondant to run smoothly down the sides of the cake.

Poured Fondant

Makes about 4 cups
Prep time: 10 minutes
Cooking time: 5 minutes
Cooling time: 5 minutes

6 cups icing sugar, sifted

½ cup water

2 Tbsp white corn syrup

2 tsp almond, vanilla or lemon extract

Gel food colouring (optional)

1. In a medium saucepan, gently stir together the icing sugar, water and corn syrup. Hook a candy thermometer over the side of the saucepan.

2. Cook over medium-low heat, without stirring, until the candy thermometer registers 115°F, about 5 minutes.

3. Immediately remove from the heat and stir to ensure all the sugar has dissolved. Stir in the extract and your food colouring of choice (if using).

4. Pour the fondant into a medium bowl and let cool for 5 minutes before using. (The fondant can be refrigerated in an airtight container for up to 3 days. Warm the fondant before using by microwaving it on high power for 30-second intervals or setting it in a bowl over a saucepan of hot, not boiling, water, until it liquefies.)

FROSTINGS, ICINGS & DECORATING BASICS

Quick Buttercream

Containing just a handful of ingredients, this is the easiest frosting of all. For the fluffiest results, beat the butter thoroughly—the more air you incorporate, the lighter and creamier the buttercream will be.

Makes about 2 cups
Prep time: 10 minutes

1 cup unsalted butter, softened

3 to 4 cups icing sugar, sifted

1 to 2 Tbsp whipping cream (35%)

1 tsp vanilla extract

1. In a large bowl and using an electric mixer, beat the butter until pale and fluffy, 3 to 5 minutes.

2. With the mixer running on low speed, gradually beat in the icing sugar, 1 cup at a time. Increase the speed to high, then beat until smooth and creamy.

3. Beat in 1 tablespoonful of the cream. For a softer buttercream, beat in the remaining cream. Beat in the vanilla extract. (The buttercream can be refrigerated in an airtight container for up to 5 days. Let it come to room temperature before using.)

CHANGE IT UP

Chocolate Buttercream: Sift ½ cup unsweetened cocoa powder into the butter along with the icing sugar in Step 2. Add up to 1 tablespoonful of additional cream, if necessary, in Step 3.

Mocha Buttercream: Sift ½ cup unsweetened cocoa powder into the butter along with the icing sugar in Step 2. Substitute 3 tablespoonfuls of strong brewed espresso (or 1 tablespoonful of instant espresso powder dissolved in 3 tablespoonfuls of hot water) for the cream.

Peanut Butter Buttercream: Beat 1 cup smooth peanut butter (not old-fashioned or all-natural) with the butter in Step 1.

French Buttercream

This variation on buttercream contains egg yolks. They give the finished frosting a rich, silky texture.

Makes about 2 cups
Prep time: 15 minutes
Cooking time: 8 to 10 minutes

²/₃ cup granulated sugar

3 Tbsp water

5 large egg yolks

Pinch of fine sea salt

1 cup unsalted butter, cut into small pieces and softened

1 tsp vanilla extract

1. In a small saucepan, combine the sugar and water. Bring to a boil over medium heat, stirring until the sugar has dissolved.

2. Hook a candy thermometer over the side of the saucepan. Boil the sugar mixture over medium heat, without stirring, until the candy thermometer registers 235°F, 8 to 10 minutes. (If you don't have a candy thermometer, drop a little of the mixture into a bowl of cold water. If it forms a soft ball, it's ready.)

3. While the syrup is cooking, combine the egg yolks and salt in a medium bowl. Using an electric mixer on high speed, beat the yolks until pale and thick.

4. When the syrup is ready, immediately remove from the heat. With the mixer still running on high speed, pour a small amount of syrup into the yolk mixture. Beat on high speed for 10 seconds to incorporate. Repeat until all the syrup is incorporated.

5. Continue to beat on high speed until the egg yolk mixture has cooled to room temperature, about 10 minutes.

6. Beat in the butter one piece at a time, beating well after each addition. Beat in the vanilla extract, then continue beating until the buttercream is smooth and slightly stiff. (The buttercream can be refrigerated in an airtight container for up to 5 days. Let it come to room temperature before using.)

CHANGE IT UP

Chocolate French Buttercream: In a small bowl set over a saucepan of hot, not boiling, water, melt 1 cup chocolate chips with 2 tablespoonfuls of hot brewed black coffee. Stir until smooth, then let cool to room temperature. Beat into the buttercream in place of the vanilla extract. Alternatively, omit the coffee and add 2 tablespoonfuls of brandy when you beat the melted chocolate into the buttercream.

Peppermint French Buttercream: Substitute ½ teaspoonful of peppermint extract for the vanilla extract.

Swiss Buttercream

This is one of our all-time favourite frostings. Swiss buttercream is glossy and holds its shape well and, while it's rich-tasting, the egg whites keep the texture light.

Makes about 4 cups
Prep time: 15 minutes
Cooking time: about 5 minutes
Cooling time: about 10 minutes

1 ¾ cups granulated sugar

6 egg whites

1 ½ cups unsalted butter, cut into small pieces and softened

2 Tbsp vanilla extract

1. In a large heatproof bowl set over a saucepan of simmering water, whisk together the sugar and egg whites until the sugar has dissolved, about 5 minutes. Test to see if the sugar has dissolved by rubbing a little of the mixture between your fingers; when it no longer feels gritty, it's ready.

2. Remove the bowl from the heat and, using an electric mixer on high speed, beat the sugar mixture until stiff peaks form and the bowl is cool to the touch, about 10 minutes.

3. Lower the speed to medium and beat in the butter one piece at a time, beating well after each addition. Beat in the vanilla extract.

4. Increase the speed to high, then beat until the buttercream thickens and begins to hold its shape. If it doesn't thicken, put the bowl in the fridge for 20 minutes, then beat the buttercream on medium speed until thickened. (The buttercream can be refrigerated in an airtight container for up to 5 days. Let it come to room temperature before using.)

CHANGE IT UP

Chocolate Swiss Buttercream: In a small bowl set over a saucepan of hot, not boiling, water, melt 8 oz chopped semi-sweet chocolate. Stir until smooth, then let cool to room temperature. Fold into the buttercream after beating it in Step 4.

Peanut Butter Swiss Buttercream: Beat ¾ cup smooth peanut butter (not old-fashioned or all-natural) and a pinch of fine sea salt into the buttercream after beating it in Step 4.

Strawberry Swiss Buttercream: Beat 2 to 4 tablespoonfuls of fresh strawberry purée (according to taste) into the buttercream after beating it in Step 4.

Basic Cream Cheese Frosting

Y ou'll find variations on this frosting throughout this book, but here's the classic version. There's no finer topping for our Carrot Cake (page 110), Simple Chocolate Cake (page 104) or your favourite cupcakes.

Makes about 2 cups

Prep time: 10 minutes

1 pkg (8 oz/250 g) brick-style cream cheese, at room temperature

¼ cup unsalted butter, softened

2 to 4 cups icing sugar, sifted

1 tsp vanilla extract

1. In a large bowl and using an electric mixer, beat together the cream cheese and butter until smooth.

2. Beat in the icing sugar, 1 cup at a time, until the frosting is the consistency you like (you may not need all of the icing sugar).

3. Beat in the vanilla extract until well blended. (The frosting can be refrigerated in an airtight container for up to 5 days. Let it come to room temperature before using.)

SWEET HISTORY

The first recorded sugar factories were in Venice in the mid-1300s. In these so-called sugar houses, the sugar was formed into cone shapes and then sold across Europe. The production techniques developed by the Venetians were considered so important that the laws of Venice made it a capital offence to reveal their details. Needless to say, Venice's sugar-making secrets got out and, within a century, sugar houses had been established in all the capitals of Europe.

Seven-Minute Frosting

Taking its name from the time needed to whip egg whites and sugar to fluffy perfection, this frosting can be used to dress up just about any cake.

Makes about 4 cups
Prep time: 15 minutes
Cooking time: 8 to 10 minutes

Syrup
1 ½ cups granulated sugar

²/₃ cup water

2 Tbsp white corn syrup

Egg Whites
6 large egg whites

2 Tbsp granulated sugar

1. For the syrup, combine the sugar, water and corn syrup in a small saucepan. Bring to a boil over medium heat, stirring until the sugar has dissolved.

2. Hook a candy thermometer over the side of the saucepan. Boil the sugar mixture over medium heat, without stirring, until the candy thermometer registers 235°F, 8 to 10 minutes. (If you don't have a candy thermometer, drop a little of the mixture into a bowl of cold water. If it forms a soft ball, it's ready.)

3. Meanwhile, for the egg whites, beat them in a large bowl, using an electric mixer on medium-high speed, until soft peaks form.

4. With the mixer running, beat the sugar into the whites.

5. When the syrup is ready, remove it from the heat immediately. With the mixer running on low speed, pour it down the side of the bowl of egg whites, adding it in a slow, steady stream.

6. Increase the speed to medium-high. Beat until the egg-white mixture has cooled completely and holds stiff peaks. (For best results, use the frosting immediately; in a pinch, it can be refrigerated overnight in an airtight container.)

Chocolate Ganache

Here's a chocolate-lover's dream. Use the ganache immediately after making it for a glossy chocolate glaze for your favourite cake. Or, let it cool then whip until fluffy (see sidebar) and use to fill a layer cake or as a topping for cupcakes.

Makes about 2 cups
Prep time: 10 minutes
Cooking time: about 3 minutes
Cooling time: about 10 minutes

1 ½ cups dark or semi-sweet chocolate chips

1 cup plus 2 Tbsp whipping cream (35%)

1. Put the chocolate chips into a medium heatproof bowl. Set aside.

2. In a small saucepan, heat the cream over medium heat until barely simmering.

3. Pour half of the hot cream over the chocolate chips. Let stand for about 30 seconds. Using a spatula and starting in the centre of the mixture, stir gently until the chocolate has melted and is combined with the cream.

4. Pour the remaining hot cream into the bowl. Starting from the centre, stir until the ganache is smooth and glossy. Let cool for 10 minutes before pouring over a cake.

WHIPPED CHOCOLATE GANACHE

Follow the recipe for Chocolate Ganache. Let the ganache cool completely at room temperature, stirring occasionally, about 2 hours. Using an electric mixer, beat the cooled ganache until light and creamy, about 3 minutes.

CHANGE IT UP

Vanilla Chocolate Ganache: In Step 2 of the recipe for Chocolate Ganache, slit a vanilla bean lengthwise then, using a small, sharp knife, scrape the seeds out into the cream. Drop in the pod. Heat the cream as for Chocolate Ganache. Remove from the heat and let stand, covered, for 5 minutes. Discard the vanilla pod before pouring the cream over the chocolate chips.

Mocha Chocolate Ganache: In Step 2 of the recipe for Chocolate Ganache, stir a shot of espresso or 1 ½ teaspoonfuls of instant espresso powder into the hot cream before pouring it over the chocolate chips.

Hazelnut Praline Powder

We love using this nutty powder as a dessert topping or sprinkled over frosting to add an extra hit of flavour to a layer cake filling.

Makes about 4 cups
Prep time: 30 minutes
Cooking time: 8 to 10 minutes

2 ½ cups hazelnuts

1 ½ cups granulated sugar

⅓ cup water

½ tsp fine sea salt

CHANGE IT UP

Other nuts—separately or in combination—work well in the praline powder: try almonds, pecans or cashews, or a combo of hazelnuts, almonds and pistachios.

1. Preheat the oven to 350°F. Spread the hazelnuts out on a large rimmed baking sheet. Bake, stirring occasionally, until fragrant, 10 to 15 minutes.

2. Immediately wrap the hazelnuts in a large, clean kitchen towel. Vigorously rub the hazelnuts through the towel to remove most of their skins. Discard the skins and set the hazelnuts aside.

3. Line the baking sheet with parchment paper or a silicone liner. Set aside.

4. In a medium, heavy-bottomed saucepan, stir together the sugar and water. Bring to a boil over medium heat, stirring until the sugar has dissolved.

5. Hook a candy thermometer over the side of the saucepan. Boil the sugar mixture, without stirring but occasionally washing down the sides of the saucepan with a clean, damp pastry brush, until the candy thermometer registers 330°F, 8 to 10 minutes. (If you don't have a candy thermometer, drop a little of the mixture into a bowl of cold water. If it forms hard, brittle threads, it's ready.)

6. Remove from the heat immediately and quickly stir in the hazelnuts. Spread the mixture out on the prepared baking sheet. Let cool completely.

7. Break the cooled praline into chunks. Place the chunks with the salt in a food processor fitted with the steel blade. Pulse until the praline is reduced to a fine powder. (The praline powder can be refrigerated in an airtight container for up to 2 months.)

Hazelnut Praline Paste

Makes about 2 cups

Praline paste is delicious mixed into buttercream or other frostings, or as a cake filling on its own. Or, swirl some through your favourite vanilla or chocolate ice cream for an indulgent treat.

Follow the directions for making Hazelnut Praline Powder but continue to pulse the mixture in the food processor until the hazelnuts release their oil and the mixture is the consistency of nut butter. If the paste is too thick, add up to 1 tablespoonful of vegetable oil. (The praline paste can be refrigerated in an airtight container for up to 2 months.)

CHANGE IT UP

Add a hit of chocolate to the Hazelnut Praline Paste by stirring in ½ cup of melted chocolate.

Easy Royal Icing

Royal icing is the frosty topping used on Christmas cakes and traditional wedding cakes, and the mortar that holds gingerbread houses together. You can also use it to add a professional touch to homemade cookies (see pages 170 to 172). And it's easy to make, too.

Makes about 2 ¼ cups
Prep time: 15 minutes

2 large egg whites

½ tsp freshly squeezed lemon juice

Pinch of fine sea salt

1 tsp almond, vanilla or lemon extract (see sidebar)

3 ¾ cups icing sugar, sifted

1. In a large bowl and using an electric mixer on medium-high speed, beat the egg whites, lemon juice and salt until foamy and white.

2. Turn down the speed to medium-low and beat in the almond extract. Still on medium-low speed, gradually beat in the icing sugar, until it's all incorporated and the mixture is smooth and glossy, about 7 minutes.

3. Increase the speed to medium-high, then beat for 2 minutes.

CHANGE IT UP

To use the royal icing for flooding cookies (see page 171), beat in 1 to 2 tablespoonfuls of water in Step 3 to thin it slightly.

BAKING DAY SECRETS

Vanilla and lemon extracts add a faint touch of colour to the icing so, if you want a pure white royal icing, use almond extract or omit the extract completely.

Vegan Royal Icing

Just as light and fluffy as regular royal icing, this vegan version is egg-free.

Makes about ½ cup
Prep time: 10 minutes

1 cup icing sugar, sifted

1 Tbsp almond milk or water

2 tsp white corn syrup

¼ tsp almond extract

1. In a medium bowl, stir together the icing sugar and almond milk until smooth.

2. Beat in the corn syrup and almond extract until the icing is smooth and glossy. If the icing is too thick, beat in a little more water ¼ teaspoon at a time.

CHANGE IT UP

Substitute your favourite flavouring—we like rum extract or rose water—for the almond extract.

Marzipan

Homemade marzipan is a cinch to prepare. Add some food colouring, a little imagination and our easy step-by-step instructions (see pages 164 and 165) and you can create marzipan flowers to dress up any cake or cupcake.

Makes about 3 ½ cups (1 ¾ lb)
Prep time: 15 minutes

3 ½ cups almond meal or almond flour

3 cups icing sugar, sifted

¼ tsp fine sea salt

4 tsp almond extract

2 tsp rose water (see sidebar)

1 tsp vanilla extract

2 large egg whites

CHANGE IT UP

If rose water is unavailable, replace it with extra almond or vanilla extract.

1. In a food processor fitted with the steel blade, combine the almond meal, icing sugar and salt. Process until the mixture is finely ground and free of lumps.

2. Add the almond extract, rose water and vanilla extract. Pulse several times until the mixture resembles coarse bread crumbs.

3. Add the egg whites. Pulse until the mixture forms a dough, scraping down the sides of the food processor bowl as necessary. If the mixture is too sticky to handle, add a little almond meal and icing sugar, then process to combine.

4. Tip the mixture out onto a clean work surface. Form it into a disc, then wrap it tightly in plastic wrap. Keep the marzipan wrapped until ready to use. (Marzipan can be refrigerated, well wrapped in plastic wrap and stored in an airtight container, for up to 2 weeks.)

BAKING DAY SECRETS

Here's how to tint marzipan before making marzipan flowers.

1. Divide the marzipan into the same number of pieces as you require colours.

2. Keeping the remaining marzipan covered with a clean, damp towel to prevent it from drying out, flatten one piece and, using a toothpick, add a few drops of gel food colouring. Always add the colouring a small amount at a time to ensure the correct colour is achieved.

3. Wearing disposable gloves, knead the colour into the marzipan until uniformly tinted. Cover the piece of tinted marzipan and repeat with the remaining pieces, tinting each a different colour.

Marzipan Flowers

For an added touch of luxe, dust the finished marzipan flowers with edible decorating dust or glitter, which can be found at a specialty food store.

ROSES *Makes 6 flowers*

1. Tint about ⅔ cup marzipan pink, peach or red.

2. Form the tinted marzipan into a log, about 4 inches long and 2 inches in diameter. For each pair of roses, cut five slices from the log, each about ⅛ inch thick.

3. Place five of the slices between two sheets of wax paper. With the underside of a spoon or your finger, thin out the edges of each slice.

4. Line the slices up in a horizontal row, slightly overlapping. Starting with the slice that was placed down first, roll up the row of slices, continuing to roll until the last sliced is reached.

5. Pick up the rolled-up slices and gently roll the middle part between your finger and thumb to form an hourglass shape. The top of the hourglass will be one rose, the bottom another. With a sharp knife or scissors, cut the marzipan close to the base of each rose to separate them.

6. Carefully flare out the petals of each rose to make them more realistic. Repeat with the remaining slices of marzipan to make three pairs of roses in all.

7. For the leaves, tint a small piece of marzipan green. On a surface lightly dusted with icing sugar, roll the marzipan out to ⅛-inch thickness. With a sharp knife, cut out leaf shapes. Use the tip of the knife to score veins in the leaves.

VIOLETS   *Makes 6 flowers*

1. Tint about 3 tablespoonfuls of marzipan purple and about 1 tablespoonful yellow.

2. Form the purple piece of marzipan into a log, about 5/8 inch long and ½ inch in diameter. For each violet, cut five slices from the log, each about 1/8 inch thick.

3. Place the slices in a single layer between two sheets of wax paper. With the underside of a spoon or your finger, thin out the edges of one side of each slice.

4. Roll the yellow piece of marzipan into a log, about ¾ inch long and ¼ inch in diameter. Cut this log into six pieces, each about 1/8 inch thick, and roll each into a teardrop shape.

5. Wrap the thicker side of one slice of marzipan around one of the teardrop shapes to form a petal, positioning the teardrop with its thicker end uppermost. Flare out the outer edges of the petal.

6. Wrap a second petal around the teardrop, just slightly overlapping the edges of the first and gently pinching the base to seal the pieces together.

7. Repeat the process with the remaining petals. With a sharp knife or scissors, cut off the excess marzipan at the base of the violet. Repeat with the remaining marzipan to make six violets in all.

Decorating Basics

With the right equipment and our straightforward instructions, it's easy to create professional-looking, decorated cupcakes, cookies and other baked goods.

Frosting flowers on cupcakes

Flower-bedecked cupcakes turn a sweet treat into something very special.

Your choice of frosting

Your choice of gel food colouring

Piping bag(s)

Piping tip(s)

Cupcakes of your choice

1. Colour the frosting to your desired shade or shades.

2. Fit a piping bag with a tip, then twist the bag just above the piping tip to temporarily close off the bag from the tip.

3. Set the bag in an empty yogurt container, glass tumbler or plastic cup. Fold the top third of the piping bag over the edge of the container.

4. Spoon one colour of frosting into the bottom of the piping bag, filling the bag about half full and pressing firmly to minimize any air pockets. Twist the bag tightly to close it.

5. Repeat with other bags, if desired, or use two or three different colours of frosting in the same bag for multicoloured flowers.

6. Pipe flowers onto cupcakes following the directions below.

SWEET HISTORY

In the 18th century, as sugar became more affordable, specialized implements for serving it became popular. From weddings to birthdays, no formal event was complete without fancy tools, such as sugar casters, nippers, tongs, crushers or cutters.

A SIMPLE ROSE

1. Fit a piping bag with a ³/₈-inch closed star tip. Fill the bag with frosting.

2. Hold the piping bag perpendicular to the centre of the cupcake and about ½ inch above the surface.

3. Squeeze a little frosting on the centre of the cupcake then, maintaining even pressure, pipe in a spiral fashion toward the edge of the cupcake.

4. As you reach the edge, lessen the pressure on the bag slightly, then gently press down and pull away to finish frosting.

A ROSE BOUQUET

1. Fit a piping bag with a small closed star tip. Fill the bag with frosting.

2. Spoon a tablespoonful of frosting onto the centre of the cupcake. With a small offset spatula, smooth the frosting to create a small mound.

3. Pipe a circle of ¾-inch rosettes around the edge of the cupcake. (To pipe a rosette, start at its centre and spiral out.)

4. Pipe a second circle of rosettes inside the first.

5. Finally, pipe one or two rosettes to fill the centre of the cupcake.

MULTICOLOURED PETALS

1. Fit three piping bags with ¼-inch plain tips. Fill each bag with a different colour of frosting.

2. Pipe a small disc of one colour of frosting near the edge of the cupcake. Pushing down with the tip, gently pull the frosting into the centre of the disc and pull away.

3. Repeat with the second colour and third colours.

4. Continue around the outer edge of the cupcake, alternating colours.

5. Pipe a second circle of rounds inside the first using the same technique. Continue until you reach the centre, alternating colours each time.

6. Finally, pipe one small round of each colour to fill the centre of the cupcake.

BEGONIA

1. Fit a piping bag with a petal tip. Fill the bag with frosting.

2. Position the piping bag ½ inch from the edge of the cupcake, with the wide end of the tip closest to the cupcake and the narrow end raised about 45 degrees.

3. Pipe petals using a teardrop motion as you squeeze and releasing the pressure as you

bring the tip back to the starting point of each petal. Continue around the entire edge of the cupcake.

4. Pipe a second layer of petals inside the first using the same technique. Continue until you reach the centre of the cupcake.

5. Finally, decorate each cupcake with three small pearl drageés in the centre.

HYDRANGEA

1. Divide the frosting among three bowls. Leaving one bowl uncoloured, colour the second bowl light purple and the third light blue. (Or choose your favourite hydrangea colour combination, such as white, deep purple and light blue; or white and two shades of pink.)

2. Fit a large piping bag with a ³⁄₈-inch closed star tip.

3. Spread the light purple frosting down one side of the bag and the light blue frosting down the other side. Spoon the white frosting into the centre of the bag. Squeeze the bag until all three colours are visible at the tip.

4. Pressing into the cupcake and releasing the pressure as you pull away, pipe small mounds of frosting on top of the cupcake, until the entire surface is covered.

RUFFLED CARNATION

1. Fit a piping bag with a petal tip. Fill the bag with frosting.

2. Position the tip so the narrow end is nearest the edge of the cupcake. Squeeze out a little frosting to stick to the cupcake, then begin creating a ruffle pattern by repeatedly pulling the tip about ½ inch away

from the cupcake and pushing it back to create small folds.

3. Continue around the cupcake in a spiral pattern toward the centre, with each circle slightly overlapping the last, until the entire cupcake is covered.

Decorating with Royal Icing 101

Decorating with royal icing is an easy way to jazz up plain sugar or gingerbread cookies.

1 batch of Easy Royal Icing
(page 162)

Your choice of gel food colouring

Piping bag(s)

Piping tip(s)

Cookies of your choice

1. Colour the icing to your desired shade or shades.

2. Fit a piping bag with a tip, then twist the bag just above the piping tip to temporarily close off the bag from the tip.

3. Set the bag in an empty yogurt container, glass tumbler or plastic cup. Fold the top third of the piping bag over the edge of the container.

4. Spoon one colour of icing into the bottom of the piping bag, filling the bag about half full and pressing firmly to minimize any air pockets. Twist the bag tightly to close it.

5. Repeat with other bags, if desired. Pipe the icing onto cookies following the directions below.

OUTLINING WITH ROYAL ICING

1. Fit a piping bag with a small plain round tip. Fill the bag with icing.

2. Firmly squeeze the top of the piping bag with one hand and direct the tip with the other. Press down on the tip, then lift the tip up, pulling the icing in the direction you want it to go. Don't hold the piping tip too close to the cookie; let the icing fall from the tip to the surface of the cookie.

3. Let each decorated cookie dry on a wire rack for several hours, or overnight.

FLOODING WITH ROYAL ICING

1. Fit a piping bag with a small plain round tip. Fill the bag with icing.

2. Follow the directions on how to outline with royal icing (see page 170).

3. Once the area is outlined, fill it with icing until only a few tiny gaps remain.

4. Holding the cookie gently on either side, shake it until the icing fills the gaps. Gently tap the cookie a few times on the counter to ensure the surface of the icing is smooth.

5. Any decorations should be added quickly while the icing is still wet (it will begin to dry almost immediately).

6. Let each decorated cookie dry on a wire rack for several hours, or overnight.

FEATHERING WITH ROYAL ICING

1. Fit one piping bag with a small plain round tip, then fill the bag with icing. Fit a second bag with another small plain round tip, then fill the bag with a second colour of icing.

2. Using the first bag, follow the directions for how to outline and flood with royal icing (see beside and above).

3. Using the second bag, pipe dots of icing across the surface of the cooled flooded cookie. You can pipe the dots in a straight line, or create different designs by piping them in a heart, circle or diamond shape.

4. Gently drag a toothpick through the piped dots to create a feathered effect.

5. Holding the cookie gently on either side, shake it to smooth out the design.

6. Let each decorated cookie dry on a wire rack for several hours, or overnight.

MARBLING WITH ROYAL ICING

1. Fit one piping bag with a small plain round tip, then fill the bag with icing. Fit a second and third bag with small plain round tips, then fill each of these bags with different colours of icing.

2. Using the first bag, follow the directions for how to outline and flood with royal icing (see page 171).

3. Using the second bag, pipe parallel lines across the surface of the cookie, leaving about ½ inch between each line.

4. Using the third bag, pipe another set of parallel lines across the cookie, piping in between the first set.

5. Gently drag a toothpick through the lines of coloured royal icing, either in alternating directions or in the same direction to create a marbled design.

6. Holding the cookie gently on either side, shake it to smooth out the design.

7. Let each decorated cookie dry on a wire rack for several hours, or overnight

BAKING DAY SECRETS

For a quick and easy way to decorate cookies, simply tint royal icing with the gel food colouring of your choice. Dip cookies in the icing or use a brush to paint the icing on the tops of the cookies. Let the cookies dry at room temperature for several hours, or overnight, before serving.

PIES, CHEESECAKES & OUR FAVOURITE FRUIT DESSERTS

Perfect Pastry

Don't be put off making pastry. Whether you mix the dough by hand or you use a food processor, our recipe is as easy as . . . well, pie. Read our handy tips, too, and you'll soon be baking up the flakiest, tastiest pies ever.

Makes enough for 2 single-crust pies or 1 double-crust pie
Prep time: 10 minutes
Chilling time: at least 1 hour

2 ½ cups all-purpose flour

1 Tbsp granulated sugar

Pinch of fine sea salt

1 cup cold unsalted butter, cut into ½-inch pieces

¼ to ½ cup ice water

To make the pastry by hand

1. In a large bowl, whisk together the flour, sugar and salt.

2. Add the butter to the flour mixture. Using a pastry cutter or your hands, work it in until pea-size lumps of butter are just visible.

3. Add ¼ cup of the water. Stir with a fork until the dough comes together. Add a little more water if the dough is dry. Don't over-work the dough, or the pastry will be tough.

4. On a clean work surface, gather the dough into a ball. Cut it in half and pat out each piece into a disc. Wrap it tightly in plastic wrap, then refrigerate for at least 1 hour. (The pastry can be refrigerated for up to 3 days. Or put the wrapped pastry in freezer bags and freeze for up to 1 month. Thaw in the fridge for 24 hours before using.)

To make the pastry using a food processor

1. In a food processor fitted with the steel blade, combine the flour, sugar and salt. Pulse two or three times just to combine.

2. Add the butter to the flour mixture. Pulse about 12 times, or until pea-size lumps of butter are just visible.

3. Add ¼ cup of the water. Pulse just until the dough comes together. Add a little more water if the dough is dry. Don't over-work the dough, or the pastry will be tough.

4. Wrap, chill and store the dough as in Step 4 of the pastry by hand method.

Perfect Pastry 101

Here's how to make perfect pastry every time:

- Use cold ingredients.

- Combine the butter with the flour mixture gently, using a pastry cutter or your hands (or a food processor), just until the butter is in pea-size lumps. Those little bits of butter melt during baking to create pockets in the flour mixture. Steam from the melted butter lifts the pockets and makes flaky, crisp layers in the pastry.

- Be gentle with the dough and don't overwork it.

- Add only enough ice water so the dough holds together. Too much liquid and the dough will be tough.

- Refrigerate the dough before rolling it out to ensure it's as cold as possible before baking.

- Roll out the dough on a lightly floured work surface, rolling in one direction from the centre to the edges and rotating the dough to make an even shape.

Decorating and Baking Pie Crusts

Lining a Pie Dish

- Roll out the pastry on a lightly floured work surface to a disc about 4 inches larger than the pie dish (for a 9-inch dish, you'll need a 13-inch disc).

- Gently ease the pastry into the pie dish.

- Trim the excess pastry, leaving a ½-inch overhang.

- Tuck the overhang under, then flute the edges decoratively, if you wish (see below).

- Refrigerate the pie crust for at least 30 minutes before adding the filling.

Fluting the Edges of a Pie Crust

- Working around the edge of the pie crust, pinch sections of the dough with the index finger and thumb or knuckles of one hand, while pushing gently from the other side with the index finger or knuckle of the other hand.

Making a Lattice Top

- For a 9-inch pie, roll out the pastry to an 11-inch disc.

- Using a pizza cutter or sharp knife, cut the pastry into ¾- to 1-inch strips.

- Lay five strips, evenly spaced, over the filling, positioning the longer strips in the centre of the pie.

- Fold back the middle strip and the two outermost strips.

- Lay another strip of pastry across the two unfolded strips and at right angles to them.

- Replace the folded strips over the new strip.

- Fold back the two strips that were not folded before. Lay another strip of dough at right angles to the first five.

- Fold the first strips over this strip.

- Repeat the process until the top of the pie is covered in a lattice of pastry.

Baking an Unfilled Pie Crust (Baking Blind)

Baking a pie crust before adding the filling is known as "baking blind" and is easy to do:

- Line a pie dish with pastry as described at the top of this page. Chill for at least 30 minutes.

- Place an oven rack in the lower-middle position of the oven. Preheat the oven to 375°F.

- Cut a disc of parchment paper or foil large enough to cover the lined pie plate right to the edges of the pastry.

- Lay the parchment or foil over the pastry. Fill the pie dish with uncooked dried beans or ceramic pie weights (look for these in your favourite kitchen supply store).

- Bake for 20 minutes. Remove the beans or weights and the parchment paper or foil. Bake until the pastry is golden all over and feels dry to the touch, about 15 minutes. If the pastry edges start to brown too quickly, cover them with strips of foil.

- Let the pie crust cool completely on a wire rack before adding the filling.

Deep-Dish Pumpkin Pie

No Thanksgiving table would be complete without a pumpkin pie as a sweet centrepiece. Our deep-dish version features a quick-to-prep crumb crust and a filling that's full of flavour.

Makes one 9-inch pie; 8 to 10 servings
Prep time: 20 minutes
Cooking time: 50 minutes

Crust

1 Graham Cracker Crust
(page 183)

Filling

2 cups fresh or canned pumpkin
purée (not pie filling)

1 cup lightly packed golden
yellow sugar

1 ¼ tsp ground cinnamon

1 tsp vanilla extract

½ tsp ground ginger

½ tsp freshly grated nutmeg

¼ tsp ground cloves

Pinch of fine sea salt

3 large eggs

1 ½ cups warm whole milk

1. Preheat the oven to 450°F.

2. Press the graham cracker crust mixture evenly over the base and up the sides of a deep 9-inch pie plate. Set aside.

3. For the filling, whisk together the pumpkin purée, sugar, cinnamon, vanilla extract, ginger, nutmeg, cloves and salt.

4. Whisk in the eggs until well combined. Whisk in the milk until the mixture is creamy and smooth.

5. Pour the pumpkin mixture into the prepared crust. Bake for 10 minutes. Turn down the oven temperature to 350°F. Bake until a wooden skewer inserted in the centre of the pie comes out clean, about 40 minutes.

6. Let cool completely. Serve cold or at room temperature.

Tarte au Sucre

This easy sugar pie from Quebec is deliciously rich. Serve slim wedges of it with dollops of softly whipped cream or scoops of vanilla ice cream.

Makes one 9-inch pie; 8 to 10 servings

Prep time: 20 minutes

Chilling time: at least 30 minutes

Cooking time: 40 to 45 minutes

Pastry

½ batch of Perfect Pastry (page 174)

Filling

1 ⅔ cups firmly packed dark brown sugar

1 tsp fine sea salt

½ cup evaporated milk

¼ cup unsalted butter, softened

1 large egg

1 tsp vanilla extract

1. On a lightly floured work surface, roll out the pastry and line a 9-inch pie dish (see page 175). Refrigerate for at least 30 minutes.

2. When ready to bake, preheat the oven to 350°F.

3. For the filling, stir together the brown sugar and salt in a large bowl.

4. In a small saucepan, heat the evaporated milk and butter over medium heat, stirring until the butter has just melted.

5. Immediately pour the milk mixture over the sugar mixture. Whisk gently for 30 seconds. (It's okay if the sugar doesn't dissolve completely.) Whisk in the egg and vanilla until smooth.

6. Holding a fine-mesh sieve over the prepared pie crust, carefully pour the sugar mixture through the sieve into the crust.

7. Place the pie plate on a rimmed baking sheet. Bake in the centre of the oven until the filling just barely jiggles in the centre, 35 to 40 minutes.

8. Let the pie cool to room temperature on a wire rack. Serve at room temperature or chilled.

BAKING DAY SECRETS

Leftovers from most types of pie (lemon meringue is an exception because the meringue tends to "weep" during storage) can be refrigerated in an airtight container for up to 4 days.

Peanut Butter Pie

If you love peanut butter, you'll adore this pie. The crust is a breeze to make and the filling whips up in next to no time.

Makes one 9-inch pie; 10 servings
Prep time: 30 minutes
Chilling time: at least 5 ½ hours
Cooking time: about 40 minutes

Brown Sugar Pie Crust

1 ¼ cups all-purpose flour

¼ cup firmly packed dark brown or demerara-style sugar

½ tsp fine sea salt

½ cup cold unsalted butter, cut into ½-inch pieces

2 to 3 Tbsp ice water

Filling

1 pkg (8 oz/250 g) brick-style cream cheese, at room temperature

1 cup icing sugar, sifted

¾ cup smooth peanut butter, at room temperature

2 tsp vanilla extract

½ tsp fine sea salt

1 ¼ cups whipping cream (35%)

½ cup chopped roasted salted peanuts

1. For the brown sugar pie crust, whisk together the flour, brown sugar and salt in a large bowl.

2. Add the butter to the flour mixture. Using a pastry cutter or your hands, work it in until pea-size lumps of butter are just visible.

3. Add 2 tablespoonfuls of the water. Stir with a fork until the dough comes together in a shaggy ball. Add a little more water if the dough is dry. Don't overwork the dough, or the pastry will be tough.

4. On a lightly floured work surface, knead the dough gently until it comes together. Pat it out into a disc, wrap tightly in plastic wrap, then refrigerate for 1 hour.

5. On a lightly floured work surface, roll out the dough and line a 9-inch pie dish (see page 175). Refrigerate for at least 30 minutes.

6. Bake the pie crust blind (see page 175). Let cool completely.

7. For the filling, in a large bowl and using an electric mixer, beat the cream cheese with the icing sugar until smooth. Beat in the peanut butter, vanilla extract and salt until smooth.

8. In a medium bowl and using clean beaters, beat the whipping cream until it holds stiff peaks.

9. Fold 1 cup of the whipped cream into the peanut butter mixture, reserving the remaining whipped cream.

10. Spoon the peanut butter filling into the prepared pie crust, smoothing the surface level. Cover with plastic wrap and chill for at least 4 hours, or up to 3 days. Refrigerate the reserved whipped cream until ready to serve.

11. When ready to serve, swirl the reserved whipped cream over the top of the pie, then sprinkle with the chopped peanuts.

Tarte Tatin

This classic French tart features juicy apples atop a puff pastry crust. Serve warm with scoops of vanilla ice cream or dollops of lightly sweetened whipped cream.

Makes one 10-inch tart; 8 servings
Prep time: 40 minutes
Chilling time: 1 hour, 15 minutes
Cooking time: about 40 minutes
Standing time: 10 minutes

Easy Puff Pastry

1 ½ cups all-purpose flour

½ tsp fine sea salt

½ cup cold unsalted butter, cut into ½-inch pieces

1 large egg, chilled

2 Tbsp ice water

Filling

7 to 8 Granny Smith or Golden Delicious apples

½ cup unsalted butter, softened

1 ¼ cups granulated sugar

1 tsp freshly squeezed lemon juice

¼ tsp fine sea salt

1. For the easy puff pastry, whisk together the flour and salt in a large bowl. Add the butter. Using a pastry cutter or your hands, work it in until pea-size lumps of butter are just visible.

2. In a small bowl, whisk together the egg and water. Drizzle the egg mixture over the flour mixture. Stir with a fork until the dough comes together in a loose ball. Don't overwork the dough, or the pastry will be tough.

3. On a lightly floured work surface, knead the dough gently until it comes together. Shape the dough into a 5- x 3-inch rectangle. Wrap it tightly in plastic then refrigerate for 15 minutes.

4. Remove the dough from the fridge. On a lightly floured work surface, roll it out to a 10- x 7-inch rectangle.

5. With one short side facing you, fold the bottom third of the dough over the centre, then fold the top third down as if you were folding a letter. Wrap the dough tightly in plastic wrap and refrigerate for 10 minutes.

6. Remove the dough from the fridge and place it on a lightly floured work surface so the opening is on the right. Roll it out to a 10- x 7-inch rectangle. Fold and chill the dough as before, making sure the opening is to the right before you roll.

7. Repeat Step 6 once more. (The puff pastry can be refrigerated for up to 3 days. Or put the wrapped pastry in a freezer bag and freeze for up to 1 month. Thaw in the fridge for 24 hours before using.)

8. When ready to use, on a lightly floured work surface, roll out the dough to a 12-inch square. Using a large plate as a guide, cut out an 11-inch circle. Cover the dough with plastic wrap and chill for at least 30 minutes.

9. For the filling, cut an ⅛-inch slice from the top and bottom of each apple to create flat ends. Peel and core the apples, then cut each into eight slices.

10. In a heavy-bottomed 10-inch ovenproof skillet, melt the butter over medium heat. Remove from the heat.

11. Sprinkle the sugar, lemon juice and salt evenly over the butter. Starting in the centre, arrange the apple slices, on their trimmed ends, in concentric circles, fitting them in a snugly as possible.

12. Return the skillet to medium heat. Cook, uncovered and without stirring, until the juice around the apples turns amber, 10 to 12 minutes. Remove from the heat.

13. Preheat the oven to 375°F.

14. Prick the chilled pastry all over with a fork. Carefully lay it over the apples in the skillet, tucking in the edges around the apples. Place the skillet on a large rimmed baking sheet.

15. Bake until the pastry is golden brown, 25 to 30 minutes.

16. Let the tart rest in the skillet on a wire rack for 10 minutes. Run a knife around the edge of the pastry to loosen it from the skillet.

17. Invert a large serving plate over the skillet. Wearing oven mitts, invert the skillet and plate together. Remove the skillet, leaving the tarte tatin on the plate. Replace any apple slices that were stuck to the bottom of the skillet. Cut the tarte tatin into wedges and serve immediately.

BAKING DAY SECRETS

If you're short of time, substitute
ready-made puff pastry for our
homemade version.

Frozen Banana-Split Pie

ere we've taken that favourite childhood treat, the banana split, and created a fabulous retro pie. This is perfect for a summer party.

Makes one 9-inch pie; 10 to 12 servings

Prep time: 40 minutes

Cooking time: about 5 minutes

Chilling time: at least 2 hours

Standing time: 30 minutes

Graham Cracker Crust

2 cups graham cracker crumbs

⅓ cup unsalted butter, melted

2 Tbsp granulated sugar

¼ tsp fine sea salt

Filling

⅓ cup cold water

1 envelope (1 Tbsp) unflavoured powdered gelatin

1 cup mashed bananas (about 2 very ripe bananas)

⅓ cup Simple Syrup (page 107)

1 ¼ pkgs (each 8 oz/250 g) brick-style cream cheese (10 oz/300 g in total), at room temperature

½ cup granulated sugar

3 large egg yolks

1 cup whipping cream (35%)

Topping

2 cups whipping cream (35%)

2 bananas

1 Tbsp freshly squeezed lemon juice

Maraschino cherries

½ cup chopped roasted, salted peanuts

½ cup Easy Chocolate Syrup (page 302)

Chocolate sprinkles

1. Line the base of a 9-inch springform pan with a circle of parchment paper. Cut a strip of parchment paper the same width as the depth of the pan and use it to line the sides of the pan.

2. For the graham cracker crust, stir together the crumbs, butter, sugar and salt in a medium bowl until well combined.

3. Press the crumb mixture evenly over the base of the prepared pan. Refrigerate while you make the filling.

4. For the filling, pour the water into a small bowl. Sprinkle the gelatin over top and set aside for 5 minutes.

5. In a small saucepan, stir together the mashed banana and simple syrup. Cook, stirring occasionally, over medium heat until the banana mixture is simmering, about 5 minutes. Remove from the heat and set aside to cool slightly.

6. In a large bowl and using an electric mixer on low speed, beat together the cream cheese, sugar and egg yolks until smooth and thick.

7. In a medium bowl and using clean beaters, beat the whipping cream until thick but not stiff. Set aside.

8. Add the gelatin mixture to the warm banana mixture, stirring well.

9. Stir ¼ cup of the cream cheese mixture into the banana mixture. Stir another ¼ cup of the cream cheese mixture into the banana mixture.

10. Add all of the banana mixture to the cream cheese mixture, folding until well combined. Fold in the whipped cream until well combined.

11. Pour the filling over the crust, smoothing the surface level with an offset spatula. Freeze for at least 2 hours or up to 24 hours.

12. Thirty minutes before serving, remove the pie from the freezer.

13. For the topping, in a large bowl and using an electric mixer, beat the whipping cream until stiff peaks form.

14. Just before serving, peel the bananas and slice them into a medium bowl. Add the lemon juice and toss gently. Release the sides of the springform pan and slide the pie onto a serving plate. Arrange a layer of sliced bananas on top of the pie. Top with whipped cream and more sliced bananas. Garnish with maraschino cherries and peanuts. Drizzle with chocolate syrup, then scatter with sprinkles.

Essential Butter Tarts

Made with simple, readily available ingredients, butter tarts date back to the days of Canada's early settlers. Everyone seems to have a favourite version of this Canadian treat—this is ours.

Makes 12 tarts
Prep time: 25 minutes
Chilling time: at least 1 hour,
  30 minutes
Standing time: 10 minutes
Cooking time: 30 to 35 minutes

Rich Pie Pastry

¾ cup unsalted butter, softened

⅓ cup granulated sugar

3 large egg yolks

2 cups all-purpose flour

Filling

¾ cup firmly packed dark brown sugar

¾ cup maple syrup

3 Tbsp unsalted butter, melted

1 tsp apple cider vinegar

1 tsp vanilla extract

2 large eggs

1 cup currants

CHANGE IT UP

Feel free to replace the currants with 1 cup of toasted chopped pecans or walnuts. Or omit both currants and nuts and enjoy the butter tarts plain.

1. For the pastry, in a medium bowl and using an electric mixer, beat together the butter and sugar until pale and fluffy. Beat in the egg yolks until well combined.

2. Add the flour, then beat on low speed just until no white streaks remain.

3. On a clean work surface, gather the dough into a ball. Pat it out into a disc, wrap tightly in plastic wrap and refrigerate for at least 1 hour. (The pastry can be refrigerated for up to 3 days. Or put the wrapped pastry in a freezer bag and freeze for up to 1 month. Thaw in the fridge for 24 hours before using.)

4. Remove the dough from the fridge and let stand at room temperature for 10 minutes.

5. Divide the dough into 12 even-sized pieces. Form each piece into a ball.

6. Press each ball of dough into the base and up the sides of each well of a 12-well muffin pan. Use the floured base of a shot glass to press the dough evenly into each well. Make sure the dough comes to just above the rim of each well, as the pastry will shrink slightly as it bakes. Put the muffin pan in the freezer for 30 minutes.

7. For the filling, whisk together the sugar, maple syrup, butter, vinegar and vanilla extract in a medium bowl. Continue whisking until the sugar has dissolved completely.

8. Whisk in the eggs until well combined. Pour the mixture through a fine-mesh sieve into a pitcher. Set aside.

9. Preheat the oven to 325°F. Sit a large paper muffin liner in each tart crust. Fill each with dried beans or ceramic pie weights.

10. Bake just until the edges of the crusts look dry, about 15 minutes. Remove the muffin liners and beans or weights. Bake until the surface of the pastry looks dry, 5 to 8 minutes.

11. Divide the currants among the tarts. Whisk the filling mixture to combine, then carefully pour it into the tarts, filling them as full as possible without spilling over.

12. Bake until the filling has puffed up but still jiggles a little in the centre, about 10 minutes. Let the tarts cool completely in the pan on a wire rack.

Fresh Fig Tart

Rich molasses flavours pair with the floral taste of fresh figs in this elegant tart. If you don't have a tart pan with a removable bottom, use a regular 9-inch pie plate, rolling out the pastry to a 13-inch disc. Serve it in slim wedges on its own or with scoops of good-quality vanilla ice cream.

Makes one 10-inch tart; 10 to 12 servings

Prep time: 25 minutes

Chilling time: 1 hour

Standing time: 10 minutes

Cooking time: about 50 minutes

Pastry

1 batch of Rich Pie Pastry (page 185)

Fig Filling

¾ cup firmly packed dark brown sugar

¾ cup golden corn syrup

3 Tbsp unsalted butter, melted

1 tsp apple cider vinegar

1 tsp vanilla extract

2 large eggs

10 to 12 medium fresh figs

GETTING A HEAD START

You can prepare and bake the tart shell up to 3 days ahead. Store it, well wrapped, at room temperature, then prepare the filling the day you plan to serve the tart.

1. Prepare the rich pie pastry and chill for 30 minutes.

2. Remove the dough from the fridge and let stand at room temperature for 10 minutes.

3. On a lightly floured work surface, roll out the pastry to a 14-inch disc. Place the pastry in a 10-inch tart pan with a removable base.

4. Starting from the centre of the pan, gently press the dough outward and up the sides of the pan. The finished pie crust should be about ¼ inch thick. Trim off any excess, and place the pan in the freezer for 30 minutes.

5. For the fig filling, whisk together the sugar, corn syrup, butter, vinegar and vanilla extract in a medium bowl. Continue whisking until the sugar has dissolved completely.

6. Whisk in the eggs until well combined. Pour the mixture through a fine-mesh sieve into a pitcher. Set aside.

7. Preheat the oven to 375°F. Bake the tart crust blind (see page 175). Let cool completely. Turn down the oven temperature to 325°F.

8. Trim the figs, then cut them vertically into thin slices (slightly less than ¼ inch thick). Working from the outside to the centre, arrange the fig slices, in a single layer, in the tart shell.

9. Whisk the filling mixture again to combine, then carefully pour it into the tart, filling it as full as possible without spilling over.

10. Bake until the filling has puffed up but still jiggles a little in the centre, 10 to 15 minutes. Let the tart cool completely in the pan on a wire rack. Remove the tart from the pan and slide onto a serving plate. Serve at room temperature or cold.

Nectarine & Cranberry Streusel Tarts

Use any fruit for these darling tarts. We love the combo of sweet nectarines and tart cranberries, but peaches, apples or pears are great choices, too.

Makes four 5-inch tarts
Prep time: 30 minutes
Chilling time: 30 minutes
Cooking time: 50 to 55 minutes

Pastry

1 batch of Perfect Pastry (page 174)

Filling

1 cup pitted and sliced nectarines

1 cup fresh or frozen cranberries

½ cup granulated sugar

¼ cup all-purpose flour

½ tsp freshly grated nutmeg

¼ tsp fine sea salt

Streusel Topping

2/3 cup all-purpose flour

½ cup firmly packed golden yellow sugar

½ tsp ground cinnamon

1/3 cup unsalted butter, softened

½ cup slivered almonds

1. On a lightly floured work surface, roll out both discs of pastry to ¼-inch thickness. Using a 7-inch plate as a guide, cut out four 7-inch rounds and line four 5-inch individual tart pans (see page 175). Refrigerate for 30 minutes.

2. When ready to bake, preheat the oven to 375°F.

3. Bake the tart crusts blind (see page 175) for 15 minutes with the parchment or foil and dried beans or pie weights, then 10 minutes without. Let cool completely.

4. For the filling, toss together the nectarines, cranberries, sugar, flour, nutmeg and salt in a large bowl.

5. Spoon the nectarine mixture into the tart crusts.

6. For the streusel topping, whisk together the flour, sugar and cinnamon in a medium bowl. Using your fingers, rub in the butter until the mixture resembles coarse meal. Stir in the almonds.

6. Sprinkle the topping evenly over the fruit filling. Bake until the pastry is golden brown and the filling is bubbly, 25 to 30 minutes. Serve warm.

Chinese Egg Tarts

With their sunny custard filling, these melt-in-the mouth tarts are popular during Lunar New Year, but we love their rich egginess all year round. If you don't have a shallow 12-well tartlet pan, use a shallow muffin pan or 12 disposable foil tartlet pans set on a rimmed baking sheet.

Makes 12 tarts
Prep time: 30 minutes
Cooking time: about 20 minutes

Crust

3 cups all-purpose flour

1 cup icing sugar, sifted

1 ¼ cups unsalted butter, softened

1 large egg

1 tsp vanilla extract

Custard Filling

¾ cup water

⅓ cup granulated sugar

5 large eggs

½ cup whole milk

1 tsp vanilla extract

1. For the crust, whisk together the flour and icing sugar in a medium bowl. Set aside.

2. In a large bowl and using an electric mixer, beat the butter until pale and fluffy.

3. Add the flour mixture to the butter. Stir with a fork until the mixture is crumbly. Using your fingers, work the butter into the flour mixture until evenly distributed.

4. In a small bowl, whisk together the egg and vanilla extract. Add to the flour mixture, stirring just until the dough comes together.

5. On a clean work surface, gather the dough into a ball. Wrap it tightly in plastic wrap, then let rest at room temperature for 15 minutes while you make the filling.

6. For the custard filling, stir together the water and sugar in a small saucepan. Cook over medium heat until the sugar has dissolved. Remove from the heat and let cool to room temperature.

7. In a medium bowl, whisk together the eggs, milk and vanilla extract.

8. Whisk in the cooled sugar mixture until smooth. Pour the egg mixture through a fine-mesh sieve into a pitcher. Set aside.

9. Preheat the oven to 450°F.

10. Pinch off about 2 tablespoonfuls of the dough and roll it into a ball. Press the ball of dough into the base and up the sides of a well of the tart pan. Use the floured base of a shot glass to press the dough evenly into the well. Make sure the dough comes to just above the rim of the pan, as the pastry will shrink slightly as it bakes.

11. Repeat with the remaining dough to make 12 tarts in all.

12. Whisk the egg mixture to combine, then carefully pour it into the lined wells, filling them almost to the top.

13. Bake for 10 minutes. Rotate the pan or baking sheet 180 degrees, then bake until the pastry is lightly browned and the custard is set, 5 to 10 minutes. Serve warm or cold.

Springtime Rhubarb Pie

We always get excited when we spot rhubarb's bright red stalks in the market in May, because it means the warm weather is finally here. And what better way to celebrate spring's arrival than with this lovely pie?

Makes one 9-inch pie; 8 to 10 servings

Prep time: 30 minutes

Chilling time: 30 minutes

Cooking time: 55 minutes

Cooling time: 1 hour

Pastry

1 batch of Perfect Pastry (page 174)

Filling

1 ¼ cups granulated sugar

2 large eggs

¼ cup all-purpose flour

2 Tbsp whipping cream (35%)

¼ to ½ tsp freshly grated nutmeg

4 cups trimmed and sliced rhubarb (½-inch slices)

Egg Wash & Topping

1 large egg whisked with 1 Tbsp water

1 Tbsp granulated sugar

1. On a lightly floured work surface, roll out half of the pastry (reserve the other half for the top of the pie) and line a 9-inch pie dish (see page 175). Refrigerate for at least 30 minutes.

2. When ready to bake, place a large rimmed baking sheet on the lowest rack of the oven, then preheat the oven to 400°F.

3. For the filling, whisk together the sugar, eggs, flour, cream and nutmeg in a large bowl until pale and thick.

4. Add the rhubarb to the sugar mixture, stirring well to combine. Pour the rhubarb mixture into the prepared pie crust.

5. On a lightly floured work surface, roll out the remaining pastry to a 10-inch disc. Using a sharp knife or a small cutter, cut five decorative holes around the centre of this piece of pastry to allow the steam to escape from the finished pie.

6. Place the pastry over the filling. Trim off the excess pastry, leaving a ½-inch overhang. Tuck the overhang under, then flute the edges decoratively, if you wish (see page 175).

7. Brush the top of the pie with egg wash. Sprinkle with sugar.

8. Place the pie dish on the hot baking sheet. Bake for 15 minutes. Turn down the oven temperature to 350°F. Bake until the pastry is golden brown and the filling is bubbly, about 40 minutes. Let cool on a wire rack for 1 hour before serving.

BAKING DAY SECRETS

Rhubarb leaves are poisonous, so always trim them off and discard them carefully in case curious pets or small children are tempted to have a taste.

Pomegranate & Chocolate Tarts

These cute little tarts have a rich chocolate filling topped with the exotic crunch of jewel-like pomegranate seeds—and they taste as good as they look.

Makes four 4 ½-inch tarts
Prep time: 30 minutes
Chilling time: 3 hours
Cooking time: about 30 minutes
Standing time: 5 minutes

Vanilla Crust

1 vanilla bean

1 ¼ cups all-purpose flour

½ cup unsalted butter, melted

3 Tbsp granulated sugar

¼ tsp fine sea salt

3 to 5 Tbsp ice water

Chocolate Filling

1 ¾ cups semi-sweet chocolate chips

¼ cup unsalted butter, softened

1 cup whipping cream (35%)

3 Tbsp granulated sugar

¼ tsp fine sea salt

1 pomegranate

BAKING DAY SECRETS

When preparing a pomegranate, wear an apron (and disposable gloves if you wish): the fruit's pink juice can stain your clothes.

1. For the vanilla crust, using a sharp knife, split the vanilla bean in half lengthwise. Scrape the seeds out into a medium bowl, reserving the pod.

2. Add the flour, butter, sugar and salt to the vanilla seeds and stir to combine.

3. Using a fork, stir in the water, 1 tablespoonful at a time, just until the dough comes together.

4. On a clean work surface, gather the dough into a ball. Divide it into four even-sized pieces and pat each piece into a disc. Wrap each disc tightly in plastic wrap and refrigerate for 30 minutes.

5. On a lightly floured work surface, roll out the pastry to ¼-inch thickness. Using a 7-inch plate as a guide, cut out four 7-inch rounds and use them to line four 5-inch individual tart pans (see page 175). Refrigerate for 30 minutes.

6. When ready to bake, preheat the oven to 350°F.

7. Bake the pie crusts blind (see page 175) for 15 minutes with the parchment or foil and dried beans or pie weights, then 10 minutes without. Let cool completely.

8. For the chocolate filling, combine the chocolate chips and butter in a medium heatproof bowl. Set aside.

9. In a small saucepan, combine the cream, sugar, salt and reserved vanilla pod. Cook over medium heat, stirring until the sugar dissolves.

10. Remove from the heat and pour the hot cream mixture over the chocolate mixture. Let stand for 5 minutes.

11. Using a rubber spatula (not a whisk), gently stir the chocolate filling until smooth, 3 to 5 minutes. Discard the vanilla pod.

12. Pour the chocolate filling into the tart shells. Refrigerate until the filling has set, about 2 hours.

13. Just before serving, score the skin of the pomegranate with a sharp paring knife to divide it into quarters. Holding it over a bowl to catch the juice, break open the pomegranate. Using your fingers, separate the flesh-covered seeds from the white membrane.

14. Top each tart with pomegranate seeds.

Lattice-Topped Apple Pie

Here's a picture-perfect pie. With its classic lattice top and shiny glaze, you'll feel so proud taking this apple pie from the oven. If Honeycrisp apples are unavailable, use all Granny Smiths, or substitute Gala apples.

Makes one 9-inch pie; 8 to 10 servings
Prep time: 30 minutes
Chilling time: 30 minutes
Cooking time: 55 minutes
Cooling time: at least 4 hours

Pastry

1 batch of Perfect Pastry (page 174)

Filling

4 cups peeled, cored and sliced Honeycrisp apples (3 to 4 apples)

3 cups peeled, cored and sliced Granny Smith apples (2 to 3 apples)

1 Tbsp freshly squeezed lemon juice

2 tsp dark rum or vanilla extract

2/3 cup lightly packed golden yellow sugar

2/3 cup all-purpose flour

1 Tbsp finely grated fresh ginger

1/4 tsp ground cinnamon

1/4 tsp fine sea salt

2 Tbsp unsalted butter, cut into 1/2-inch pieces and softened

Topping

1 large egg

1 Tbsp whole milk or cream

1 Tbsp turbinado or granulated sugar

1. On a lightly floured work surface, roll out half of the pastry (reserve the other half for the lattice top) and line a 9-inch pie dish (see page 175). Refrigerate for at least 30 minutes.

2. When ready to bake, place a large baking sheet on the lower rack of the oven, then preheat the oven to 425°F.

3. For the filling, combine the apples, lemon juice and rum in a large bowl. Toss until the apples are evenly coated. Set aside.

4. In a medium bowl, whisk together the sugar, flour, ginger, cinnamon and salt until well combined. Add the sugar mixture to the apples and toss until the apples are evenly coated with the sugar mixture.

5. Tip the apple mixture into the prepared pie crust, jiggling the pie plate so the apples settle into the crust. Scatter the butter over the apples.

6. Cover the pie with a lattice top (see page 175).

7. For the topping, whisk together the egg and milk in a small bowl. Brush the lattice top with the egg mixture. Sprinkle with turbinado sugar.

8. Place the pie dish on the hot baking sheet. Bake for 5 minutes. Turn down the oven temperature to 350°F. Bake until the crust is deep golden brown and the filling is bubbly, about 50 minutes. Check the pie after 25 minutes. If the crust is browning too much, cover the pie loosely with foil.

9. Let the pie cool completely on a wire rack for at least 4 hours. (This will allow the juices in the pie to thicken.) Serve cold or at room temperature.

SWEET HISTORY

As "sugar houses" to process sugar opened up throughout Europe in the 1400s, the demand for sugar rose. As well as being a sweetener, sugar was prized for its role in food preservation, beer-making and distilling. Sugar growers and manufacturers needed to expand their supply options and look for new locations to source sugar cane. In October 1493, on his second voyage to the Americas, Christopher Columbus took with him sugar cane plants, creating a whole new industry in the New World.

Luscious Banana Cream Pie

Here's the benchmark banana cream pie. Sweet, creamy and oh, so good, it's a great treat for a crowd.

Makes one 9-inch pie; 8 to 10 servings
Prep time: 40 minutes
Chilling time: 4 hours, 45 minutes
Cooking time: 45 minutes
Steeping time: 20 minutes

Pastry

½ batch of Perfect Pastry (page 174)

Filling

1 vanilla bean

1 ½ cups whole milk

¾ cup whipping cream (35%)

¾ cup granulated sugar

1 Tbsp finely grated lime zest (2 to 3 limes)

5 large egg yolks

¼ cup cornstarch

½ tsp fine sea salt

3 Tbsp cold unsalted butter

2 Tbsp freshly squeezed lime juice (about 4 limes)

2 large firm, ripe bananas

Topping

1 cup whipping cream (35%)

2 Tbsp icing sugar

1 tsp vanilla extract

1. On a lightly floured work surface, roll out the pastry and line a 9-inch pie dish (see page 175). Refrigerate for at least 30 minutes.

2. When ready to bake, preheat the oven to 375°F.

3. Bake the pie crust blind (see page 175). Let cool completely.

4. For the filling, using a sharp knife, split the vanilla bean in half lengthwise. Scrape the seeds out into a medium, heavy-bottomed saucepan, then drop in the pod.

5. Add the milk, cream, ½ cup of the sugar and the lime zest to the saucepan. Cook over medium heat until the mixture is just starting to simmer, about 3 minutes. Remove from the heat, cover and set aside for 20 minutes to steep.

6. In a large bowl, whisk together the egg yolks, cornstarch, salt and the remaining ¼ cup of sugar.

7. Reheat the milk mixture over medium heat until just beginning to steam. Gradually whisk the hot milk mixture into the egg yolk mixture, ½ cup at a time, whisking constantly.

8. Pour the milk-egg mixture back into the saucepan. Cook over medium heat, stirring constantly, until the mixture begins to simmer. Cook, still stirring constantly, 1 minute.

9. Remove from the heat. Discard the vanilla pod. Whisk in the butter, then 1 tablespoonful of the lime juice. Lay a piece of plastic wrap directly on the surface of the filling and let cool for 15 minutes.

10. Pour the remaining 1 tablespoonful of lime juice into a medium bowl. Cut off one-third of one unpeeled banana, wrap it

tightly in plastic wrap and refrigerate to use as garnish.

11. Peel the remaining bananas, then slice them on the diagonal to create ovals about 2 inches long, dropping the slices in the bowl of lime juice as you work. Toss the banana slices with the lime juice to coat them completely.

12. Spoon half of the filling into the prepared pie crust, smoothing the surface level. Top the filling with half of the banana slices, arranging them in concentric circles.

13. Spoon the remaining filling over the bananas, smoothing the surface level. Lay a piece of plastic wrap directly over the filling. Refrigerate for at least 4 hours, or up to 24 hours.

14. Just before serving, make the topping by beating the cream and icing sugar in a medium bowl until medium peaks form. Beat in the vanilla extract until stiff peaks form.

15. Peel and slice the reserved piece of banana. Garnish the pie with whipped cream and the sliced banana. Serve immediately.

CHANGE IT UP

Substitute finely grated orange zest and freshly squeezed orange juice for the lime zest and juice.

Coconut Cream Pie

Another family favourite, this creamy, tropical-tasting pie would be the ideal dessert for a summer barbecue.

Makes one 9-inch pie; 8 to 10 servings
Prep time: 30 minutes
Chilling time: 4 hours, 30 minutes
Cooking time: 45 minutes

Pastry

½ batch of Perfect Pastry
(page 174)

Filling

1 can (13 ½ oz/400 mL)
unsweetened coconut milk

¾ cup granulated sugar

⅔ cup whole milk

5 large egg yolks

¼ cup cornstarch

½ tsp fine sea salt

1 Tbsp cold unsalted butter

2 tsp dark rum

1 tsp vanilla extract

½ tsp coconut extract

Topping

1 cup whipping cream (35%)

2 Tbsp icing sugar

1 tsp vanilla extract

½ cup sweetened flaked coconut,
toasted

1. On a lightly floured work surface, roll out the pastry and line a 9-inch pie dish (see page 175). Refrigerate for at least 30 minutes.

2. When ready to bake, preheat the oven to 375°F.

3. Bake the pie crust blind (see page 175). Let cool completely.

4. For the filling, combine the coconut milk, ½ cup of the sugar and the whole milk in a medium, heavy-bottomed saucepan.

5. Cook over medium heat until the mixture is just starting to simmer, about 3 minutes.

6. In a large bowl, whisk together the egg yolks, cornstarch, salt and the remaining ¼ cup of sugar.

7. Gradually whisk the hot milk mixture into the egg yolk mixture, ½ cup at a time, whisking constantly.

8. Pour the milk-egg mixture back into the saucepan. Cook over medium heat, stirring constantly, until the mixture begins to simmer. Cook, still stirring constantly, 1 minute.

9. Remove from the heat. Whisk in the butter, rum and vanilla and coconut extracts. Lay a piece of plastic wrap directly on the surface of the filling and let cool for 15 minutes.

10. Spoon the filling into the prepared pie crust, smoothing the surface level. Lay a piece of plastic directly on the surface of the filling. Refrigerate for at least 4 hours, or up to 24 hours.

11. Just before serving, make the topping by beating the cream and icing sugar in a medium bowl until medium peaks form. Beat in the vanilla extract until stiff peaks form.

12. Garnish the pie with whipped cream and flaked coconut. Serve immediately.

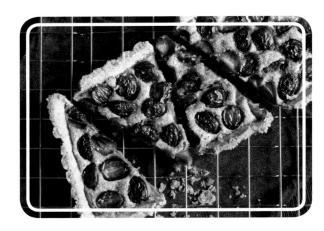

Grape-Pecan Tart

The combo of fragrant grapes, nutty pecans and an un-usual rosemary-flecked oat crust works surprisingly well in this elegant tart. Concord, Fredonia or Autumn Royal are all good grapes for this. If you don't have a 14- x 4-inch tart pan, substitute a 9-inch tart pan with a removable base.

Makes one 14-inch tart;
  10 servings
Prep time: 30 minutes
Chilling time: 30 minutes
Cooking time: 60 to 70 minutes
Cooling time: at least 30 minutes

Oat Crust

²/₃ cup oat flour (see sidebar on page 101)

½ cup pecan pieces

¹/₃ cup all-purpose flour

3 Tbsp granulated sugar

1 Tbsp fresh rosemary needles

½ tsp fine sea salt

¹/₃ cup cold unsalted butter, cut into ½-inch pieces

Filling

¾ cup pecan pieces

¼ cup granulated sugar

2 Tbsp all-purpose flour

½ tsp ground cinnamon

¼ tsp fine sea salt

¼ cup unsalted butter, softened

1 large egg

1 ¼ cups black seedless table grapes, cut in half

1 Tbsp turbinado sugar

1. For the oat crust, place the oat flour, pecan pieces, all-purpose flour, sugar, rosemary and salt in a food processor fitted with the steel blade. Pulse until the mixture resembles fine crumbs.

2. Add the butter, then pulse 10 or 12 times just until the dough begins to clump.

3. Tip the dough onto a clean work surface and gather it into a ball. Set the bowl of the food processor aside but don't wash it.

4. Place the dough in a 14- x 4-inch tart pan with a removable base. Press the dough evenly over the bottom and up the sides of the pan. Prick the pie crust all over with a fork, then place the pan in the freezer for 30 minutes.

5. When ready to bake, preheat the oven to 350°F.

6. Put the tart pan on a baking sheet. Bake until golden and dry to the touch, 20 to 25 minutes.

Let cool completely. Leave the oven on.

7. For the filling, combine the pecan pieces, granulated sugar, flour, cinnamon and salt in the food processor. Pulse until the mixture resembles fine crumbs.

8. Add the butter and egg, then pulse until smooth.

9. Spread the filling evenly over the prepared tart crust. Top the filling with the grape halves (it doesn't matter which way up they're facing), pressing them down slightly into the filling. Sprinkle evenly with the turbi-nado sugar.

10. Bake until the filling is lightly browned and dry to the touch, about 45 minutes, rotating the pan 180 degrees halfway through baking time.

11. Let the tart cool on a wire rack for at least 30 minutes. Serve warm or at room temperature.

Québécois Sugar Cream Pie

This authentic French-Canadian pie features a comforting custard filling. It's undoubtedly rich, but we love it served in slim wedges with fresh blueberries on the side.

Makes one 9-inch pie; 8 to 10
   servings
Prep time: 30 minutes
Chilling time: 30 minutes
Cooking time: 35 to 50 minutes

Pastry

1 batch of Perfect Pastry
   (page 174)

Filling

2 cups whipping cream (35%)

1 cup lightly packed golden
   yellow sugar

½ cup unsalted butter, cut into
   ½-inch pieces and softened

⅓ cup all-purpose flour

1. On a lightly floured work surface, roll out half of the pastry (reserve the other half for the top of the pie) and line a 9-inch pie dish (see page 175). Refrigerate for at least 30 minutes.

2. When ready to bake, preheat the oven to 350°F.

3. Bake the pie crust blind (see page 175) with the parchment or foil and beans or pie weights for just 10 to 15 minutes. Remove the parchment and beans or pie weights and let cool completely. Leave the oven on.

4. For the filling, combine the cream, sugar, butter and flour in a medium saucepan. Cook over medium heat, whisking constantly, until the mixture is

smooth and has thickened, about 7 minutes. Pour the filling into the prepared pie crust.

5. On a lightly floured work surface, roll out the remaining pastry to a 9-inch disc. Using a sharp knife, cut out a fleur-de-lys shape (or other shape of your choice) from the centre of the piece of pastry to allow the steam to escape from the finished pie. Carefully place the pastry over the filling (there is no need to seal the edges of the pie).

6. Bake until the pastry is golden brown and the filling is bubbly, 25 to 35 minutes. Let the pie cool to room temperature on a wire rack before slicing.

Lemony Lemon Meringue Pie

We're sure this is the lemoniest lemon meringue pie you'll ever taste. Lemon extract, as well as fresh lemon, adds zestiness to the filling, and a fluffy meringue top provides the finishing touch.

For best results, make the filling and meringue, and assemble the pie the day you plan to serve it (so start early!). You can also bake the pastry up to 3 days ahead.

Makes one 9-inch pie; 8 to 10 servings
Prep Time: 40 minutes
Chilling time: 4 hours, 30 minutes
Cooking time: about 1 hour, 35 minutes
Cooling time: 1 hour

Pastry

½ batch of Perfect Pastry (page 174)

Lemon Filling

1 ¼ cups granulated sugar

⅓ cup cornstarch

¼ tsp fine sea salt

½ cup whole milk

⅓ cup water

4 large egg yolks

1 tsp vanilla extract

½ tsp lemon extract

¾ cup freshly squeezed lemon juice (about 4 lemons)

3 Tbsp cold unsalted butter

1 Tbsp finely grated lemon zest (1 to 2 lemons)

Lemon Meringue

4 large egg whites

1 tsp freshly squeezed lemon juice

Pinch of fine sea salt

6 Tbsp instant-dissolving sugar

1. On a lightly floured work surface, roll out the pastry and line a 9-inch pie dish (see page 175). Refrigerate for at least 30 minutes.

2. When ready to bake, preheat the oven to 375°F.

3. Bake the pie crust blind (see page 175). Let cool completely but leave the oven on.

4. For the lemon filling, whisk together the sugar, cornstarch and salt in a medium, heavy-bottomed saucepan until well combined.

5. In a small bowl, stir together the milk and water. Gradually whisk the milk mixture into the sugar mixture, continuing to whisk until no lumps remain.

6. Cook over medium heat, stirring constantly, until the mixture begins to thicken and boil. Boil, stirring constantly, for 1 minute. Remove from the heat.

7. In a medium bowl, whisk together the egg yolks and the vanilla and lemon extracts.

8. Gradually whisk the hot milk mixture into the egg yolk mixture, a little at a time, whisking constantly. Whisk in the lemon juice.

9. Strain the milk-egg mixture through a fine-mesh sieve back into the saucepan. Cook over medium heat, stirring constantly, until the mixture begins to simmer. Cook, stirring constantly, 1 minute.

10. Remove from the heat. Whisk in the butter and lemon zest. Pour the hot filling into the prepared pie crust. Set aside.

11. For the lemon meringue, in a large bowl and using an electric mixer on medium speed, beat the egg whites, lemon juice and salt until foamy and white.

12. Beat in the sugar, about 1 tablespoonful at a time. Continue beating until the egg whites are glossy and stiff peaks form, about 5 minutes. Do not overbeat.

13. Spoon the meringue over the hot filling, spreading the meringue right to the edges of the pie crust.

14. Bake until the meringue is light golden brown, 10 to 12 minutes.

15. Let the pie cool completely on a wire rack, about 1 hour. Refrigerate for 4 hours before slicing.

BAKING DAY SECRETS

For the best-ever lemon meringue pie, spread the meringue over the hot filling and make sure the meringue touches the pastry edges all the way around the pie. This prevents the meringue from shrinking.

Rosemary-Plum Mascarpone Tart

U se firm black plums for this elegant tart, as overripe fruit will lose its shape during cooking.

Makes one 8-inch tart; 8 servings
Prep time: 40 minutes
Chilling time: at least 2 hours
Cooking time: about 35 minutes

Rosemary Crust

1 cup all-purpose flour

3 Tbsp lightly packed golden yellow sugar

1 ½ tsp finely chopped fresh rosemary

½ tsp fine sea salt

¼ cup plus 3 Tbsp cold unsalted butter, cut into ½-inch pieces

2 tsp apple cider vinegar

2 to 3 Tbsp ice water

Filling

3 to 4 black plums

½ cup mascarpone cheese

½ cup plus 1 Tbsp icing sugar, sifted

2 tsp finely grated lemon zest

1 tsp vanilla extract

¼ tsp fine sea salt

Egg Wash & Topping

1 large egg whisked with 1 Tbsp water

1 Tbsp turbinado or granulated sugar (optional)

2 Tbsp apple jelly

Fresh rosemary for garnish

CHANGE IT UP
Firm red plums, pluots, nectarines or peaches can be substituted for the black plums.

1. For the rosemary crust, combine the flour, sugar, rosemary and salt in a food processor fitted with the steel blade. Pulse several times until well combined.

2. Add the butter and pulse until the mixture resembles coarse crumbs.

3. Add the vinegar. Pulse just until combined. Gradually add the water, 1 teaspoonful at a time, pulsing after each addition until the dough starts to form a ball. Do not overprocess.

4. Tip the dough onto a clean work surface and gather it into a ball. Wrap it tightly in plastic wrap, then refrigerate for at least 2 hours, or up to 24 hours.

5. When ready to bake, preheat the oven to 375°F. Line a large baking sheet with parchment paper. Set aside.

6. On a large sheet of parchment paper, roll out the chilled dough to a 10-inch disc. Carefully slide the parchment and the dough onto a large baking sheet. Cover tightly with plastic wrap and set aside.

7. For the filling, line a second baking sheet with paper towels. Cut the plums in half and remove the pits. Cut the plum halves lengthwise into ¼-inch slices. Spread the plum slices out on the paper towels to remove any excess moisture. Set aside.

8. In a small bowl and using a spatula, beat together the mascarpone cheese, icing sugar, lemon zest, vanilla extract and salt until smooth.

9. Spread the mascarpone mixture evenly over the dough, leaving a 1-inch border around the edge.

10. Starting at the outer edge and working toward the centre, arrange the plum slices, in concentric circles and slightly overlapping, on top of the mascarpone mixture.

11. Fold the pastry border over the plums, creating overlapping folds as you work your way around the tart.

12. Brush the pastry edges with egg wash. Sprinkle with turbinado sugar (if using). Bake until the pastry is golden brown and the plum filling is bubbly, 30 to 35 minutes.

13. In a small microwave-safe bowl, microwave the apple jelly on high power until melted, 10 to 30 seconds.

14. Place the baking sheet on a wire rack. Brush the pastry with the melted apple jelly. Let the tart cool to room temperature. Serve garnished with fresh rosemary.

Autumn Sweet Potato Pie

Why not mix it up come Thanksgiving and serve this spicy sweet potato pie in place of pumpkin?

Makes one 9-inch pie; 8 to 10 servings
Prep time: 30 minutes
Chilling time: 30 minutes
Cooking time: about 2 hours

Pastry

½ batch of Perfect Pastry (page 174)

Filling

2 large sweet potatoes (about 1 ½ lb/750 g)

¾ cup whole milk

½ cup whipping cream (35%)

⅓ cup granulated sugar

2 large eggs

¼ tsp freshly grated nutmeg

¼ tsp ground cloves

¼ tsp ground cinnamon

¼ tsp fine sea salt

¼ cup crystallized ginger, finely chopped

Cinnamon Whipped Cream

1 cup whipping cream (35%)

5 Tbsp granulated sugar

1 ½ tsp vanilla extract

¼ tsp ground cinnamon

1. On a lightly floured work surface, roll out the pastry and line a 9-inch pie dish (see page 175). Refrigerate for at least 30 minutes.

2. When ready to bake, preheat the oven to 375°F.

3. Blind bake the pie crust (see page 175). Let cool completely. Increase the oven temperature to 400°F.

4. For the filling, pierce the sweet potatoes in several places with a fork. Place them on a baking sheet, then bake until very tender, about 1 hour, 15 minutes.

5. Remove the sweet potatoes from the oven. Leave the oven on.

6. When the sweet potatoes are cool enough to handle, cut them in half and scoop out the flesh.

7. In a food processor fitted with the steel blade, pulse the sweet potato flesh until smooth. Add the milk, cream, sugar, eggs, ground spices and salt. Pulse until smooth and well combined.

8. Scrape the sweet potato mixture into a medium bowl. Stir in the ginger.

9. Pour the sweet potato mixture into the prepared pie crust. Bake for 10 minutes. Turn down the oven temperature to 375°F. Bake until the pastry is golden brown and a wooden skewer inserted in the centre of the filling comes out clean, about 30 minutes. Let the pie cool to room temperature on a wire rack.

10. For the cinnamon whipped cream, in a medium bowl and using an electric mixer, beat the cream, sugar, vanilla extract and cinnamon until stiff peaks form. Garnish the pie with the whipped cream.

Summer Peach Pie

This is the perfect summer pie for any occasion. And it can be changed up depending on what fruit is at its freshest best. Nectarines and apricots are both fantastic fillings. Or, try replacing 2 cups of the peaches with fresh raspberries or blackberries.

Makes one 9-inch pie; 8 to 10 servings
Prep time: 30 minutes
Chilling time: 4 hours, 30 minutes
Standing time: 1 hour
Cooking time: about 1 hour

Pastry

1 batch of Perfect Pastry (page 174)

Filling

6 cups peeled, pitted and sliced freestone peaches (about 2 lb peaches)

2/3 cup firmly packed demerara-style sugar

1/3 cup granulated sugar

2 Tbsp freshly squeezed lemon juice

1/4 cup all-purpose flour

1/4 cup cornstarch

1/2 tsp ground cardamom

1/4 tsp ground cinnamon

1/4 tsp fine sea salt

Pinch of ground cloves

1 Tbsp finely grated lemon zest (1 to 2 lemons)

1 tsp almond extract

1/2 tsp vanilla extract

1 Tbsp unsalted butter, cut into 1/2-inch pieces and softened

Topping

1 large egg

1 Tbsp whole milk or cream

1 Tbsp turbinado sugar or granulated sugar

1. On a lightly floured work surface, roll out half of the pastry (reserve the other half for the top of the pie) and line a 9-inch pie dish (see page 175). Refrigerate for at least 30 minutes.

2. When ready to bake, place a large baking sheet on the lowest rack of the oven, then preheat the oven to 425°F.

2. For the filling, toss the sliced peaches with both sugars and the lemon juice in a large bowl. Let stand for about 1 hour.

3. Strain the peach mixture through a large fine-mesh sieve, reserving the juices. Return the peaches to the bowl. Set the juices aside.

4. In a small saucepan, whisk together the flour, cornstarch, cardamom, cinnamon, salt and cloves. Whisk in the reserved peach juices until no lumps remain.

5. Cook over medium heat, stirring constantly, until the mixture boils and thickens, about 2 minutes. Remove from the heat. Stir in the lemon zest and almond and vanilla extracts.

6. Pour the thickened juices over the peaches and toss to coat evenly.

7. Tip the peach mixture into the prepared pie crust, jiggling the pie plate so the peaches settle into the crust. Scatter the butter over the peaches.

8. On a lightly floured work surface, roll out the remaining pastry to a 10-inch disc. Using a sharp knife or a small cutter, cut five decorative holes around the centre of the piece of pastry to allow the steam to escape from the finished pie.

9. Place the pastry over the filling. Trim the excess pastry, leaving a 1/2-inch overhang. Tuck the overhang under, then flute the edges decoratively, if you wish (see page 175).

10. For the topping, whisk together the egg and milk in a small bowl. Brush the top of the pie with the egg mixture. Sprinkle with turbinado sugar.

11. Place the pie dish on the hot baking sheet. Bake for 10 minutes. Turn down the oven temperature to 350°F. Bake until the crust is deep golden brown and the filling is bubbly, about 50 minutes. Check the pie after 20 minutes. If the crust is browning too much, cover the pie loosely with foil.

12. Let the pie cool completely on a wire rack for at least 4 hours. (This will allow the juices in the pie to thicken.) Serve cold or at room temperature.

Chocolate Fantasy Cheesecake

If you're a chocolate lover, this is the cheesecake you've been waiting for. With a chocolate crust, filling and topping, it's a chocoholic's dream.

Makes one 9-inch cheesecake;
   10 to 12 servings
Prep time: 40 minutes
Cooking time: about 1 hour
Chilling time: at least 4 hours,
   30 minutes

Chocolate Wafer Crust

20 chocolate wafers, crushed into crumbs

1 Tbsp granulated sugar

¼ cup unsalted butter, melted

Filling

10 oz dark or semi-sweet chocolate, chopped

4 pkgs (each 8 oz/250 g) brick-style cream cheese, at room temperature and cut into ½-inch pieces

1 cup granulated sugar

1/3 cup unsweetened cocoa powder

4 large eggs

Ganache Topping

½ cup whipping cream (35%)

5 oz dark or semi-sweet chocolate, chopped

1 tsp granulated sugar

1. Preheat the oven to 350°F. Line the base of a 9-inch springform pan with parchment paper. Set aside.

2. For the chocolate wafer crust, stir together the chocolate wafer crumbs and sugar in a medium bowl. Stir in the butter until well combined.

3. Press the crumb mixture evenly over the base of the prepared pan. Bake until firm, 5 to 7 minutes. Let cool completely. Turn down the oven temperature to 325°F.

4. For the filling, put the chocolate in a medium bowl set over a saucepan of hot, not boiling, water. Stir until almost completely melted. Remove the bowl from the heat and stir until completely smooth. Set aside to cool.

5. Put the cream cheese in a food processor fitted with the steel blade (or use a large bowl and a hand-held electric mixer). Pulse until smooth and creamy. Add the sugar and cocoa powder, then pulse until well combined.

6. With the food processor running, gradually pour in the cooled melted chocolate. Process until smooth, creamy and well combined.

7. Add the eggs one at a time, pulsing to combine after each addition.

8. Pour the filling over the prepared crust. Bake until the centre is set, about 50 minutes. Let the cheesecake cool in the pan on a wire rack, then refrigerate for at least 4 hours.

9. For the ganache topping, combine the cream, chocolate and sugar in a medium saucepan. Cook over low heat, stirring gently, until the chocolate has melted and the mixture is completely smooth.

10. Pour the topping evenly over the cheesecake. Refrigerate until the topping has set, at least 30 minutes.

11. When ready to serve, hold a large, slim knife under hot water, then run it around the edge of the cheesecake to loosen it from the pan. Release the sides of the pan and slide the cheesecake onto a serving plate.

New York–Style Cheesecake
with Mixed Berry Coulis

I f you prefer, serve this classic cheesecake topped with some fresh berries on the side.

Makes one 9-inch cheesecake;
  10 to 12 servings
Prep time: 30 minutes
Cooking time: about 1 hour
Cooling time: 30 minutes
Chilling time: 5 hours

Crust

1 Graham Cracker Crust
  (page 183)

Cream Cheese Filling

3 pkgs (each 8 oz/250 g) brick-
  style cream cheese, at room
  temperature

1 ¼ cups granulated sugar

½ cup sour cream (14%)

2 Tbsp all-purpose flour

2 tsp vanilla extract

1 tsp freshly squeezed lemon
  juice

4 large eggs

1 large egg yolk

Mixed Berry Coulis (page 299)

Fresh berries for garnish (optional)

1. Preheat the oven to 325°F. Grease a 9-inch springform pan, then set aside.

2. Press the graham cracker crust mixture evenly over the base and 3 inches up the sides of the prepared pan. Bake until firm, about 12 minutes. Let cool completely. Leave the oven on.

3. For the cream cheese filling, in a large bowl and using an electric mixer, beat the cream cheese and sugar until smooth, scraping down the sides of the bowl as necessary.

4. Beat in the sour cream, flour, vanilla extract and lemon juice just until combined.

5. Beat in the eggs and egg yolk, in three additions, beating just until combined. Do not overmix. (Too much air in the batter can make the top of the cheesecake crack during baking.)

6. Pour the filling over the cooled crust, smoothing the top level.

7. Place the springform pan in a roasting pan and set the roasting pan on a baking sheet. Pull the oven rack partway out of the oven and put the roasting pan containing the cheesecake on the rack. Pour hot, not boiling, water into the roasting pan to come halfway up the side of the springform pan.

Carefully place the baking sheet and roasting pan into the oven.

8. Bake until the centre jiggles slightly when the pan is tapped and an instant-read thermometer inserted in the centre of the cheesecake registers 150°F, about 50 minutes.

9. Remove the cheesecake from the oven. Remove the springform pan from the roasting pan and put it on a wire rack. Cover the pan with a cold baking sheet and let stand for 5 minutes.

10. Remove the baking sheet and carefully run a paring knife around the edge of the cheese-cake. Replace the baking sheet on top of the pan and let the cheesecake cool on the rack for 30 minutes. Remove the baking sheet and let the cheesecake cool to room temperature.

11. Cover the pan tightly with plastic wrap and refrigerate for at least 5 hours before serving. (The undecorated cheesecake can be refrigerated, covered with plastic wrap, for up to 3 days.)

12. Just before serving, release the sides of the springform pan and slide the cheesecake onto a serving plate. Cut into wedges and serve with the mixed berry coulis. Garnish with fresh berries (if using).

Gluten-Free Carrot Cake Cheesecake

We love cheesecake and we love carrot cake, so we thought we'd combine the two. Even better? This dessert is gluten-free.

Makes one 9-inch cheesecake;
* 10 to 12 servings*
Prep time: 1 hour
Cooking time: 1 ½ to 2 hours
Cooling time: 30 minutes
Chilling time: 5 hours

Roasted Carrot Purée

3 to 4 large carrots, trimmed and peeled

¼ cup firmly packed dark brown sugar

2 Tbsp unsalted butter, melted

Pecan Crust

¾ cup unsweetened shredded coconut

½ cup pecan halves

⅓ cup unsalted butter, melted

3 Tbsp granulated sugar

Filling

3 pkgs (each 8 oz/250 g) brick-style cream cheese, at room temperature

1 cup granulated sugar

2 tsp vanilla extract

1 tsp ground cinnamon

½ tsp ground ginger

½ tsp ground cloves

¼ tsp freshly grated nutmeg

3 large eggs

¾ cup whipping cream (35%)

Toasted pecan halves for garnish (optional)

1. Preheat the oven to 400°F. Line a large rimmed baking sheet with parchment paper.

2. For the roasted carrot purée, spread the carrots out in a single layer on the prepared baking sheet. Sprinkle with the sugar, then drizzle with the butter.

3. Roast the carrots until they are golden brown and feel very tender when pierced with a fork, 20 to 35 minutes (cooking time will depend on the thickness of the carrots). Let the carrots cool completely on the baking sheet.

4. Put the carrots, along with any juices that have accumulated on the baking sheet, in a food processor fitted with the steel blade or a blender. Pulse until a smooth purée forms. Measure and set aside 1 cup of the carrot purée. (Save any remaining purée to serve as a vegetable dish or add to a soup.) Turn down the oven temperature to 325°F and clean the food processor bowl.

5. For the pecan crust, in a food processor, pulse the coconut and pecans until finely ground.

6. Tip the pecan mixture into a medium bowl. Stir in the butter and sugar until well combined. Press the pecan mixture over the base of a 9-inch springform pan. Bake until firm, about 10 minutes. Let cool completely in the pan on a wire rack. Leave the oven on.

7. For the filling, in a large bowl and using an electric mixer, beat the cream cheese and sugar until smooth, scraping down the sides of the bowl as necessary. Beat in the vanilla extract and spices.

8. Beat in the eggs one at a time, beating just until combined after each addition. Beat in the cream just until combined. Do not overmix. (Too much air in the batter can make the top of the cheesecake crack during baking.) Fold in the reserved carrot purée until well combined.

9. Pour the filling over the prepared crust, smoothing the top level.

10. Place the springform pan in a roasting pan. Pull the oven rack partway out of the oven and put the roasting pan containing the cheesecake on the rack. Pour hot, not boiling, water into the roasting pan to come halfway up the sides of the springform pan. Carefully slide the oven rack back into the oven.

11. Bake until the centre jiggles slightly when the pan is tapped and an instant-read thermometer inserted in the centre registers 150°F, 1 to 1 ¼ hours.

12. Remove the cheesecake from the oven. Remove the springform pan from the roasting pan and put it on a wire rack. Cover the pan with a cold baking sheet and let stand for 5 minutes.

13. Remove the baking sheet and carefully run a paring knife around the edge of the cheese-cake. Replace the baking sheet on top of the pan and let the cheesecake cool on the rack for 30 minutes. Remove the baking sheet and let the cheesecake cool to room temperature.

14. Cover the pan tightly with plastic wrap and refrigerate for at least 5 hours before serving. (The undecorated cheesecake can be refrigerated, covered with plastic wrap, for up to 3 days.)

15. Just before serving, release the sides of the springform pan and slide the cheesecake onto a serving plate. Garnish with toasted pecan halves (if using).

Key Lime Cheesecake

Key limes are smaller than regular limes and have a sweeter, punchier flavour. They add a great kick of citrus to this dessert, which combines the best of two wonderful worlds: cheesecake and key lime pie! If you can't find key limes, use regular ones.

Makes one 9-inch cheesecake;
  10 to 12 servings
Prep time: 1 hour
Cooking time: about 50 minutes
Cooling time: 30 minutes
Chilling time: 5 hours

Crust
1 Graham Cracker Crust (page 183)

Filling
1 cup granulated sugar

Finely grated zest of 5 key limes
  (or 1 regular lime)

3 pkgs (each 8 oz/250 g) brick-style cream cheese, at room temperature

1 ½ Tbsp all-purpose flour

2 tsp vanilla extract

3 large eggs

Topping
½ cup water

8 Tbsp granulated sugar

1 Tbsp cornstarch

3 large egg whites

¼ tsp cream of tartar

¼ tsp fine sea salt

½ tsp vanilla extract

1 batch of Key Lime Curd
  (recipe follows)

1. Preheat the oven to 350°F.

2. Press the graham cracker crust mixture evenly over the base and 2 inches up the sides of a 9-inch springform pan. Place the pan in the freezer while you make the filling.

3. For the filling, stir together the sugar and lime zest in a large bowl. Using your fingers, rub the ingredients together to infuse the sugar with the lime zest.

4. Using an electric mixer, beat the cream cheese into the sugar until the mixture is smooth. Beat in the flour and vanilla extract just until combined.

5. Beat in the eggs one at a time, beating just until combined after each addition. Do not overmix. (Too much air in the batter can make the top of the cheesecake crack during baking.)

6. Pour the filling over the prepared crust, smoothing the top level.

7. Place the springform pan in a roasting pan. Pull the oven rack partway out of the oven and put the roasting pan containing the cheesecake on the rack. Pour hot, not boiling, water into the roasting pan to come halfway up the sides of the springform pan. Carefully slide the oven rack back into the oven.

8. Bake until the centre jiggles slightly when the pan is tapped and an instant-read thermometer inserted in the centre registers 150°F, about 50 minutes.

9. Remove the cheesecake from the oven. Remove the springform pan from the roasting pan and put it on a wire rack. Cover the pan with a cold baking sheet and let stand for 5 minutes.

10. Remove the baking sheet and carefully run a paring knife around the edge of the cheese-cake. Replace the baking sheet on top of the pan and let the cheesecake cool on the rack for 30 minutes. Remove the baking sheet and let the cheesecake cool to room temperature.

11. Cover the pan tightly with plastic wrap and refrigerate for at least 5 hours before serving. (The undecorated cheesecake can be refrigerated, covered in plastic wrap, for up to 3 days.)

12. For the topping, stir together the water, 2 tablespoonfuls of the sugar and all the cornstarch in a small saucepan. Cook over low heat, stirring constantly, until the sugar has dissolved, about 10 minutes. Remove from the heat and set aside.

13. In a large bowl and using an electric mixer, beat together the egg whites, cream of tartar and salt until foamy. Beat in the vanilla extract.

14. Gradually beat in the remaining 6 tablespoonfuls of sugar, continuing to beat on medium-high speed until soft peaks form.

15. Gradually beat in the cornstarch mixture. Increase the speed to high and beat until stiff peaks form. Set aside.

16. Release the sides of the springform pan and slide the cheesecake onto a serving plate. Spread the key lime curd over the top of the cheesecake (you may not need all of the curd).

17. Pile the meringue over the curd, spreading gently with a knife or offset spatula.

18. Light a butane kitchen torch following the manufacturer's instructions (see sidebar if you don't have a butane torch). Using small, circular motions, torch the meringue until the peaks are golden brown. If the meringue darkens too quickly, hold the torch further away; if the meringue isn't darkening, hold the torch closer to it. (The key lime cheesecake is best served the day it's made but can be covered and refrigerated for up to 2 days, although the longer you store it the more moist the meringue will become.)

Key Lime Curd

Makes about ¾ cup
Prep time: 15 minutes
Cooking time: about 8 minutes
Cooling time: 40 minutes

¼ cup unsalted butter, cut into ½-inch pieces and softened

¾ cup granulated sugar

3 large eggs

¼ cup fresh key lime juice (about 10 key limes or 2 regular limes)

1. Place the butter in a large bowl and set a fine-mesh sieve over the bowl. Set aside.

2. In a large nonreactive saucepan, whisk together the sugar, eggs and lime juice. Cook over medium heat, whisking constantly, until the mixture just begins to thicken, about 8 minutes. (Do not let the mixture boil or the eggs will scramble.)

3. Remove from the heat, then pour the lime mixture through the sieve into the bowl of butter.

4. Remove the sieve. Stir the lime mixture until the butter has completely melted. Let the lime curd cool at room temperature for about 40 minutes before spooning it into a container. (The lime curd can be refrigerated in an airtight container for up to 1 week.)

BAKING DAY SECRETS

If you don't have a butane kitchen torch, you can toast the meringue in the oven. Leave the cheesecake in the springform pan. Spread the top with the key lime curd, then cover with the meringue. Bake in a preheated 350°F oven until the meringue is golden brown, 10 to 12 minutes.

All-Season Fruit Crisp

You can use almost any fresh or frozen fruit in this easy crisp (see sidebar). It's perfect for a crowd, and can be prepped in one large dish or individual gratin dishes or ramekins. Serve it with vanilla ice cream, softly whipped cream or thick Greek yogurt.

Makes 10 to 12 servings
Prep time: 20 minutes
Standing time: 5 to 15 minutes
Cooking time: about 45 minutes

Fruit Filling

8 cups prepared fresh or frozen fruit (see sidebar)

⅓ to ½ cup granulated sugar (depending on type of fruit)

1 tsp cornstarch

Crisp Topping

1 ⅓ cups all-purpose flour

⅔ cup firmly packed golden yellow sugar

1 cup large-flake rolled oats

1 tsp baking soda

1 tsp fine sea salt

½ cup cold unsalted butter, cut into ½-inch pieces

1. For the fruit filling, toss together the fruit, sugar and cornstarch in a large bowl. Let stand, stirring occasionally, until the sugar dissolves and the mixture is juicy, about 5 minutes for fresh fruit, 10 to 15 minutes for frozen fruit.

2. Preheat the oven to 375°F.

3. For the crisp topping, stir together the flour, sugar, oats, baking soda and salt in a medium bowl.

4. Add the butter to the flour mixture. Using a pastry cutter or your hands, work it in until the mixture is crumbly.

5. Spoon the fruit mixture into a 13- x 9-inch baking dish or divide evenly among ten ¾-cup gratin dishes or ramekins. Scatter the topping evenly over the fruit.

6. Bake in the centre of the oven until the fruit filling is bubbly and the topping is golden and crisp, about 45 minutes. Let cool to room temperature before serving.

BAKING DAY SECRETS

Choose any fresh or frozen fruit for our All-Season Fruit Crisp or Cobbler.

There's no need to thaw frozen fruit first. Fresh or frozen berries can be added whole, but slice or chop larger fresh fruits, removing their peel, pits or cores if necessary.

Some of our favourites are:

- apples
- apricots
- peaches
- blueberries
- pears
- mangoes
- plums
- raspberries
- rhubarb
- nectarines
- blackberries
- strawberries

We also like to include combos of fruit. For **Strawberry-Rhubarb Crisp** or **Cobbler** use 4 cups each trimmed, chopped rhubarb and hulled, chopped strawberries. For **Mixed Berry Crisp** or **Cobbler** use 2 cups each blackberries, blueberries, raspberries and hulled, chopped strawberries.

All-Season Fruit Cobbler

Makes 10 servings

Prep time: 20 minutes

Standing time: 5 to 15 minutes

Cooking time: 35 to 50 minutes

While a fruit crisp is topped with a crumbly, buttery topping, a cobbler features a fluffy biscuit topping. If you find it hard to decide which you prefer, make both! Again, vanilla ice cream, softly whipped cream or thick Greek yogurt are all perfect accompaniments.

Fruit Filling

1 batch of Fruit Filling from All-Season Fruit Crisp (page 215)

Cobbler Topping

2 cups all-purpose flour

½ cup granulated sugar

1 tsp baking powder

½ tsp baking soda

½ tsp fine sea salt

⅔ cup buttermilk (see page 11)

½ cup unsalted butter, melted and cooled

Additional granulated sugar for sprinkling

1. Preheat the oven to 400°F.

2. Prepare the fruit filling following the instructions for All-Season Fruit Crisp.

3. Spoon the fruit mixture into a 13- x 9-inch baking dish. Bake, uncovered, until the fruit begins to release its juices, 20 to 30 minutes.

4. For the cobbler topping, while the fruit filling bakes, whisk together the flour, sugar, baking powder, baking soda and salt in a large bowl. Set aside.

5. In a small bowl, stir together the buttermilk and melted butter. Set aside.

6. Just before the fruit filling is ready, add the buttermilk mixture to the flour mixture. Toss the ingredients together with a fork until the dough comes together in moist clumps. Do not overmix, or the cobbler topping will be dry.

7. Gather the dough into a ball. Form the dough into 12 even-sized pieces and form each piece into a shaggy ball. Place the balls, about ½-inch apart, on top of the hot fruit filling. Sprinkle a little additional sugar over the cobbler topping.

8. Bake until the cobbler topping is golden brown, 15 to 20 minutes. Let the cobbler cool to room temperature before serving.

HOLIDAYS & SPECIAL OCCASIONS

Yule Log

Burning a yule log in the hearth to celebrate the winter solstice was a tradition for hundreds of years. This classic holiday cake, shaped like the famous log, is an even sweeter way to bring friends and family together.

Makes 14 servings
Prep time: 1 hour
Cooking time: 12 to 16 minutes
Chilling time: at least 4 hours

Cake

½ cup cake-and-pastry flour

¼ cup cornstarch

½ tsp ground mace

¾ cup granulated sugar

3 large eggs

3 large egg yolks

Pinch of fine sea salt

Brandied Whipped Cream

1 cup whipping cream (35%)

2 Tbsp brandy

1 ½ Tbsp granulated sugar

Brandied Chocolate Buttercream

½ cup unsalted butter, softened

1 ¼ cups icing sugar, sifted

½ cup unsweetened cocoa powder

2 Tbsp brandy

Meringue mushrooms, marzipan decorations (pages 163–65), sugared rosemary (recipe follows) and/or icing sugar for decorating

1. Place the oven rack in the centre of the oven, then preheat the oven to 400°F. Butter a 15- x 10-inch jelly roll pan, line it with parchment paper, then butter the parchment paper. (Buttering the pan helps the parchment stick to it.) Set aside.

2. For the cake, whisk together the flour, cornstarch and mace in a medium bowl Set aside.

3. In a large heatproof bowl, whisk together the sugar, eggs, egg yolks and salt. Set the bowl over a saucepan of simmering water, then whisk gently until the mixture is just lukewarm (about 100°F on an instant-read thermometer), about 4 minutes.

4. Remove from the heat. Using an electric mixer on medium-high speed, beat the sugar mixture until it has cooled (touch the outside of the bowl to check) and tripled in volume. (The egg foam will be thick and will form a slowly dissolving ribbon when the beaters are lifted.)

5. Sift one-third of the flour mixture over the sugar mixture. Using a rubber spatula, fold in the flour mixture, making sure to scrape all the way to the bottom of the bowl to prevent the flour mixture from accumulating there and forming lumps. Repeat with half of the remaining flour mixture, making sure the ingredients are well combined before adding the remainder of the flour mixture.

6. Scrape the batter into the prepared pan and smooth the top level. Bake until the cake springs back when lightly pressed in the centre and a wooden skewer inserted in the cake comes out clean, 8 to 12 minutes. Let the cake cool in the pan on a wire rack for 10 to 15 minutes.

7. Run a sharp knife around the edge of the cake to loosen it from the pan. Invert the pan onto a clean cutting board or a sheet of parchment paper. Remove the pan, then peel away the parchment paper lining from the bottom of the cake.

8. Using a serrated knife, trim off and discard the edges of the cake to neaten it up. Carefully invert the cake onto a fresh piece of parchment paper so that it's right side up. Set aside.

9. For the brandied whipped cream, in a medium bowl and using an electric mixer, whip together the cream, brandy and sugar until stiff peaks form.

10. Spread the brandied whipped cream over the top of the cake. Starting from one long edge, gently roll up the cake into a tight cylinder, using the parchment paper to help you. Wrap the cake tightly in parchment paper or plastic wrap, then refrigerate for at least 4 hours, or overnight.

11. For the brandied chocolate buttercream, in a large bowl and using an electric mixer, beat the butter until pale and fluffy. Beat in the icing sugar until the mixture is creamy and smooth. Sift the cocoa powder over the mixture, then beat until smooth and combined. Stir in the brandy.

12. Trim the ends of the cake, cutting them on the diagonal. Set these trimmed ends aside.

13. Spread the cake with most of the chocolate buttercream, covering it completely. Position the reserved slices on the top and side of the cake to resemble cut branches. Spread the remaining buttercream over them.

14. Using the blade of a knife or the tines of a fork, make streaks in the buttercream along the length of the cake to resemble tree bark.

Decorate the cake with meringue mushrooms, marzipan decorations, sugared rosemary or a light dusting of icing sugar. (The cake can be refrigerated in an airtight container for up to 2 days.)

Sugared Rosemary

Makes 6 to 8 sprigs
Prep time: 15 minutes
Cooking time: about 3 minutes
Drying time: 1 to 2 hours

1 cup granulated sugar

⅓ cup water

6 to 8 rosemary sprigs, washed and dried well

1. Set a wire rack over a baking sheet. Spread ½ cup of the sugar out on a large plate. Set aside.

2. In a small saucepan, stir together the remaining ½ cup of sugar and the water. Bring to a boil over medium heat, stirring until the sugar dissolves. Remove from the heat and let cool to room temperature.

3. Holding a rosemary sprig by its stem, dip it into the sugar syrup to coat the leaves completely. Shake off the excess, then roll the rosemary sprig in the sugar to coat completely.

4. Lay the sprig on the wire rack, then repeat with the remaining rosemary sprigs. Let the sprigs dry at room temperature before using, 1 to 2 hours.

Rich, Dark Fruitcake

The longer you allow this dense, dark fruitcake to mature, the better it will be. Trust us—it's worth the wait. If you opt to mature it for longer than 3 months, you may need extra rum for drizzling.

Makes one 9-inch cake; 16 servings
Prep time: 30 minutes
Soaking time: 30 minutes
Cooking time: about 2 hours
Maturing time: at least 3 months

Cake

1 vanilla bean

2 ¼ cups dried figs, finely chopped

2 cups dried cranberries

2 cups dried apricots, finely chopped

1 ½ cups dark or golden raisins

1 ½ cups chopped mixed candied or dried fruit (cherries, pineapple and/or dates)

1 cup firmly packed demerara-style sugar

1 cup crystallized ginger, finely chopped

1 cup plus 2 Tbsp unsalted butter, softened

1 cup spiced dark rum

1 Tbsp finely grated orange zest

½ cup freshly squeezed orange juice (about 2 oranges)

1 Tbsp finely grated lemon zest (1 to 2 lemons)

¼ cup freshly squeezed lemon juice (about 2 lemons)

2 tsp almond extract

1 ⅓ cups plus 1 Tbsp all-purpose flour

1 cup almond meal or almond flour

½ cup hazelnuts, toasted (see page 22) and finely ground

2 tsp mixed spice or pumpkin pie spice

1 ¼ tsp ground cinnamon

½ tsp baking powder

½ tsp fine sea salt

¼ tsp ground cloves

¼ tsp ground ginger

¼ tsp freshly grated nutmeg

4 large eggs

1 Tbsp vanilla extract

Additional spiced dark rum

For Maturing the Cake

¾ cup spiced dark rum

Almond Icing

1 ½ cups icing sugar, sifted

Pinch of fine sea salt

4 tsp white corn syrup

1 Tbsp almond extract

6 to 7 tsp whipping cream (35%)

BAKING DAY SECRETS

Any dried fruit can be used in this classic fruitcake, so feel free to change up the combo according to what you have in your cupboard. As for nuts, almonds, pecans or walnuts can be substituted for the hazelnuts.

1. Using a sharp knife, split the vanilla bean in half lengthwise. Scrape the seeds out into a large saucepan, then drop in the pod.

2. Add all the dried and candied fruits, sugar, crystallized ginger, butter, the 1 cup of rum, orange zest and juice, and lemon zest and juice to the saucepan. Bring to a boil over medium heat. Turn down the heat to medium-low and simmer for 5 minutes.

3. Remove from the heat and stir in the almond extract. Tip the mixture into a large bowl. Set aside to soak, uncovered, for about 30 minutes, then discard the vanilla pod.

4. Preheat the oven to 300°F. Grease a deep 9-inch round baking pan. Line the bottom of the pan with a double-layered circle of parchment paper, then line the sides with a double-layered strip of parchment paper that extends 2 inches above the edge of the pan. Set aside.

5. In a large bowl, whisk together the flour, almond meal, ground hazelnuts, mixed spice, cinnamon, baking powder, salt, cloves, ginger and nutmeg. Set aside.

6. In a small bowl, whisk together the eggs and vanilla extract. Add the flour and egg mixtures to the cooled fruit mixture. Using a spatula or wooden spoon, stir until well combined.

7. Scrape the batter into the prepared pan, tapping the pan lightly on the work surface to eliminate any pockets of air. Use an offset spatula to smooth the top level.

8. Wrap the outside of the pan with a double layer of brown paper or newspaper, then tie the paper securely with kitchen twine. (This prevents the sides of the cake from overcooking.) Bake until a wooden skewer inserted in the centre of the cake comes out with only a few moist crumbs attached, about 2 hours, rotating the pan 180 degrees halfway through baking time.

9. Remove the cake from the oven. Using a skewer, poke several holes in the top. Pour over about 2 tablespoonfuls of additional spiced dark rum. Let the cake cool completely in the pan on a wire rack before unmoulding.

10. To mature the cake, wrap it tightly in plastic wrap then in foil. Store in a cool, dry, dark place for at least 3 months. Every other week, unwrap the cake, drizzle it with about 2 tablespoonfuls of rum, then rewrap it. (You can reuse the same plastic and foil for this.)

11. When ready to serve, unwrap the cake and place it on a serving plate.

12. For the almond icing, whisk together the icing sugar and salt in a medium bowl. Stir in the corn syrup and almond extract.

13. Stir in the cream, about 1 teaspoonful at a time, until the icing is a pourable consistency. Pour the icing over the top of the fruit cake. Using a small offset spatula, spread it to the edges of the cake, letting it drizzle down the side. Serve immediately, or allow the icing to harden before serving, about 15 minutes. (The iced cake can be stored refrigerated in an airtight container for up to 2 weeks.)

Old-Fashioned Gingerbread Cake

D ark, most and spicy, this cake has it all. It keeps well, too, so it's ideal when you're feeding a crowd at holiday time. We love the rich molasses glaze on this cake, but feel free to use your favourite glaze (the one from the Hot Cross Buns recipe on page 262 would be a simple substitute) or just serve the cake plain, if you prefer.

Makes one 9-inch Bundt cake; 10 to 12 servings
Prep time: 20 minutes
Cooking time: 40 to 45 minutes

Cake

2 ¾ cups all-purpose flour

1 ½ tsp baking soda

1 tsp ground ginger

1 tsp ground cinnamon

½ tsp ground cloves

½ tsp fine sea salt

Pinch of freshly grated nutmeg

½ cup unsalted butter, softened

½ cup granulated sugar

1 large egg

1 cup fancy molasses

1 cup hot water

Molasses Glaze

¼ cup icing sugar, sifted

2 Tbsp unsalted butter, melted

2 Tbsp fancy molasses

1 Tbsp whole milk

1 tsp vanilla extract

1. Preheat the oven to 350°F. Grease a 9-inch Bundt pan, then dust it with flour. Set aside.

2. For the cake, whisk together the flour, baking soda, ginger, cinnamon, cloves, salt and nutmeg in a medium bowl. Set aside.

3. In a large bowl and using an electric mixer, beat together the butter and sugar until pale and fluffy. Beat in the egg, then beat in the molasses.

4. Add the flour mixture to the sugar mixture alternately with the hot water, making three additions of flour and two of water, and beginning and ending with the flour. Stir until well combined.

5. Scrape the batter into the prepared pan. Bake until a wooden skewer inserted in the cake comes out clean, 40 to 45 minutes.

6. Let the cake cool in the pan for 5 to 10 minutes. Invert a serving plate on top of the pan. Flip over the plate and pan to remove the cake from the pan. Remove the pan, then let the cake cool completely on the plate.

7. For the molasses glaze, whisk together the icing sugar, butter, molasses, milk and vanilla extract in a small bowl until smooth.

8. Pour the glaze over the cake, letting it drizzle down the side. Let the glaze set before serving. (The cake can be refrigerated in an airtight container for up to 3 days.)

CHANGE IT UP

If you're not a fan of cloves or nutmeg, simply omit them. The cake will still taste spicy good.

Add a touch of citrus to this spicy cake by adding the finely grated zest of 1 orange along with the molasses in Step 3.

Holiday Gingerbread

What's a holiday cookie tray without gingerbread? This recipe makes a big batch of spicy dough that you can form into gingerbread men or women, or any festive shape you wish.

Makes about 48 cookies
Prep time: 25 minutes
Chilling time: 1 hour, 20 minutes
Cooking time: 10 to 15 minutes

6 ½ cups all-purpose flour

1 tsp fine sea salt

1 cup unsalted butter, softened

1 cup firmly packed dark brown sugar

2 Tbsp finely grated fresh ginger

4 tsp ground cinnamon

1 Tbsp ground ginger

1 tsp ground cloves

2 large eggs

1 cup fancy molasses

Easy Royal Icing (page 162)

1. In a medium bowl, whisk together the flour and salt. Set aside.

2. In a large bowl and using an electric mixer, beat the butter with the sugar on medium speed until light and fluffy, about 4 minutes.

3. Beat in the fresh ginger and ground spices.

4. Beat in the eggs one at a time, beating well after each addition. Beat in the molasses.

5. With the mixer running on low speed, beat the flour mixture into the sugar mixture 1 cup at a time, beating after each addition just until no white streaks remain.

6. Turn out the dough onto a clean work surface and cut it in half. Pat out each piece of dough into a disc. Wrap each piece of dough tightly in plastic wrap, then refrigerate until firm, about 1 hour. (The dough can be refrigerated for up to 3 days. Remove it from the fridge about 30 minutes before rolling it out.)

7. When ready to bake, preheat the oven to 350°F. Line two large baking sheets with parchment paper, then set aside.

8. On a lightly floured work surface (or between two large sheets of parchment paper), roll out one piece of dough to about ¼-inch thickness. (If the dough cracks, let it stand at room temperature until it softens enough to roll.)

9. Using a 3 ½-inch-tall ginger-bread person cutter (or decorative

cutter of your choice), cut out cookies, rerolling the dough scraps once. (Rerolling the scraps more than once makes the cookies tough.) Repeat with the remaining dough.

10. Place the cookies, 2 inches apart, on the prepared baking sheets. Place the baking sheets in the freezer for 20 minutes. (Don't be tempted to skip this step. Freezing the cookies briefly helps them keep their shape, as it prevents them from spreading too much during baking.)

11. Bake the cookies on two separate racks of the oven until they're firm and starting to brown at the edges, 10 to 15 minutes, rotating the baking sheets and switching their positions halfway through the cooking time.

12. Remove the cookies to wire racks and let cool completely. Decorate them with royal icing (see page 170). (The cookies can be stored in an airtight container at room temperature for up to 4 days, or frozen for up to 2 months.)

Galette des Rois

Galette des rois (the name translates as "kings' cake") is a French puff pastry cake served on the feast of the Epiphany (January 6). By tradition, a dried bean or tiny figurine is hidden in the cake. Whoever finds it in their slice is crowned king for the day. Even if you don't celebrate Epiphany, you'll love the rich almond filling sandwiched between light layers of crisp puff pastry.

Makes 10 servings
Prep time: 1 hour
Chilling time: up to 3 hours
Cooking time: 30 to 40 minutes

Quick Puff Pastry

3 ½ cups all-purpose flour

Pinch of fine sea salt

2 cups cold unsalted butter, cut into small pieces

1 ¾ cups whipping cream (35%)

Frangipane Filling

3 large egg yolks

⅓ cup granulated sugar

2 Tbsp all-purpose flour

1 ¾ cups whole milk

½ cup icing sugar, sifted

⅓ cup ground almonds

3 Tbsp unsalted butter, softened

1 large egg

½ tsp almond extract

Egg Glaze

1 large egg, beaten

BAKING DAY SECRETS

You won't need all of the frangipane filling for the galette, but it's too good to waste. Spoon any leftovers into baked mini tart shells and top with fresh berries, or spread it on split Strawberry Shortcakes (page 126) before adding the whipped cream and strawberries.

1. For the quick puff pastry, whisk together the flour and salt in a large bowl. Add the butter and toss to coat with the flour mixture. Using your hands, work the butter into the flour slightly to ensure each piece of butter is coated with flour. Add the cream, then stir to form a loose dough.

2. Turn the dough out onto a lightly floured work surface. Using your hands, press the dough into a square shape.

3. Using a rolling pin, press down on the dough and roll it out to the length of the rolling pin.

4. Fold each short end toward the centre so the edges meet. Roll out the dough a second time to the length of the rolling pin. Fold the dough again, then make an indentation on one side of it with your finger. Wrap the dough tightly in plastic and refrigerate for 30 minutes.

5. Remove the dough from the fridge. Place it on the work surface and rotate it so that the indented side has turned through 90 degrees. Do the rolling and folding process two more times, marking the dough and rotating it through 90 degrees each time. Wrap the dough tightly in plastic wrap and refrigerate it for 30 minutes.

6. Do the rolling and folding process two more times, marking the dough and rotating it through 90 degrees each time again. Wrap the dough tightly in plastic wrap and refrigerate it for another 30 minutes, or until you're ready to use the pastry.

7. For the frangipane filling, whisk together the egg yolks, granulated sugar and flour in a medium bowl. Set aside.

8. In a medium saucepan, heat the milk over medium heat until it's hot but not boiling.

9. Whisking constantly, slowly add the hot milk to the egg yolk mixture. Pour the mixture back into the saucepan. Cook over low heat, whisking constantly, until the mixture thickens, about 7 minutes. Scrape the mixture into a clean medium bowl and set aside to cool to room temperature.

10. In a medium bowl and using an electric mixer, beat together the icing sugar, ground almonds and butter until smooth and fluffy. Beat in the whole egg and almond extract.

11. Gradually stir the icing sugar mixture into the cooled egg yolk mixture until well combined. Lay a piece of plastic wrap directly on the surface of the frangipane filling to prevent a skin from forming. Refrigerate until firm, 15 to 30 minutes.

12. Line a baking sheet with parchment paper.

13. To assemble the galette, cut the puff pastry in half. On a lightly floured work surface, roll out one half of the pastry to a 10-inch disc, about ⅛ inch thick. Transfer the disc to the prepared baking sheet.

14. Spread ⅓ cup of the frangipane filling over the pastry, leaving a 1-inch border around the edge. Lightly brush the border with water. (Refrigerate the remaining frangipane filling and see the sidebar for ways to use it.)

15. Roll out the remaining puff pastry to a 10-inch disc. Carefully place it over the frangipane-covered pastry.

16. Pinch the pastry edges together to seal the dough. Using a sharp knife, carefully score a design into the top of the galette, making it as fancy or as simple as you like. Using a paring knife, poke five holes around the top of the tart to allow the steam to escape during baking.

17. For the egg glaze, brush the top of the galette with beaten egg.

18. Refrigerate the galette for 1 hour or freeze it for 30 minutes.

19. When ready to bake, preheat the oven to 450°F. Bake the chilled galette for 10 minutes. Turn down the oven temperature to 375°F, then bake until the pastry is golden brown and has puffed up so its layers are visible, 15 to 25 minutes.

20. Let the galette cool completely on the baking sheet. Cut into wedges to serve. (Any leftovers can be stored in an airtight container at room temperature for up to 3 days.)

TOOL KIT

If you don't have a panettone mould, grease a deep 6-inch round baking pan. Line the pan with a double thickness of parchment paper large enough to extend 4 inches above the sides of the pan. Tie a piece of kitchen twine around the paper extension. Follow the recipe as above, but instead of suspending the baked panettone in the saucepan, cool it right-side up in the pan on a wire rack. The texture of the finished panettone will be denser, but it will still taste wonderful.

Chocolate-Cranberry Panettone

This fruit-studded sweet bread hails originally from the Italian city of Milan. It is enjoyed at Christmas and New Year throughout southern Europe and as far afield as South America. Stale panettone can be used to make a fruit-filled bread pudding, and is fantastic toasted and spread with butter.

Makes one 7-inch loaf
Prep time: 40 minutes
Soaking time: at least 2 hours
Rising time: 4 hours
Cooking time: 35 minutes

Panettone

1 cup dried cranberries

2 Tbsp dark rum

2 Tbsp cold water

$2/3$ cup warm water (about 110°F)

$1/3$ cup granulated sugar

2 ¼ tsp active dry yeast

3 ½ cups bread flour

½ cup unsalted butter, softened

1 large egg

3 large egg yolks

1 Tbsp finely grated lemon zest (1 to 2 lemons)

1 ½ tsp fine sea salt

1 tsp vanilla extract

1 cup chopped semi-sweet chocolate

Egg Wash

1 large egg whisked with 1 Tbsp water

1. In a medium bowl, toss the cranberries with the rum and cold water. Set aside to soak at room temperature for at least 2 hours, or overnight.

2. Pour the warm water into a medium bowl. Sprinkle 1 tablespoonful of the sugar and the yeast over the water. Let stand until puffy, about 5 minutes.

3. Stir in ¾ cup of the flour. Cover tightly with plastic wrap and set aside in a warm place until doubled in size, about 30 minutes.

4. In the bowl of a stand mixer fitted with the paddle attachment (or in a large bowl and using a hand-held electric mixer), beat together the butter and remaining sugar until smooth and pale.

5. Beat in the egg and egg yolks until well combined. Beat in the yeast mixture, lemon zest, salt and vanilla extract.

6. Beat in the remaining 2 ¾ cups of flour, in three additions, until a shaggy dough forms.

7. Fit the stand mixer (if using) with the dough hook attachment. Mix on medium speed for 5 minutes. Turn down the speed to low and mix in the cranberry mixture and chocolate until evenly distributed through the dough.

8. Turn out the dough onto a lightly floured work surface and knead it a few times to bring it together into a ball. (If not using a stand mixer, mix in the flour until combined, then turn out the dough onto a lightly floured work surface and knead until smooth. Knead in the cranberry mixture and chocolate until evenly distributed through the dough.)

9. Place the dough in a lightly oiled large bowl, turning the dough to coat it evenly with oil. Cover the bowl with a damp towel, or loosely with plastic wrap. Let stand in a warm place until the dough has doubled in size, about 2 hours.

10. On a lightly floured work surface, punch down the dough to remove the air. Shape it into a smooth ball, then place it in a 7-inch diameter paper panettone mould. Cover the mould loosely with plastic wrap. Let stand in a warm place until doubled in size, about 1 ½ hours. Meanwhile, place the oven rack in the centre position and preheat the oven to 350°F.

11. Have ready a large saucepan at least 8 inches in diameter and 8 inches deep. (You'll hang the finished panettone in it to cool.)

12. Brush the egg wash over the top of the panettone. Bake until the panettone is golden brown on top, a wooden skewer inserted in the centre comes out clean and an instant-read thermometer inserted in the centre registers 200°F, 30 to 35 minutes.

13. Immediately push two long wooden skewers horizontally and at right angles to each other through the paper mould at the base of the panettone so that they poke out the other side. Invert the panettone inside the large saucepan so the skewers support the panettone on the edge of the saucepan and the panettone is suspended inside it. Let the panettone cool completely. (The panettone is best served the day it's baked, but can be stored at room temperature, tightly wrapped in plastic wrap, for up to 3 days.)

Steamed Christmas Pudding

Don't let the lengthy list of ingredients put you off trying this holiday classic. It isn't a pudding as we know it in Canada, but rather a richly spiced, steamed dessert made from dried fruit. And it's utterly delicious. It keeps well, so you can make it weeks ahead of the holidays (see sidebar for storage tips). We love it served with Delectable Caramel Sauce (page 298) and/or Crème Anglaise (page 300).

Makes 8 to 10 servings
Prep time: 30 minutes
Soaking time: 24 hours
Cooking time: 4 ½ to 5 hours

¾ cup currants

½ cup dried cranberries

½ cup chopped dried apples

½ cup golden raisins

½ cup chopped pitted prunes

¼ cup chopped candied citrus peel

⅓ cup freshly squeezed orange juice (1 to 2 oranges)

¼ cup whisky

1 ¼ cups all-purpose flour

½ cup dry bread crumbs

1 tsp baking soda

½ tsp ground cinnamon

½ tsp freshly grated nutmeg

½ tsp ground cloves

½ tsp ground ginger

½ tsp ground allspice

½ tsp fine sea salt

½ cup unsalted butter, softened

⅔ cup firmly packed dark brown sugar

2 large eggs

2 Tbsp fancy molasses

1 Tbsp finely grated orange zest

1 tsp vanilla extract

½ cup chopped pecans

Delectable Caramel Sauce (page 298; optional)

1. In a large bowl, toss together the dried fruit and peel, orange juice and whisky. Cover and let soak at room temperature for 24 hours.

2. Grease an 8-cup heatproof bowl (slightly larger is fine). Line the bottom with a small disc of parchment paper, then grease the paper. Set aside.

3. In a second large bowl, whisk together the flour, bread crumbs, baking soda, spices and salt. Set aside.

4. In a third large bowl and using an electric mixer, beat the butter with the sugar until smooth. Beat in the eggs one at a time, beating well after each addition. Beat in the molasses, orange zest and vanilla extract.

5. Using a wooden spoon or spatula, stir the flour mixture into the sugar mixture in two additions. Stir in the dried fruit, along with any liquid that remains in the bowl. Stir in the pecans.

6. Spoon the batter into the prepared bowl, packing it firmly. Cut a disc of parchment paper the same size as the top of the bowl. Grease it and place, greased side down, directly on the batter.

7. Cut a second disc of parchment paper 4 inches larger than the diameter of the bowl. Make a ½-inch pleat across the centre of the parchment disc, then place it over the bowl, pressing down to fold the excess paper around the sides of the bowl. Tie the paper around the bowl tightly with kitchen twine.

8. Repeat the previous step with a disc of foil 6 inches larger than the diameter of the bowl.

9. Loop a piece of kitchen twine around the twine holding the foil and tie it on the opposite side to create a small handle.

10. Place the pudding in a saucepan large enough to accommodate both its height and diameter. Boil a full kettle of water and pour enough water into the saucepan to reach halfway up the sides of the bowl. Cover the saucepan and place it over low heat.

BAKING DAY SECRETS

No time to soak the dried fruit mixture overnight? Simply combine the orange juice and whisky in a small saucepan, then bring to a simmer over medium heat. Pour over the fruit in a large bowl, then cover with a towel and let stand at room temperature for 2 hours.

11. Steam the pudding until a large skewer inserted through the foil and parchment paper and into the centre of the pudding comes out clean, 4 ½ to 5 hours. If the pudding isn't done when tested, patch the testing hole in the coverings with a small piece of foil and continue to steam the pudding. When the pudding is done, use the twine handle to carefully remove the bowl from the saucepan.

12. To serve the pudding immediately, carefully remove the foil and parchment paper. Run a knife around the edge of the bowl, then invert the pudding onto a warm serving plate. Drizzle over some caramel sauce (if using). Cut into wedges to serve. If making ahead, see the sidebar for storage and serving instructions.

GET A HEAD START

If making the pudding ahead, remove the foil and parchment paper and let the pudding cool completely in the bowl. Wrap the bowl tightly in plastic wrap and store in a cool, dark place for up to 3 months.

Every 2 weeks, unwrap the pudding. Drizzle with 1 tablespoonful of whisky or brandy (using the same liquor each time), then rewrap tightly in the plastic wrap.

Alternatively, let the pudding cool and turn it out as described in Step 12 of the recipe. Wrap it tightly in plastic wrap and seal in a freezer bag. Freeze for up to 6 months. Thaw at room temperature for 3 hours before reheating.

To reheat the pudding, place it back in its steaming bowl (if necessary), rewrap as before with parchment and foil, then steam for 2 hours.

Christmas Stollen

Packed with spices and fruit and covered with snowy icing sugar, stollen is a traditional holiday bread from Germany. Feel free to use your favourite dried fruit in the fruit mixture.

Makes one 11- x 9-inch loaf
Prep time: 1 hour
Soaking time: at least 2 hours
Rising time: 2 ½ hours
Cooking time: 35 to 40 minutes

Fruit Mixture

⅓ cup spiced dark rum

⅓ cup freshly squeezed orange juice (1 to 2 oranges)

½ cup finely chopped crystallized ginger

½ cup finely chopped dried apricots

½ cup finely chopped dried cherries

¼ cup chopped candied citrus peel

¼ cup golden raisins

¼ cup currants

2 Tbsp unsalted butter, melted

Yeast Sponge

½ cup warm whole milk (about 110°F)

2 tsp liquid honey

1 Tbsp plus 1 tsp dry active yeast

1 cup plus 2 Tbsp all-purpose flour

Dough

2 large eggs

2 large egg yolks

2 Tbsp finely grated orange zest

2 Tbsp finely grated lemon zest (about 3 lemons)

2 Tbsp liquid honey

2 tsp almond extract

1 tsp vanilla extract

3 ¼ cups bread flour

⅓ cup lightly packed golden yellow sugar

1 tsp fine sea salt

½ tsp ground cardamom

¼ tsp ground cinnamon

½ cup unsalted butter, cut into small pieces and softened

1 cup icing sugar for dusting

---

1. For the fruit mixture, stir together the rum and orange juice in a small bowl. Set aside.

2. In a large bowl, combine the ginger and all the dried fruit and peel. Pour the rum mixture over the fruit, stirring to combine. Set aside to soak, uncovered, for at least 2 hours, or overnight, stirring occasionally.

3. For the yeast sponge, pour the warm milk into a medium bowl. Stir in the honey. Sprinkle the yeast over the milk. Let stand until puffy, about 5 minutes.

4. Stir in the all-purpose flour. Cover the bowl tightly with plastic wrap and set aside in a warm place until doubled in size, about 30 minutes.

5. For the dough, whisk together the eggs, egg yolks, orange and lemon zests, honey and almond and vanilla extracts in a small bowl. Set aside.

6. In the bowl of a stand mixer fitted with the whisk attachment (or in a large bowl), whisk

together the bread flour, sugar, salt, cardamom and cinnamon. Fit the mixer with the paddle attachment (or use a hand-held electric mixer). Gradually beat the egg mixture into the flour mixture until well combined.

7. Add the yeast sponge and beat until a rough dough forms with the yeast mixture scattered through it.

8. Fit the stand mixer (if using) with the dough hook. Knead the dough, gradually adding the softened butter, one piece at a time, until the dough pulls away from the sides of the bowl and leaves it clean. Knead until the dough is smooth and shiny, about 3 minutes.

9. Turn out the dough onto a lightly floured work surface and knead a few times to bring it together into a ball. (If not using a stand mixer, mix in the egg mixture until well combined, then mix in the softened butter, one piece at a time. Turn out the dough onto a lightly floured work surface and knead until smooth and shiny.)

10. Place the dough in a lightly oiled large bowl, turning the dough to coat it evenly with oil. Cover the bowl with a damp towel, or loosely with plastic wrap. Let stand in a warm place until the dough has doubled in size, about 1 hour.

11. Meanwhile, drain the fruit mixture, reserving the fruit and rum mixture separately. Whisk the melted butter into the rum mixture until well combined. Set aside.

12. Line a large baking sheet with parchment paper. Set aside.

13. On a lightly floured work surface, punch down the dough to remove the air. Pat the dough out into a 12-inch disc. Scatter the drained fruit mixture evenly over the dough. Roll up the dough like a jelly roll, pinching the ends to prevent the fruit from escaping.

14. Fold the rolled-up dough into thirds, then transfer it to the prepared baking sheet. Pat or roll it out to an 11- x 9-inch oval.

15. Make an indentation with a rolling pin or a dowel, slightly off-centre along the length of the oval. Fold the dough along the indent, folding the narrower side over the wider side. Gently press down to seal the edges.

16. Cover the baking sheet loosely with plastic wrap. Let stand in a warm place until almost doubled in size, about 1 hour.

17. When ready to bake, preheat the oven to 375°F.

18. Bake the stollen until it's a deep, golden brown and an instnt-read thermometer inserted in the centre registers 190°F, 35 to 40 minutes.

19. Remove the stollen to a wire rack and let cool for about 5 minutes. If the butter in the reserved rum mixture has solidified, microwave the mixture on high power for 10-second intervals until the butter melts. Brush the stollen with the rum-butter mixture.

20. Sift half of the icing sugar over the stollen to coat it generously. Let the stollen cool completely, then sift the remaining icing sugar over it. Use a sharp serrated knife to slice the stollen.

BAKING DAY SECRETS

If you prefer, the shaped stollen can be left overnight to rise in the fridge in Step 16. Cover the stollen and baking sheet completely with plastic wrap to ensure the stollen doesn't dry out. The next day, let the stollen come to room temperature for 45 to 60 minutes before baking as described in the recipe.

Chocolate-Orange Babka

This sweet loaf, with its rich chocolate filling, is a traditional Jewish recipe and is popular at Hanukkah. Try it with a cup of strong coffee: bliss!

Makes one 8-inch loaf
Prep time: 1 hour
Rising time: 26 hours
Chilling time: about 10 minutes
Cooking time: about 30 minutes

Dough

⅓ cup warm whole milk (about 110°F)

⅓ cup lightly packed golden yellow sugar

2 tsp active dry yeast

2 ⅓ cups all-purpose flour

⅓ cup unsalted butter, softened

2 Tbsp vegetable oil

1 large egg

2 large egg yolks

2 Tbsp finely grated orange zest

1 Tbsp vanilla extract

½ tsp fine sea salt

Chocolate-Orange Filling (recipe follows)

½ cup finely chopped dark chocolate or mini chocolate chips

Orange Syrup

1 large orange

⅓ cup granulated sugar

1 Tbsp maple syrup or liquid honey

1. For the dough, pour the warm milk into a medium bowl. Sprinkle 1 teaspoonful of the sugar and the yeast over the milk. Let stand until puffy, about 5 minutes.

2. Stir in ½ cup of the flour. Cover tightly with plastic wrap and set aside in a warm place until doubled in size, about 20 minutes.

3. In the bowl of a stand mixer fitted with the paddle attachment (or in a large bowl and using a hand-held electric mixer), beat together the butter, oil and remaining sugar until fluffy, about 2 minutes.

4. With the mixer running on medium speed, beat in the egg and egg yolks until well combined. Beat in the orange zest and vanilla extract.

5. Fit the stand mixer (if using) with the dough hook and turn the speed to low. Beat in the remaining flour in two additions, beating to incorporate after each addition. Beat for 1 minute.

6. Beat in the yeast mixture. Beat just until the dough starts to come together, about 2 minutes.

7. Sprinkle the salt over the dough. Increase the speed to medium-low. Beat until the dough is smooth and soft and pulls away from the sides of the bowl, leaving it clean.

8. Turn out the dough onto a lightly floured work surface and knead it a few times to bring it together into a ball. (If not using a stand mixer, mix in the flour, yeast mixture and salt until combined, then turn out the dough onto a lightly floured work surface and knead until a smooth, soft dough forms.)

9. Place the dough in a lightly oiled large bowl, turning the dough to coat it evenly with oil. Cover the bowl with a damp towel, or loosely with plastic wrap. Refrigerate until the dough has doubled in size, 24 hours.

10. On a lightly floured work surface, punch down the dough to remove the air. Grease a deep 8-inch round baking pan, then line the bottom and sides with parchment paper. Set aside.

11. Roll out the dough to an 18- x 14-inch rectangle, arranging the dough so that one long end is parallel to the edge of your work surface. (The dough will be quite thin.)

12. Using a rubber spatula, carefully spread the cooled chocolate-orange filling over the dough, leaving a ½-inch border along each long edge. Sprinkle the chocolate evenly over the filling.

13. Lightly brush water along the border of the long side furthest from you. Starting with the long side nearest you, roll up the dough to form a rope, pressing down gently to seal the dampened edge to the dough.

14. Using your palms, gently roll the rope of dough back and forth on the work surface until it has an even thickness of 2 to 2 ½ inches. Carefully place the rope of dough on a large baking sheet,

continued . . .

coiling it loosely to fit. Cover with plastic wrap and refrigerate for about 10 minutes. (This will make it easier to slice.)

15. Return the rope to the work surface with the seam side underneath. Using a sharp, serrated knife, carefully slice the rope in half lengthwise.

16. With the cut sides facing up, join the ends of the two pieces together to form an inverted V. Take the left arm of the V and lift it over the right. Repeat the process until the end is reached, twisting the two pieces into a braid. Gently press the ends together to seal.

17. Coil the braided dough into the prepared pan, making sure the cut sides are facing up. It should look almost like a knot. Cover the pan loosely with plastic wrap. Let stand in a warm place until doubled in size, 1 ½ to 2 hours.

18. When ready to bake, preheat the oven 375°F.

19. Bake until the babka is golden brown and an instant-read thermometer inserted in the centre registers 190°F, 25 to 30 minutes.

20. While the babka is baking, make the orange syrup. Using a vegetable peeler, pare three strips of rind from the orange, avoiding the white pith. Cut the orange in half and squeeze out ⅓ cup of the juice.

21. In a small saucepan, combine the orange rind and juice, sugar and maple syrup. Bring to a simmer over medium heat, stirring to dissolve the sugar. Remove from the heat and discard the orange rind. Set aside until the babka is ready.

22. Remove the babka from the oven. Immediately brush all of the orange syrup over the top of the loaf. Let the babka cool completely in the pan on a wire rack before unmoulding. (The babka can be stored, well wrapped in plastic wrap, at room temperature for up to 4 days, or wrapped in foil and frozen for up to 2 months. Thaw it at room temperature before serving.)

BAKING DAY SECRETS

Make sure the babka has cooled completely before removing it from the pan. If it's still even slightly warm, it may fall apart.

Makes enough filling for one babka
Prep time: 5 minutes
Cooking time: about 1 minute

Chocolate-Orange Filling for Babka

½ cup finely chopped dark chocolate or mini dark chocolate chips

½ cup firmly packed dark brown sugar

2 Tbsp unsweetened cocoa powder

1 tsp ground cinnamon

¼ tsp fine sea salt

⅓ cup unsalted butter, softened

2 Tbsp freshly squeezed orange juice

2 Tbsp finely grated orange zest

2 tsp vanilla extract

1. In a medium bowl, whisk together the chocolate, sugar, cocoa powder, cinnamon and salt. Set aside.

2. In a small saucepan over medium heat, melt the butter with the orange juice just until it begins to simmer, 30 to 60 seconds.

3. Remove from the heat and stir in the orange zest and vanilla extract.

4. Pour the butter mixture over the chocolate mixture and stir to combine. Some of the chocolate will melt but the filling won't be completely smooth. Let cool slightly before using.

Homemade Mincemeat Pie

Sure, you can pick up mincemeat at your local grocery store for this delectable holiday pie, but once you've enjoyed the rich flavours of homemade mincemeat, you may never buy another jar again.

Makes one 9-inch double-crust pie; 10 servings
Prep time: 30 minutes
Chilling time: 30 minutes
Cooking time: 55 to 60 minutes

2 large Golden Delicious apples, peeled, cored and cut into ½-inch pieces

1 ½ cups fresh or frozen cranberries

½ cup firmly packed dark brown sugar

½ cup golden raisins

½ cup sultana raisins

½ cup currants

½ cup dried cranberries

¼ cup unsalted butter, softened

¼ cup apple juice

¼ cup brandy or dark rum

1 Tbsp finely grated lemon zest (1 to 2 lemons)

2 Tbsp freshly squeezed lemon juice

2 Tbsp cornstarch

1 tsp ground cinnamon

½ tsp freshly grated nutmeg

½ tsp ground allspice

¼ tsp ground cloves

1 batch of Perfect Pastry (page 174)

Egg Wash

1 large egg whisked with 1 Tbsp water

1. In a large, heavy-bottomed saucepan, mix together the apples, fresh or frozen cranberries, sugar, golden and sultana raisins, currants, dried cranberries, butter, apple juice, brandy, lemon zest and juice, cornstarch and spices.

2. Bring to a simmer over medium-low heat. Cook, uncovered and stirring often, until the apples are soft, the fresh or frozen cranberries have popped and the mixture thickens, about 20 minutes. Remove from the heat and let cool completely.

3. Divide the pastry in half and shape each piece into a disc. On a lightly floured work surface, roll out one piece of pastry to a 13-inch disc about ¼ inch thick.

4. Roll the pastry around the rolling pin, then place it in a deep 9-inch pie dish.

5. Roll out the second piece of pastry to the same dimensions. Cut out and reserve a ¾-inch circle from the centre.

6. Fill the pie shell with the cooled mincemeat. Brush the edge of the crust with the egg wash. Cover the pie with the second piece of pastry. Trim the edges, leaving a ½-inch overhang. Fold the extra pastry under and crimp the edges to seal it (see page 175).

7. On a lightly floured work surface, reroll the small, reserved piece of pastry. Cut out leaf shapes to decorate the pie. Stick the leaves to the pie with egg wash, then brush egg wash all over the top of the pie. Refrigerate for 30 minutes.

8. When ready to bake, preheat the oven to 375°F.

9. Bake the pie until the pastry is golden brown and the filling is hot and bubbling, 35 to 40 minutes. Let the pie cool slightly on a wire rack. Serve warm or at room temperature.

Stunning Chocolate Croquembouche

Traditional croquembouche is a spectacular French dessert—the name comes from the French for "crunches in the mouth"—that piles choux pastry puffs in a tower anchored by strands of caramelized sugar. Our version is a little simpler but just as impressive: we dip the choux puffs in a dark chocolate topping then garnish them with a little spun sugar.

Makes 12 to 15 servings
Prep time: 30 minutes
Cooking time: about 40 minutes

Choux Puffs

1 ½ cups water

¾ cup unsalted butter, cut into small pieces and softened

¼ tsp fine sea salt

2 cups all-purpose flour

5 large eggs

Filling & Topping

4 cups whipping cream (35%)

½ cup icing sugar, sifted

1 tsp vanilla extract

8 oz dark or semi-sweet chocolate, chopped

Spun Sugar (optional; recipe follows)

---

1. Preheat the oven to 450°F. Line two large baking sheets with parchment paper, then set aside.

2. For the choux puffs, combine the water, butter and salt in a medium saucepan. Bring to a boil, without stirring, over high heat.

3. Immediately remove from the heat and add the flour all at once. Using a wooden spoon, stir the mixture vigorously until it forms a thick, smooth dough and pulls away from the side of the saucepan, about 2 minutes.

4. Return the saucepan to medium heat. Cook, stirring constantly, until the dough looks drier, about 2 minutes.

5. Scrape the dough into a medium bowl. Using an electric mixer, beat the dough until it has cooled to room temperature.

6. Beat in the eggs one at a time, beating well after each addition. Beat the dough vigorously until it's thick, shiny and smooth. (This strengthens the gluten in the flour and helps the puffs rise during baking.)

7. Dip two tablespoons in water, then shake off the excess water. Scoop up a walnut-size piece of dough with one damp spoon. With the other, scrape the dough onto the prepared baking sheets, arranging the pieces about 1 inch apart.

8. Bake for 10 minutes, then turn down the oven temperature to 350°F. Bake until the choux puffs have risen and are a deep golden brown, 10 to 15 minutes. Carefully remove the choux puffs from the baking sheets and let cool completely on a wire rack. (The choux puffs can be stored in an airtight container at room temperature for up to 24 hours, or frozen for up to 1 month. Thaw at room temperature before proceeding with the recipe.)

9. For the filling and topping, combine the cream, icing sugar and vanilla extract in a large bowl. Using an electric mixer on high speed, beat the cream mixture until stiff peaks form. Cover and refrigerate until needed.

10. In a microwave-safe bowl, microwave the chocolate on high power for 30-second intervals, stirring after each, until the chocolate is melted and smooth.

11. Using a small knife, cut a small opening in each of the choux puffs. Fit a piping bag with a wide circular or star tip, then twist the bag just above the piping tip to temporarily close off the bag from the tip.

12. Set the bag in an empty yogurt container, glass tumbler or plastic cup. Fold the top third of the piping bag over the edge of the container.

13. Spoon the whipped cream into the bottom of the piping bag, filling the bag about half full. Twist the bag tightly to close it.

14. Gently insert the piping tip into the opening in one of the puffs, then squeeze the piping bag gently to fill the puff with whipped cream, being careful not to overfill it. Repeat with the remaining choux puffs.

15. Dip each filled choux puff into the melted chocolate, then arrange them carefully on a plate or cake stand. Start by placing them in a circle, then stack the remaining choux puffs on top. Once the choux puffs are stacked, set aside at room temperature until the chocolate has set, 15 to 20 minutes. Decorate with spun sugar (if using) and serve within 2 hours.

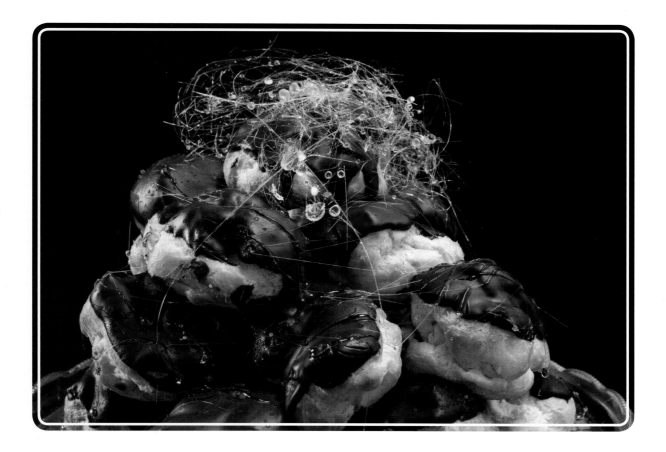

Spun Sugar

Makes enough to top one dessert
Prep time: 20 minutes
Cooking time: 10 to 12 minutes

2 cups granulated sugar

½ cup water

½ tsp freshly squeezed lemon juice

1. Have ready a large bowl of ice water. Combine the sugar, water and lemon juice in a medium saucepan, swirling gently to combine.

2. Hook a candy thermometer over the side of the saucepan. Bring to a boil over medium heat, then cook the sugar mixture, without stirring but occasionally washing down the sides of the saucepan with a damp, clean pastry brush, until the caramel is light amber and the candy thermometer registers 300°F, 10 to 12 minutes. (If you don't have a candy thermometer, drop a little of the mixture into a bowl of cold water. If it forms hard, brittle threads, it's ready.)

3. Immediately remove from the heat and place the saucepan in the bowl of ice water. This will prevent the caramel from overcooking.

4. Grease the handle of a wooden spoon, then place it on the edge of a counter or table, allowing the handle to stick out over the edge. Place newspaper or a large piece of parchment paper on the floor below it to catch any drips.

5. Dip a fork into the caramel, then, working quickly, drizzle the caramel over the spoon handle, flicking the fork back and forth like a pendulum. Light, web-like strands of sugar will form over the spoon handle, hanging down from it like threads.

6. Once you've covered the spoon handle with a few layers of spun sugar, detach it gently from the handle and wind it into a circle to form a nest. Place the spun sugar on top of the croquembouche. Continue to create more spun sugar, if liked. Any leftover caramel can be drizzled over the croquembouche.

Strawberry-Rose Profiteroles

Profiteroles—aka cream puffs—make a head-turning summer dessert. Our version features a rich pastry cream flavoured with exotic rose water and juicy strawberries.

Makes about 30 profiteroles
Prep time: 1 hour
Cooking time: about 45 minutes
Chilling time: 1 hour
Setting time: about 15 minutes

Profiteroles

1 cup water

½ cup whole milk

¾ cup unsalted butter, cut into small pieces and softened

¼ tsp fine sea salt

1 cup all-purpose flour

1 cup bread flour

5 large eggs

Strawberry-Rose Pastry Cream

½ cup whole hulled strawberries

1 tsp freshly squeezed lemon juice

½ vanilla bean

2 cups whole milk

½ cup granulated sugar

5 large egg yolks

5 Tbsp cornstarch

1 Tbsp unsalted butter, cut into small pieces and softened

⅓ cup whipping cream (35%)

¼ cup hulled and finely chopped strawberries

1 to 3 Tbsp rose water (see page 10)

Red gel food colouring (optional)

White Chocolate Glaze

½ cup finely chopped white chocolate

1 tsp white corn syrup

2 Tbsp whipping cream (35%)

½ cup shelled pistachios, finely chopped

1. For the profiteroles, follow Steps 1 through 7 of the Stunning Chocolate Croquembouche recipe (page 236), heating the milk with the water, butter and salt and adding the bread flour along with the all-purpose flour.

2. Bake for 10 minutes, then turn down the oven temperature to 350°F. Bake until the profiteroles have risen and are a deep golden brown, 10 to 15 minutes.

3. Remove the profiteroles from the oven. Using a wooden skewer, poke a hole in the bottom or side of each one to release the steam. Return the profiteroles to the oven to dry, with the oven door ajar, for 5 minutes.

4. Carefully remove the profiteroles from the baking sheets and let cool completely on a wire rack. (The profiteroles can be stored in an airtight container at room temperature for up to 24 hours, or frozen for up to 1 month. Crisp up the frozen profiteroles in a 375°F oven for 8 to 10 minutes, then let cool completely before proceeding with the recipe.)

5. For the strawberry-rose pastry cream, combine the whole strawberries and lemon juice in a food processor fitted with the steel blade. Pulse until smooth. (If you prefer a super-smooth purée, strain the strawberry mixture through a fine-mesh sieve.) Set aside.

6. Using a sharp knife, split the vanilla bean in half lengthwise. Scrape the seeds out into a medium saucepan, then drop the pod into the saucepan.

7. Add the milk and ⅓ cup of the sugar to the saucepan. Bring to a simmer over medium heat, stirring until the sugar has dissolved, about 3 minutes. Remove from the heat, cover and let stand for about 5 minutes.

8. In a medium bowl, whisk together the remaining sugar, the egg yolks and cornstarch until well combined.

9. Whisk the hot milk into the egg-yolk mixture, a little at time.

10. Strain the egg yolk mixture through a fine-mesh sieve back into the saucepan. Cook over medium heat, stirring constantly with a rubber spatula, until the mixture starts to thicken, about 7 minutes.

11. Turn down the heat to medium-low and switch the spatula for a whisk. Cook, whisking constantly, until the mixture starts to bubble, about 1 ½ minutes.

12. Remove from the heat and whisk until smooth. Whisk in the butter, one piece at a time, until it melts. Fold in the strawberry purée.

13. Scrape the pastry cream into a medium bowl. Place a piece of plastic wrap directly on the surface of the pastry cream. Refrigerate until chilled, at least 1 hour.

14. In a separate medium bowl, whip the cream until stiff peaks form.

15. Gently stir the cold pastry cream until slightly softened. Fold in the chopped strawberries, then fold in one-third of the whipped cream to lighten the pastry cream. Fold in the remaining whipped cream. Fold in the rose water, 1 tablespoonful at a time, until flavoured to your taste. Add enough food colouring (if using) to tint the pastry cream pale pink.

16. Spoon the pastry cream into a large piping bag fitted with a plain or star tip. Chill until ready to serve the profiteroles.

17. For the white chocolate glaze, melt the white chocolate with the corn syrup in a medium heatproof bowl set over a saucepan of hot, not boiling, water. Remove from the heat and stir until the mixture is smooth.

18. Stir in the cream. Set aside until cooled and thickened slightly, about 10 minutes.

19. Just before serving, using a sharp serrated knife, cut the tops off the profiteroles. Pipe a rosette of pastry cream in the bottom half of each profiterole.

20. Dip the tops of the profiteroles in the white chocolate glaze. Replace the tops of the profiteroles. Sprinkle each profiterole with pistachios. Set aside until the glaze has hardened, about 15 minutes. Serve immediately.

BAKING DAY SECRETS

If you prefer, substitute ¼ cup of strawberry jam for the fresh strawberry purée in the pastry cream.

Peppermint Pinwheels

These festive cookies are sure to brighten up any holiday table. Even better at such a busy time of year, the dough can be made up to a month before baking day.

Makes 48 cookies

Prep time: 30 minutes

Freezing time: at least 2 hours

Cooking time: about 7 minutes

1 ¾ cups all-purpose flour

½ tsp baking soda

¼ tsp fine sea salt

½ cup unsalted butter, softened

1 cup granulated sugar

1 large egg

½ tsp vanilla extract

½ tsp peppermint extract

Green gel food colouring

1. Line a large baking sheet with parchment paper. Set aside.

2. In a medium bowl, whisk together the flour, baking soda and salt. Set aside.

3. In a large bowl and using an electric mixer, beat the butter with the sugar until pale and fluffy. Beat in the egg and vanilla extract.

4. Gradually add the flour mixture to the sugar mixture, stirring until well combined.

5. Divide the dough in half. Place one half on a large piece of plastic wrap. Sprinkle this piece of dough with the peppermint extract and enough green food colouring to tint it to your liking. Gently knead the extract and colouring into the dough until it's evenly coloured. Set aside.

6. On a lightly floured work surface, roll out the white cookie dough to a 12- x 8-inch rectangle. Carefully transfer it to the prepared baking sheet.

7. On a lightly floured work surface, roll out the green dough to a 12- x 8-inch rectangle. Carefully place it on top of the white dough.

8. Starting from one long edge, roll up the two layers of dough as tightly as possible. Don't worry if the dough rips a little.

9. Cut the log in half crosswise. Wrap each piece in parchment paper or plastic wrap and freeze

for at least 2 hours, or overnight. (The dough can be frozen for up to 1 month. Let stand at room temperature for 30 minutes before proceeding with the recipe.)

10. When ready to bake, preheat the oven to 350°F. Line two large baking sheets with parchment paper. Set aside.

11. Cut the logs of cookie dough into ¼-inch slices and place, about 1 inch apart, on the prepared baking sheets. Bake on two separate racks of the oven, rotating positions halfway through cooking time, until the centre of each cookie is set, about 7 minutes. Remove the cookies to wire racks and let cool completely. (The cookies can be stored in an airtight container at room temperature for up to 4 days, or frozen for up to 2 months.)

Maple-Cream Cookie Sandwiches

These cookies are great for any celebration, but with their rich maple filling, they're the perfect finale for a Canada Day barbecue.

Makes 16 sandwich cookies
Prep time: 30 minutes
Chilling time: about 1 hour
Cooking time: 8 to 10 minutes

Cookies

3 ¼ cups all-purpose flour

½ tsp fine sea salt

1 cup unsalted butter, softened

½ cup granulated sugar

½ cup firmly packed dark brown sugar

¼ cup maple syrup

1 large egg

Maple Cream Filling

2 cups icing sugar, sifted

¼ tsp fine sea salt

¼ cup unsalted butter, softened

5 Tbsp maple syrup (approx.)

1. For the cookies, whisk together the flour and salt in a medium bowl. Set aside.

2. In a large bowl and using an electric mixer, beat together the butter and both sugars until fluffy. Beat in the maple syrup and egg until well combined.

3. Beat the flour mixture into the butter mixture, a little at a time, until a smooth dough forms. If the dough is crumbly, turn it out onto a lightly floured work surface and knead gently until it comes together.

4. Divide the dough in half. Pat out each piece into a disc about ½ inch thick. Wrap each piece of dough tightly in the plastic wrap, then refrigerate until firm, about 1 hour. (The dough can be refrigerated for up to 3 days. Remove it from the fridge about 1 hour before rolling it out.)

5. When ready to bake, preheat the oven to 350°F. Line a large baking sheet with parchment paper, then set aside.

6. On a lightly floured work surface, roll out the dough to ⅛ inch thickness. Using a 2 ½-inch maple leaf cookie cutter (or a shape of your choice), cut out cookies, rerolling the dough scraps once. (Rerolling the scraps more than once makes the cookies tough.)

7. Place the cookies, 1 inch apart, on the prepared baking sheet. Bake until golden brown, 8 to 10 minutes. Remove the cookies to wire racks and let cool completely.

8. For the maple cream filling, whisk together the icing sugar and salt in a medium bowl.

9. In a separate medium bowl, beat the butter until pale and fluffy. Beat in the icing sugar mixture, ½ cup at a time, adding 1 tablespoonful of maple syrup after each addition, until the consistency of the filling is to your liking (you may not need all of the maple syrup).

10. Spread half of the cookies with the maple cream filling, using about 2 teaspoonfuls per cookie. Top with the remaining cookies, squeezing them together gently. (The cookies can be stored in an airtight container at room temperature for up to 4 days.)

Easter Paska

Paska is a yeast-raised bread enjoyed at Eastertime in some countries of Eastern Europe. It's richly decorated, then topped with a shiny glaze.

Makes one 9-inch loaf
Prep time: 1 ½ hours
Rising time: about 2 hours, 45 minutes
Cooking time: about 1 hour

Dough

1 ¼ cups warm whole milk (about 110°F)

²/₃ cup granulated sugar

1 Tbsp instant dry yeast

7 cups all-purpose flour

1 ¼ cups unsalted butter, softened

2 large eggs

4 large egg yolks

1 Tbsp finely grated lemon zest (1 to 2 lemons)

1 Tbsp finely grated orange zest

1 Tbsp dark rum

2 tsp fine sea salt

1 tsp vanilla extract

Egg Wash

1 large egg whisked with 1 Tbsp water

1. Pour the warm milk into a medium bowl. Sprinkle 1 tablespoonful of the sugar and the yeast over the milk. Let stand until puffy, about 5 minutes.

2. Stir in 1 ½ cups of the flour. Cover tightly with plastic wrap and set aside in a warm place until doubled in size, about 45 minutes to 1 hour.

3. In the bowl of a stand mixer fitted with the paddle attachment (or in a large bowl and using a hand-held electric mixer), beat together the butter and the remaining sugar on medium-low speed until smooth.

4. Beat in the eggs and egg yolks one at a time, beating until well combined. Beat in the yeast mixture, lemon and orange zests, rum, salt and vanilla extract.

5. Turn down the speed to low and start beating in the remaining flour, 1 cup at a time. Once a loose dough begins to form (after about 3 cups of flour have been added), fit the stand mixer (if using) with the dough hook and continue adding the remaining flour.

6. Increase the speed to medium-high and mix until an elastic, slightly sticky dough forms, about 8 minutes.

7. Turn out the dough onto a lightly floured work surface and knead it a few times to bring it together into a ball. (If not using a stand mixer, mix in the flour until combined, then turn out the dough onto a lightly floured work surface and knead until an elastic, slightly sticky dough forms.)

8. Place the dough in a lightly oiled large bowl, turning the dough to coat it evenly with oil. Cover the bowl with a damp towel, or loosely with plastic wrap. Let stand in a warm place until the dough has doubled in size, about 1 hour.

9. Grease a 9-inch springform pan. Line the bottom of the pan with a circle of parchment paper, then line the sides with a strip of parchment paper that extends 2 inches above the edge of the pan. Set aside.

10. On a lightly floured work surface, punch down the dough to remove the air. Cut off one-third of the dough, wrap in plastic wrap and set aside for the decorations.

11. Pat the remaining dough into an 8-inch disc, then gently press it evenly into the prepared pan. Brush the dough with egg wash, cover the pan with plastic wrap and set aside.

12. From the piece of dough saved for the decorations, cut off one-third and rewrap this smaller piece in plastic wrap. From the larger piece, pinch off 1 tablespoonful of dough and roll it into a small rope about ¼ inch in diameter. Coil the rope into a spiral and set aside.

13. Cut the rest of the larger piece of dough in half. Roll each half into a rope about 22 inches long. Twist the two ropes together to form a long, twisted rope.

14. Place this rope of dough on top of the dough in the pan in a wreath shape, gently stretching the rope to press the ends together.

15. Cut the reserved piece of dough (the one you wrapped in plastic wrap earlier) in half. Roll each half into a rope about 12 inches long. Twist the two ropes together to form a long, twisted rope as before. Place this 12-inch rope of dough inside the wreath-shape on top of the dough in the pan, stretching the ends to meet the ends of the outside rope.

16. Brush the spot where the ropes meet with the egg wash and place the reserved spiral of dough on top.

17. Brush the entire loaf with egg wash. Cover the pan loosely with plastic wrap. Let stand in a warm place until doubled in size, about 30 to 45 minutes.

18. When ready to bake, preheat the oven to 400°F.

19. Place the paska in the oven, then turn down the temperature to 350°F. Bake until the paska is a deep golden brown and an instant-read thermometer inserted in the centre registers 200°F, about 1 hour, rotating the pan 180 degrees after 30 minutes. If the top begins to brown too much, lightly tent the paska with foil.

20. Let the paska cool in the pan on a wire rack for 10 minutes. Remove from the pan and and let cool completely on the wire rack.

Spooky Ghost Meringues

These ghost meringues are so cute they're far from scary. Perfect for a Halloween party, they're also great to crunch on while you watch a spooky movie from behind the couch.

Makes 15 to 20 meringues
Prep time: 25 minutes
Cooking time: 1 ½ hours
Drying time: at least 6 hours

3 large egg whites

Pinch of cream of tartar

Pinch of fine sea salt

½ cup granulated sugar

30 to 40 white sugar pearl candies

Edible colour marker (optional)

1. Place the oven racks on the bottom and top third positions. Preheat the oven to 200°F. Line two large baking sheets with parchment paper, then set aside.

2. In a large bowl and using an electric mixer, beat the egg whites on medium-high speed until foamy.

3. Beat in the cream of tartar and salt. Continue beating until soft peaks form, about 2 minutes.

4. Increase the speed to high and beat in the sugar, a few spoonfuls at a time until everything is incorporated.

5. Continue beating until the meringue is thick and holds stiff peaks.

6. Fit a large piping bag with a large circular tip, then twist the bag just above the piping tip to temporarily close off the bag from the tip. Set the bag in an empty yogurt container, glass tumbler or plastic cup. Fold the top third of the piping bag over the edge of the container. Spoon the meringue into the piping bag. Twist the bag to close it.

7. Using about 2 tablespoonfuls of meringue for each ghost, pipe swirls of meringue, 2 inches apart, on the prepared baking sheets, squeezing the piping bag firmly at the base with one hand and using the other to guide the tip. Place two white sugar pearl candies on each meringue for eyes.

8. Bake the meringues for 1 hour. Leaving the oven switched on, open the oven door. Bake for 30 minutes.

9. Switch the oven off but leave the meringues in the oven to dry, with the door open, for at least 6 hours, or overnight. When dried, they will sound hollow when you tap on the bottoms.

10. Remove the meringues from the oven. If you wish, use an edible colour marker to add detail to the eyes. (The meringues can be stored in an airtight container at room temperature, with wax paper between the layers, for up to 1 week.)

Tarantula Cupcakes

Spook your Halloween guests with these fun spider-topped cupcakes. They're sca-a-a-rily good.

Makes 24 cupcakes

Prep time: 40 minutes

Cooking time: about 20 minutes

Chocolate Cupcakes

2 ¼ cups all-purpose flour

2 cups granulated sugar

1 cup unsweetened cocoa powder

2 tsp baking soda

½ tsp fine sea salt

2 cups cold brewed black coffee or water

²/₃ cup vegetable oil

1 Tbsp vanilla extract

2 tsp white vinegar

Chocolate Frosting

½ cup unsalted butter, softened

2 cups icing sugar, sifted

¼ cup unsweetened cocoa powder

1 tsp vanilla extract

2 Tbsp whole milk (optional)

Decorations

Black, brown or orange and yellow sprinkles

Black gum balls

Black jelly beans

Black licorice laces

Round licorice allsorts

1. Preheat the oven to 350°F. Line two muffin pans with 24 large paper liners, then set aside.

2. For the chocolate cupcakes, whisk together the flour, sugar, cocoa powder, baking soda and salt in a large bowl. Set aside.

3. In a medium bowl, whisk together the coffee, oil, vanilla extract and vinegar.

4. Slowly whisk the coffee mixture into the flour mixture until well combined.

5. Fill the paper liners about two-thirds full with batter. Bake until the cupcakes spring back when lightly touched and a wooden skewer inserted in the centre of a cupcake comes out clean, about 20 minutes.

6. Let the cupcakes cool in the pans for 10 minutes, then remove to a wire rack and let cool completely. (The undecorated cupcakes can be refrigerated in an airtight container for up to 4 days.)

7. For the chocolate frosting, in a large bowl and using an electric mixer, beat the butter until pale and fluffy.

8. Beat in the icing sugar, 1 cup at a time, until the frosting is thick and creamy.

9. Beat in the cocoa powder and vanilla extract until well combined. If the frosting is too thick, stir in the milk, 1 tablespoonful at a time, until the frosting is a spreadable consistency.

10. Using an offset spatula or a piping bag, swirl the frosting on top of the cupcakes.

11. Put the sprinkles in individual bowls. If you're using orange and yellow sprinkles, mix these together in one bowl. Dip the cupcakes in the sprinkles.

12. For scary spiders, decorate the cupcakes with a gum ball for the body, a black jelly bean for the head and licorice laces for the legs. For cute spiders, decorate with licorice allsorts for the eyeballs and licorice laces for the legs. (The decorated cupcakes can be refrigerated in an airtight container for up to 3 days. Bring them to room temperature before serving.)

Show-Stopping Vanilla-Apricot Wedding Cake

A very special day calls for an extraordinary cake. This is it. A light-as-air tiered sponge is layered with rich apricot buttercream and decorated with real flowers for a head-turning centrepiece.

Makes one 3-tiered cake; 50 to 60 servings

Prep time: 3 days

Cooking time: 40 to 75 minutes

Chilling time: about 8 hours

Cake

6 ¾ cups cake-and-pastry flour

3 Tbsp plus 2 tsp baking powder

1 ½ tsp fine sea salt

2 ⅔ cups whole milk

7 large eggs

2 Tbsp vanilla extract

2 Tbsp almond extract

1 ¾ cups plus 2 Tbsp unsalted butter, softened

3 ¾ cups granulated sugar

3 cardboard cake circles (10 inches, 8 inches and 6 inches)

1 batch of Apricot-Almond Simple Syrup (page 251)

1 batch of Vanilla Buttercream (page 251)

1 batch of Apricot Buttercream (page 251)

1 jar (8 oz/250 mL) 100% apricot spread

Decoration

Edible flowers (see sidebar on page 48; optional)

Crystallized flowers (page 252)

Marzipan flowers (page 164; optional)

1. Preheat the oven to 350°F. Grease a 6-, an 8-, and a 10-inch round baking pan (all 3 inches deep), then line the bottom of each with parchment paper. Dust the pans with flour, then shake out the excess. Set aside.

2. In a large bowl, whisk together the flour, baking powder and salt. Set aside.

3. In a large measuring cup or medium bowl, whisk together 1 cup of the milk with the eggs and vanilla and almond extracts. Set aside.

4. In a second large bowl and using an electric mixer, beat the butter until creamy. Add the sugar and beat until pale and fluffy, about 3 minutes.

5. Add half of the flour mixture to the butter mixture. Beat on low speed just until combined.

6. Add the remaining flour mixture and half of the remaining 1 ⅔ cups of the milk. Beat on low speed until the dry ingredients are moistened. Increase the speed to medium and beat mixture until the ingredients are well combined, about 30 seconds.

7. Scrape down the sides of the bowl, then add the remaining milk. Starting on low speed, then increasing the speed to medium, beat for 1 minute.

8. Turn down the mixer speed to low, then gradually beat in half of the egg mixture. Increase the speed to medium and beat until the ingredients are well combined. Repeat with the remaining egg mixture.

9. Divide the batter evenly among the prepared pans. Bake the cakes until the tops are golden brown and a wooden skewer inserted in the centre of each cake comes out clean: 35 to 40 minutes for the 10-inch cake, 30 to 35 minutes for the 8-inch cake and 25 to 30 minutes for the 6-inch cake. (If your oven won't accommodate all three pans at once, bake the 10-inch cake first, covering the other pans with plastic wrap and letting them stand at room temperature until the 10-inch cake is baked.)

10. Let the cakes cool in their pans on wire racks: the 10-inch cake for 10 to 15 minutes, the 8- and 6-inch cakes for 5 minutes. Lay the 10-inch cardboard cake circle on top of the 10-inch cake. Holding the circle gently against the cake, invert the pan to unmould the cake. Invert the cake again onto a wire rack, remove the circle and let cool completely. Repeat with the other cakes. Reserve the cake circle. (The cakes can be frozen, double-wrapped in plastic wrap and foil, for up to 2 weeks. Thaw them in the fridge overnight before decorating.)

11. While the cakes are cooling, prepare the apricot-almond simple syrup, vanilla and apricot buttercreams and decorations.

12. To assemble the wedding cake, use a long serrated knife to slice the tops of the three cakes and make them level.

13. To make stacking the cakes easier, make a shallow vertical cut in the side of each cake (this will act as a marker). Place one cake on a cake turntable. Using a ruler and a long serrated knife, cut through the cake horizontally to make three even layers. Set aside. Repeat with the remaining cakes.

14. Put the reserved 10-inch cake circle on the turntable. Spoon a small amount of the vanilla buttercream onto the circle. Centre the levelled top of the 10-inch cake upside-down on the circle.

15. Using a pastry brush, coat the cake layer with the apricot-almond simple syrup, covering the surface completely. Fill a piping bag fitted with a plain, round tip with vanilla buttercream and pipe a ring around the edge of the cake layer. (This will prevent any apricot spread from seeping out.)

16. Using a small offset spatula, spread an 1/8-inch layer of apricot spread within the circle of buttercream.

17. Pipe concentric circles of the apricot buttercream over the spread until the centre of the cake layer is filled. Smooth the apricot buttercream with an offset spatula.

18. Gently place the second 10-inch cake layer on top, using the vertical cut in the cake to line up the layers. Repeat Steps 14 to 17.

Top with the third 10-inch cake layer. Remove the 10-inch cake on its cardboard circle from the turntable and set aside.

19. Repeat the stacking and filling process with the remaining cakes and cardboard circles.

20. Next, apply a crumb coat to each cake. (This will seal in any stray crumbs that may mar the final layer of buttercream.) Place the 10-inch cake on the turntable. Using an offset spatula, spread a very thin layer of vanilla buttercream over the top and sides of each cake. Rotate the turntable to check that the 10-inch cake tier is level. If one side looks higher, gently pressing down may fix the problem, or add more buttercream to a lower area to even out the tier. Remove the 10-inch cake tier from the turntable and refrigerate it to set the crumb coat, at least 1 1/2 hours. Repeat with the remaining cake tiers.

21. When the crumb coat is set, place the 10-inch cake tier on the turntable. Spoon about 1 1/2 cups of vanilla buttercream on the top of the cake. Using a straight or offset spatula, spread the buttercream over the top of the cake, being careful not to scrape off the crumb coat.

22. Without pressing down too hard, draw a straight spatula across the surface of the cake to produce a smooth top.

23. To frost the side of the cake, use a straight or offset spatula to spread 3 1/2 cups of vanilla buttercream onto the side of the cake tier then, rotating the turntable and using the cardboard cake circle to guide the spatula, smooth the buttercream as evenly

as possible. Return the 10-inch cake tier to the fridge to set, about 2 hours.

24. Repeat with the remaining cake tiers, using about 4 cups of vanilla buttercream for the 8-inch cake and 2 cups for the 6-inch cake.

25. Spread a little vanilla buttercream on the serving base you have chosen for the wedding cake (a platter or wooden board sturdy enough to hold the weight of the finished three-tier cake). Centre the 10-inch cake tier, still on its cardboard cake circle, on the base. Gently press down on the centre of the cake to make sure it adheres to the base (any marks on the cake will be covered by the second tier).

26. Take the 8-inch baking pan and centre it on the 10-inch cake tier, pressing down gently to mark the buttercream and indicate where the second tier will be placed. Remove the pan. Return the 10-inch cake tier, on the serving base, to the fridge to set the "glue" holding the cake to the base, about 30 minutes.

27. Take the 6-inch baking pan and centre it on the 8-inch cake tier, pressing down gently to mark the buttercream and indicate where the third tier will be placed. Remove the pan. Return the 8-inch cake tier to the fridge until you're ready to assemble the cake.

28. Assemble the cake following the instructions on page 252. Decorate the cake with piped vanilla buttercream, edible flowers, crystallized flowers, marzipan flowers and/or ribbon.

Apricot-Almond Simple Syrup

Makes about 2 cups
Prep time: 5 minutes
Cooking time: about 3 minutes

1 cup apricot nectar

⅔ cup granulated sugar

½ cup freshly squeezed lemon juice (about 3 lemons)

¼ cup almond liqueur or 4 tsp almond extract

1. In a small saucepan, combine the apricot nectar, sugar and lemon juice. Bring to a boil over medium heat, stirring until the sugar has dissolved.

2. Remove from the heat, then stir in the almond liqueur. Set aside to cool completely. (The syrup, without the liqueur, can be refrigerated in an airtight container for up to 1 week. Add the liqueur before using.)

Vanilla Buttercream

Makes 18 cups
Prep time: 30 minutes

1. Prepare nine batches of the recipe for Quick Buttercream (page 154), increasing the vanilla extract to 2 ½ teaspoons per batch and adding ¼ teaspoonful of fine sea salt per batch.

2. Set aside 6 cups of the vanilla buttercream for the apricot buttercream (recipe follows). Spoon some of the remaining buttercream into a large piping bag fitted with a medium plain, round tip. Refrigerate the remaining buttercream, tightly covered, until needed. (The buttercream can be frozen in an airtight container for up to 1 month. Thaw it in the fridge before using.)

Apricot Buttercream

Makes about 7 cups
Prep time: 10 minutes
Cooking time: about 12 minutes
Standing time: 15 minutes

1 ¼ cups dried apricots, coarsely chopped

1 cup apricot nectar

⅓ cup granulated sugar

1 Tbsp finely grated lemon zest (1 to 2 lemons)

¼ cup freshly squeezed lemon juice (about 2 lemons)

¼ tsp fine sea salt

6 cups Vanilla Buttercream (recipe above)

1. In a small saucepan, combine the apricots, apricot nectar, sugar, lemon zest and juice and salt. Bring to a simmer over medium heat.

2. Turn down the heat to low, simmer, uncovered and stirring occasionally, until the apricots are almost tender, about 10 minutes. Remove from the heat, cover and let stand at room temperature until the apricots are tender and have absorbed most of the liquid, about 15 minutes.

3. Using a hand-held blender in the saucepan (or in a food processor fitted with the steel blade), purée the apricot mixture until smooth. Let cool completely.

4. Scrape the apricot mixture into a large bowl. Fold in 1 cup of the vanilla buttercream.

5. Fold in the remaining 5 cups of buttercream until well combined. Spoon half of the apricot buttercream into a large piping bag fitted with a large plain, round tip. Refrigerate the remaining buttercream, tightly covered, until needed. (The buttercream can be frozen in an airtight container for up to 1 month. Thaw it in the fridge before using.)

Crystallized Flowers

Prep time: 30 minutes
Drying time: 12 to 36 hours

1 cup granulated sugar

1 large egg white

1 tsp vodka or water

Edible flowers or petals (see
    Edible Flower Primer, page 49)

1. Set a wire rack over a large baking sheet.

2. In a food processor fitted with the steel blade or a blender, process the sugar until finely ground. Pour the processed sugar into a shallow dish.

3. In a small bowl, whisk the egg white and vodka until frothy.

4. Use tweezers to hold each flower, if necessary. Using a clean paintbrush, gently brush both sides of a flower with the egg white mixture.

5. Holding the flower over the dish of sugar, use a spoon to sprinkle sugar over the flower to coat it completely. Gently shake off any excess. Place the flower on the wire rack. Repeat with the remaining flowers.

6. Let the flowers stand at room temperature until they feel dry and are almost brittle, 12 to 36 hours (in humid weather, the flowers will take longer to dry). (The crystallized flowers can be stored in an airtight container at room temperature for up to 1 year.)

WEDDING CAKE TO-DO LIST

Many of the components of our wedding cake can be prepared in advance (see the individual recipes for storage instructions). However, if you're a last-minute kind of person, here's what you need to prep and when.

At least 3 days before the wedding: make the crystallized flowers or petals.

At least 2 days before the wedding: bake the cakes.

While cakes are baking: prep the Apricot-Almond Simple Syrup and Vanilla and Apricot Buttercreams.

One day before the wedding: assemble the cake (minus the top tier) and add any decorations.

The day of the wedding: add the top tier (if necessary) and any additional decorations.

How to Assemble Vanilla-Apricot Wedding Cake

- For a three-tier wedding cake, you'll need nine wedding cake dowels (¼ inch in diameter) from a cake decorating store.

- On the 10-inch cake tier, use one dowel to mark the places where five of the dowels will go. Space the dowel marks 1 to 2 inches apart and about 1 inch inside the perimeter of the baking pan mark.

- Press the dowel into one of the marks until it reaches the cardboard cake circle. Using a pencil, mark on the dowel where the top of the cake is.

- Remove the dowel and line it up with four other dowels, marking them all at the same place. Cut all five dowels the same length.

- Insert the dowels in the cake, ensuring that they're level with the cake's surface or slightly below.

- Repeat with the remaining four dowels and the 8-inch cake tier. (No dowels are needed for the top tier.)

- Spoon 2 tablespoonfuls of vanilla buttercream in the centre of the 10-inch cake tier.

- Using a large offset spatula and the palm of your hand to support the base, align and place the 8-inch cake tier on top of the 10-inch tier, sliding your hand and then the spatula out from under the cake. Repeat the process with the 6-inch cake tier.

- If you need to transport the finished cake to the wedding venue, either delay putting the 6-inch cake tier in place until you reach the venue, or hammer a long dowel with a sharpened end through all three cake tiers and cardboard cake circles right to the serving base to secure the cake. Leave this long dowel uncut so you can remove it when the cake arrives at the wedding venue. Take along some extra vanilla buttercream to patch the hole left by the dowel, or any damage that might have occurred en route to the venue.

BREADS, QUICK BREADS & DOUGHNUTS

Cinnamon-Raisin Bread

The aroma wafting from your oven while this spicy raisin bread bakes will have mouths watering all through the house.

Makes one 9- x 5-inch loaf
Prep time: 45 minutes
Rising time: about 2 hours
Cooking time: about 1 hour

Yeast Sponge

¾ cup warm whole milk (about 110°F)

1 Tbsp granulated sugar

1 ½ tsp active dry yeast

Dough

2 large eggs, lightly beaten

3 ¾ cups bread flour

¼ cup granulated sugar

2 tsp ground cinnamon

1 ½ tsp fine sea salt

¼ cup unsalted butter, cut into ¼-inch cubes and softened

²/₃ cup sultana raisins

1 tsp finely grated lemon zest

Egg Wash

1 large egg whisked with 1 Tbsp water

CHANGE IT UP

For a spicy cranberry-orange loaf, swap the raisins for dried cranberries and the lemon zest for 2 teaspoonfuls of finely grated orange zest.

1. For the yeast sponge, pour the warm milk into the bowl of a stand mixer (or a large bowl). Sprinkle the sugar and yeast over the milk. Let stand until puffy, about 5 minutes.

2. For the dough, add the eggs to the yeast sponge. Fit the stand mixer with the dough hook attachment (or use a hand-held electric mixer). Mix on low speed for 1 minute.

3. In a separate large bowl, whisk together the flour, sugar, cinnamon and salt. Add the butter and toss gently.

4. Add the flour mixture to the yeast sponge. Mix on medium speed for 4 minutes. (If not using a stand mixer, mix in the flour until combined, then turn out the dough onto a lightly floured work surface and knead until smooth.)

5. Turn out the dough onto a lightly floured work surface and knead a few times to bring it together into a ball. Pat it into a disc about 1 inch thick.

6. Sprinkle with the sultanas and lemon zest. Knead thoroughly until well distributed throughout the dough and the dough forms a ball.

7. Place the dough in a lightly oiled large bowl, turning the dough to coat it evenly with oil. Cover the bowl with a damp towel, or loosely with plastic wrap. Let stand in a warm place until the dough has doubled in size, about 1 hour.

8. On a lightly floured work surface, punch down the dough to remove the air. Roll out the dough to an 11- x 10-inch rectangle. With one of the longer edges facing you, fold in both sides by 1 inch. Roll up the dough tightly away from you. Pinch to seal the seam.

9. Thoroughly grease a 9- x 5-inch loaf pan. Place the loaf, seam side down, in the pan. Cover the pan with a damp towel, or loosely with plastic wrap. Let stand in a warm place until doubled in size, 45 to 60 minutes.

10. When ready to bake, preheat the oven to 400°F.

11. Brush the egg wash over the top of the loaf. Bake until the loaf is browned on top, about 1 hour. (If it appears to be browning too quickly, tent the top loosely with foil.)

12. Let the loaf cool in the pan on a wire rack for 10 minutes. Remove the loaf from the pan and let cool completely on the wire rack.

Orange-Scented Brioche

Brioche is a rich bread popular in France. Letting the dough rise in the fridge for several hours helps develop its traditional flavour.

Makes one 9-inch round loaf or two 8- x 4-inch loaves
Prep time: 30 minutes
Rising time: at least 9 hours
Cooking time: 20 to 30 minutes

2 cups bread flour

2 cups all-purpose flour

⅓ cup granulated sugar

1 Tbsp instant yeast

2 tsp fine sea salt

4 large eggs

⅓ cup plus 4 tsp warm whole milk (about 110°F)

1 Tbsp finely grated orange zest

1 cup plus 1 Tbsp unsalted butter, cut into small pieces and softened

Egg wash

1 large egg whisked with 1 Tbsp water

CHANGE IT UP

Peppery Brioche: Add 2 teaspoonfuls of freshly ground black pepper to the flour mixture. Omit the orange zest if you wish.

Rosemary Brioche: Add 1 tablespoonful of finely chopped fresh rosemary or 1 ½ teaspoonfuls of crumbled dried rosemary to the flour mixture. Omit the orange zest, if you wish, or replace it with lemon zest.

1. Line a large baking sheet with parchment paper. Set aside.

2. In the bowl of a stand mixer (or a large bowl), whisk together both flours, the sugar, yeast and salt. Fit the stand mixer with the dough hook attachment (or use a hand-held electric mixer).

3. In a small bowl, lightly beat the 4 eggs, then whisk in the milk. With the mixer running on low speed, gradually add the egg mixture to the flour mixture. Add the orange zest and mix just until combined.

4. Increase the speed to medium. Add the butter in three even additions, incorporating well between additions.

5. Mix the dough until it pulls away from the sides of the bowl and forms a ball around the hook, 5 to 8 minutes. It should be satiny, soft and smooth. (If not using a stand mixer, turn out the dough onto a lightly floured work surface and knead until satiny, soft and smooth.)

6. Turn out the dough onto a clean surface and knead it a few times until it forms a smooth ball. Place on the prepared baking sheet. Cover the baking sheet loosely but securely with plastic wrap. Refrigerate for at least 8 hours, or preferably overnight, until doubled in size.

7. Remove the dough from the fridge and let stand at room temperature for 45 minutes. Preheat the oven to 350°F. Grease a 9-inch round baking pan or two 8- x 4-inch loaf pans.

8. Using a pastry scraper or sharp knife, divide the dough into 12 even-sized pieces. (If you have a kitchen scale, weigh the pieces of dough for extra accuracy.)

9. Shape each piece of dough into a ball. If using a 9-inch pan, arrange the balls in circles in the pan. If using loaf pans, arrange the balls in pairs, six to a pan.

10. Cover the pan(s) loosely but securely with plastic wrap. Let stand in a warm place until doubled in size, about 50 minutes.

11. Brush the egg wash over the top of the loaf (or loaves), ensuring it doesn't run down the sides of the brioche, as this will make the brioche stick to the pan.

12. Bake the brioche until an instant-read thermometer inserted in the centre registers 190°F and the top is a deep golden brown, 20 to 30 minutes.

13. Let the brioche cool in the pan(s) on a wire rack for 15 minutes. Remove from the pan(s) and let cool completely on the wire rack.

256   **THE REDPATH CANADIAN BAKE BOOK**

Zucchini Bread

E asy zucchini bread is the perfect go-to snack. Try it for breakfast, team it with cheese or enjoy it with a cup of coffee or tea.

Makes two 8- x 4-inch loaves
Prep time: 20 minutes
Cooking time: about 1 hour

2 cups granulated sugar

2 cups peeled and shredded zucchini (about 3 medium zucchini)

1 cup unsalted butter, melted and cooled

3 large eggs

3 cups all-purpose flour

1 tsp baking soda

1 tsp baking powder

½ tsp fine sea salt

1 cup pecan halves, coarsely chopped (optional)

1. Preheat the oven to 300°F. Grease two 8- x 4-inch loaf pans, then dust the pans with flour. Set aside.

2. In a large bowl and using an electric mixer, beat together the sugar, zucchini, butter and eggs for 5 minutes.

3. In a medium bowl, whisk together the flour, baking soda, baking powder and salt.

4. Add the flour mixture to the zucchini mixture and stir until the flour is just moistened and combined with the batter. Do not overmix or the loaf will be tough. Stir in the pecans (if using).

5. Divide the batter evenly between the prepared pans. Bake until a skewer inserted in the centre of each loaf comes out clean, about 1 hour.

6. Let the loaves cool in the pans for 15 minutes. Remove the loaves from the pans and let cool completely on a wire rack. (The bread can be stored at room temperature, tightly wrapped in plastic wrap, for up to 3 days.)

CHANGE IT UP

Try making the zucchini loaf with walnuts instead of pecans.

Butterscotch-Cinnamon Swirl Coffee Cake

Although this spicy yeast-raised coffeecake is best eaten the day it's baked, it can be made a day ahead. Let it cool completely in the pan, then cover the pan tightly with plastic wrap. To reheat the cake, remove the plastic wrap and warm in a 300°F oven for about 20 minutes to liquefy the glaze before turning the cake out as described in the recipe.

Makes one 9-inch cake; 10 to 12 servings
Prep time: 1 hour
Rising time: 1 hour, 30 minutes
Cooking time: about 35 minutes

Dough

2 ½ to 2 ¾ cups all-purpose flour

⅓ cup granulated sugar

2 ¼ tsp instant yeast

½ tsp fine sea salt

½ tsp ground cardamom

¼ tsp ground cinnamon

Pinch of freshly grated nutmeg

⅓ cup whole milk

¼ cup unsalted butter, softened

¼ cup water

2 large eggs

1 large egg yolk

1 Tbsp vanilla extract

Butterscotch Glaze

½ cup lightly packed dark brown sugar

¼ cup unsalted butter, softened

2 Tbsp white corn syrup

1 Tbsp maple syrup

¼ tsp fine sea salt

2 tsp whisky, rum or apple juice

Butterscotch-Cinnamon Filling

¼ cup unsalted butter, melted

1 tsp ground cinnamon

½ cup butterscotch chips, chopped

1. For the dough, in the bowl of a stand mixer fitted with the dough hook attachment (or in a large bowl and using a whisk), combine 2 cups of the flour with the sugar, yeast, salt and spices.

2. In a small saucepan, heat the milk and butter over low heat just until the butter melts. Add the water. Set aside until the mixture registers 110°F on an instant-read thermometer, about 1 minute.

3. Add the milk mixture to the flour mixture. Mix on low speed (or use a hand-held mixer) until combined. Add the eggs and egg yolk one at a time, beating well after addition. Beat in the vanilla extract.

4. Add ½ cup of the remaining flour. Mix on low speed until the dough is smooth, 30 to 45 seconds. Add 2 tablespoons of the remaining flour. Mix on medium speed until the dough is smooth but still slightly sticky. (If not using a stand mixer, mix in the flour until combined, then turn out the dough onto a lightly floured work surface and knead until smooth but still slightly sticky.)

5. Turn out the dough onto a lightly floured work surface and knead the dough gently until smooth and no longer sticky, adding an additional 1 to 2 tablespoons of flour if needed.

6. Place the dough in a lightly oiled large bowl, turning the dough to coat it evenly with oil. Cover the bowl with a damp towel, or loosely with plastic wrap. Let stand in a warm place until the dough has doubled in size, about 1 hour.

7. For the butterscotch glaze, lightly butter a 9-inch round baking pan. In a small saucepan, combine the sugar, butter, both syrups and salt. Heat over low heat, stirring occasionally, until the butter has melted.

8. Remove from the heat and stir in the whisky. Pour the butter mixture into the prepared pan, tilting the pan to cover the base evenly. Set aside.

9. For the butterscotch-cinnamon filling, stir together the butter and cinnamon in a small bowl. Set aside.

10. On a lightly floured work surface, punch down the dough to remove the air. Roll it out to a 16- x 12-inch rectangle.

11. With one of the longer edges facing you, use a pastry brush to spread the cinnamon-butter mixture evenly over the dough. Sprinkle the dough with the butterscotch chips.

12. Cut the dough vertically into six 2-inch wide strips. Loosely (so the dough has room to expand

during baking) roll up one strip and place it in the centre of the prepared pan.

13. Working with one strip at a time and with the cinnamon-butter side toward the centre of the pan, coil the remaining dough strips around the rolled-up strip. Start each strip at the end of the previous one to make a single large spiral.

14. Cover the pan with a damp towel, or loosely with plastic wrap. Let stand in a warm place until it has almost doubled in size, 30 minutes.

15. When ready to bake, place the oven rack in the centre of the oven and preheat the oven to 350°F.

16. Bake until the top of the cake is a deep golden brown, about 35 minutes. Check after 20 minutes to make sure the top isn't browning too quickly. If it is, cover the cake loosely with a piece of foil for the last 10 to 15 minutes. Let the cake cool in the pan on a wire rack for 10 minutes.

17. Gently tilt the pan and tap the side on the counter to release the sides of the cake. Invert a plate on top of the cake, then invert the pan and the plate together. Leave the pan on the cake for 1 minute so the glaze transfers to the cake, then gently remove the pan. Using a rubber spatula, scrape out any glaze still in the pan and spread it over the warm surface of the cake. Serve the cake warm or at room temperature, cutting it into wedges with a serrated knife.

Frosted Cinnamon Buns

Few home bakes taste finer than a cinnamon bun still warm from the oven. For breakfast, brunch or just when you need a sweet treat with a cup of coffee, these will fit the bill.

Makes 12 buns
Prep time: 45 minutes
Rising time: about 1 hour,
  45 minutes
Cooking time: 35 to 40 minutes

Dough

3 ¾ cups all-purpose flour

1 Tbsp instant yeast

½ cup granulated sugar

7 Tbsp unsalted butter, softened

1 Tbsp finely grated orange zest

½ tsp fine sea salt

½ tsp vanilla extract

1 large egg

1 cup warm whole milk
  (about 110°F)

Filling

⅔ cup lightly packed dark brown
  sugar

2 tsp ground cinnamon

½ tsp freshly grated nutmeg

¼ tsp ground cloves

Pinch of fine sea salt

½ cup unsalted butter, softened

Cinnamon Icing

1 ½ cups icing sugar, sifted

½ tsp ground cinnamon

Pinch of fine sea salt

1 tsp vanilla extract

1 to 2 Tbsp milk or cream

CHANGE IT UP

For nutty cinnamon buns, add ⅓ cup finely chopped toasted pecans or walnuts to the sugar mixture in the filling.

1. For the dough, whisk together the flour and yeast in a medium bowl. Set aside.

2. In the bowl of a stand mixer (or in a large bowl) and using a spatula, cream together the sugar, butter, orange zest, salt and vanilla extract until well combined. Add the egg and mix well. Slowly add the milk until well combined.

3. Fit the mixer with the dough hook attachment (or use a hand-held electric mixer). With the mixer running on low speed, add half of the flour mixture. Gradually increase the speed to medium.

4. Add the remaining flour mixture, mixing until the dough pulls away from the sides of the bowl and starts to form a smooth ball. (If not using a stand mixer, mix in the flour until combined, then turn out the dough onto a lightly floured work surface and knead until smooth.)

5. Place the dough in a lightly oiled large bowl, turning the dough to coat it evenly with oil. Cover the bowl with a damp towel, or loosely with plastic wrap. Let stand in a warm place until the dough has doubled in size, about 1 hour.

6. For the filling, mix together the sugar, spices and salt in a small bowl until well combined. Set aside.

7. On a lightly floured work surface, punch down the dough to remove the air. Roll it out to an 18- x 12-inch rectangle. Turn the dough, if necessary, so that one of the longer sides is facing you.

8. Spread the softened butter over the dough, leaving a ½-inch border along the long side furthest from you. Sprinkle the brown sugar mixture evenly over the buttered dough. Gently pat the sugar mixture into the dough so that it adheres.

9. Starting at the long edge nearest you and using even pressure, carefully roll the dough toward the unbuttered edge. (If you roll too tightly, the centres of the buns will pop up during baking; too loosely and the buns will be dry.)

10. Making sure the seam is underneath, trim off and discard a thin slice from one end of the roll. Using a large, serrated knife, cut the roll into 12 even-sized slices.

11. Thoroughly grease a 10-inch round baking pan. Arrange the slices, cut sides up, in the pan, starting from the outside and working toward the centre. Cover the pan with a damp towel, or loosely with plastic wrap. Let stand in a warm place until doubled in size, 30 to 45 minutes.

12. When ready to bake, preheat the oven to 350°F.

13. Bake the buns until the tops are golden brown, 35 to 40 minutes.

14. Let the buns cool in the pan on a wire rack for 10 minutes. Remove the buns from the pan and let cool slightly on the wire rack.

15. For the cinnamon icing, gently whisk together the icing sugar, cinnamon and salt in a medium bowl. Stir in the vanilla extract.

16. Gradually add the milk, stirring until the icing is smooth. For a thinner icing, stir in more milk; for a thicker icing, stir in more icing sugar.

17. Drizzle the icing over the warm buns. Serve immediately, or at room temperature.

GET A HEAD START

Fresh cinnamon buns for brunch? Why not? Prep the cinnamon buns up to the end of Step 11. Cover the pan tightly with plastic wrap and refrigerate overnight. The next morning, remove the pan of buns from the fridge and let stand at room temperature for 15 minutes. Bake and ice the buns as directed.

Hot Cross Buns

We love making batches of hot cross buns to give away—especially since, legend has it, sharing a hot cross bun with a friend guarantees a year of good friendship.

Makes 12 buns
Prep time: 30 minutes
Rising time: 1 ½ to 2 hours
Cooking time: about 30 minutes
Setting time: 40 minutes

Buns

¾ cup warm whole milk (about 110°F)

4 tsp active dry yeast

3 large eggs

½ cup vegetable oil

⅓ cup granulated sugar

Finely grated zest of 1 lemon

¾ tsp fine sea salt

½ tsp ground cinnamon

¼ tsp freshly grated nutmeg

¼ tsp ground cloves

3 to 3 ¾ cups all-purpose flour

⅓ cup currants

¼ cup finely chopped crystallized ginger or candied orange peel

Glaze

½ cup granulated sugar

3 Tbsp water

1 tsp vanilla extract

Frosting

¾ cup icing sugar, sifted

1 Tbsp milk or cream

1. For the buns, mix together the warm milk and yeast in a large bowl. Let stand until puffy, about 5 minutes.

2. Whisk in the eggs, oil, sugar, lemon zest, salt and spices until well combined.

3. Gradually add the flour, 1 cup at a time, stirring well after each addition. Use only as much flour as is necessary to form a dough that pulls away from the sides of the bowl.

4. Turn out the dough onto a lightly floured work surface and knead well until the dough is smooth, 5 to 10 minutes. Knead in the currants and crystallized ginger.

5. Place the dough in a lightly oiled large bowl, turning the dough to coat it evenly with oil. Cover the bowl with a damp towel, or loosely with plastic wrap. Let stand in a warm place until the dough has doubled in size, 45 to 60 minutes.

6. On a lightly floured work surface, punch down the dough to remove the air. Divide it into 12 even-sized pieces and shape each piece into a ball.

7. Grease a 13- x 9-inch baking pan. Place the balls of dough, in a single layer, in the pan. Cover the pan with a damp towel, or loosely with plastic wrap. Let stand in a warm place until doubled in size, 45 to 60 minutes.

8. When ready to bake, preheat the oven to 350°F.

9. Bake the buns until browned on the top, 25 to 30 minutes. Put the pan on a wire rack and set aside while you make the glaze.

10. For the glaze, combine the sugar, water and vanilla extract in a small saucepan. Bring to a simmer over medium heat, stirring just until the sugar has dissolved. Remove the saucepan from the heat.

11. Brush the glaze generously over the tops of the warm buns, using up all of the glaze. Let the buns cool completely in the pan on a wire rack.

12. For the frosting, whisk together the icing sugar and milk until thick and creamy. Spoon the frosting into a piping bag (see sidebar) and pipe a cross on top of each bun. Let the frosting set before removing the buns from the pan. If well wrapped, the buns will keep fresh for up to 24 hours at room temperature.

TOOL KIT

If you don't have a piping bag, spoon the frosting into a large freezer bag. Snip off one of the corners and squeeze gently to pipe the frosting.

Almond Bear Claws

Don't be daunted by the length of this recipe: These almond-filled Danish are simple to prep, and you'll be rewarded with a delectable treat. If the dough is difficult to roll out, let it rest in the fridge for 5 minutes. Chilling it relaxes the gluten in the flour and makes it easier to roll.

Makes 12 bear claws
Prep time: 1 hour
Rising time: 1 hour, 15 minutes
Chilling time: 2 hours, 20 minutes
Cooking time: 15 to 18 minutes

Dough

2 ¼ cups all-purpose flour

1 ½ tsp instant yeast

½ cup whole milk

1 large egg

3 Tbsp granulated sugar

2 Tbsp unsalted butter, melted and cooled

¾ tsp fine sea salt

¾ cup unsalted butter, cut into 1-inch pieces and softened

Almond Filling

¼ cup all-purpose flour

½ tsp ground cinnamon

½ cup granulated sugar

½ cup unsalted butter, softened

¼ tsp fine sea salt

1 large egg

½ tsp vanilla extract

½ tsp almond extract

1 ½ cups ground almonds, toasted

To Assemble

1 large egg, beaten

½ cup sliced almonds

1. For the dough, whisk together the flour and yeast in a medium bowl. Set aside.

2. In the bowl of a stand mixer fitted with the dough hook attachment (or in a large bowl and using a hand-held electric mixer), combine the milk, egg, sugar, melted butter and salt. Mix on low speed for 2 minutes.

3. Add the flour mixture to the milk mixture. Mix on low speed until well combined, about 3 minutes. (If not using a stand mixer, mix in the flour until combined, then turn out the dough onto a lightly floured work surface and knead until smooth.)

4. Turn out the dough onto a lightly floured work surface and knead a few times to bring it together into a ball. Place it in a lightly oiled large bowl, turning the dough to coat it evenly with oil. Cover the bowl with a damp towel, or loosely with plastic wrap. Let stand in a warm place until the dough has doubled in size, about 45 minutes.

5. When the dough has risen, put the bowl in the fridge for 30 minutes to chill.

6. Meanwhile, draw a 9- x 6-inch rectangle in the centre of a piece of parchment paper. Flip the paper so the rectangle is underneath. Fold the paper along each long side of the rectangle, in toward the centre, pressing down

on each fold to make a sharp crease.

7. Open the folded paper and scatter the pieces of softened butter over the drawn rectangle, staying within the lines. Fold the paper over the butter, folding along crease lines you made earlier, then flatten it gently with your hands.

8. Using a rolling pin, roll out the butter to fill the drawn rectangle and make an even 9- x 6-inch shape. Chill in the fridge for 20 minutes.

9. On a lightly floured work surface, roll out the chilled dough to a 16- x 8-inch rectangle. Make sure one of the shorter sides is facing you. Brush any excess flour from the dough.

10. Unwrap the chilled butter and place it on the top two-thirds of the dough, leaving a 1-inch border around the top and two sides.

11. Fold the uncovered bottom third of the dough up over the butter, then fold the top third down (as if you were folding a letter). Gently press the edges with the rolling pin and turn the dough through 90 degrees to the left, so the seam is to the right.

12. Roll out the folded dough to a 16- x 8-inch rectangle. Repeat the folding and turning process. This completes one turn of the dough. Chill the dough in the fridge for

30 minutes. Work through the folding, turning and chilling process two more times to complete a total of three turns.

13. While the dough is chilling the final time, make the almond filling. Sift the flour and cinnamon into a medium bowl. Set aside.

14. In the bowl of a stand mixer filled with the paddle attachment (or in a large bowl and using an electric hand mixer), cream together the sugar, butter and salt on medium speed. Beat in the egg. Beat in the vanilla and almond extracts.

15. With the mixer running on low speed, add the ground almonds until well combined. Add the flour-cinnamon mixture and mix just until combined.

16. Spoon the almond filling into a pastry bag fitted with a ¾-inch plain round tip. Set aside. Grease a large baking sheet or line it with parchment paper. Set aside.

17. To assemble the bear claws, on a lightly floured work surface, roll out the dough to a 16- x 12-inch rectangle and cut it into twelve 4-inch squares.

18. Pipe a line of almond filling across each square, about 1 inch down from the top edge. Brush the top inch of each square with beaten egg and fold over the filling, pressing firmly to seal and leaving the bottom inch of each square uncovered.

19. Using a sharp knife, cut five evenly spaced, ½-inch deep, vertical slits in the bottom edge of each square. Curve the sides

of each square upward slightly so the slits open up.

20. Place the bear claws on the prepared baking sheet. Cover the baking sheet with a damp towel, or loosely with plastic wrap. Let stand in a warm place until doubled in size, about 30 minutes.

21. When ready to bake, preheat the oven to 400°F.

22. Brush the bear claws gently with the remaining beaten egg. Sprinkle the tops evenly with most of the sliced almonds. If liked, press one of the remaining almond slices onto ends of each "claw."

23. Bake the bear claws until golden brown, 15 to 18 minutes. Transfer to a wire rack to cool for 15 minutes. Serve warm.

Traditional Bannock

Bannock is one of the oldest types of bread around and has been baked in Canada for hundreds of years. It's an easy no-yeast, quick bread that's particularly tasty served warm with butter.

Makes one 10-inch loaf
Prep time: 20 minutes
Cooking time: 25 to 35 minutes

2 ½ cups all-purpose flour

¼ cup whole wheat flour

¼ cup lightly packed golden yellow sugar

2 Tbsp baking powder

1 ½ tsp fine sea salt

1 cup water

⅓ cup vegetable oil

Egg wash

1 large egg whisked with 1 Tbsp water

1. Preheat the oven to 400°F. Line a baking sheet with parchment paper.

2. For the dough, whisk together both flours, the sugar, baking powder and salt in a medium bowl until well combined.

3. Make a well in the flour mixture. Pour the water and oil into the well. Using a fork or your hands, mix the ingredients together until the dough forms a sticky ball.

4. Turn out the dough onto a lightly floured work surface. Knead several times just until the dough is no longer sticky.

5. Put the dough on the prepared baking sheet. Pat into a 10-inch oval about ½ inch thick. Brush the dough with egg wash. Using a sharp knife, score several slashes in the top of the dough.

6. Bake the bannock until golden brown on all sides, 25 to 35 minutes.

7. Remove the bannock from the baking sheet and let cool on a wire rack. Serve warm or at room temperature.

CHANGE IT UP

For a basic bannock, omit the whole wheat flour and add an extra ¼ cup all-purpose flour.

For a healthier bannock, omit the all-purpose flour and add an extra 2 ½ cups whole wheat flour.

For a richer flavour, use melted butter or lard in place of the vegetable oil.

For individual bannocks, divide the dough into four or six even-sized pieces, shape them into small ovals or rounds and bake for just 20 minutes.

Rum-Spiked Banana Bread

This classic banana bread gets an extra hit of flavour from the addition of spiced rum. If you prefer not to use rum, substitute orange juice—the bread will be just as dee-lish.

Makes one 9- x 5-inch loaf
Prep time: 15 minutes
Cooking time: about 1 hour

2 ¼ cups all-purpose flour

1 tsp baking powder

1 tsp baking soda

1 tsp ground cinnamon

½ tsp freshly grated nutmeg

½ tsp fine sea salt

½ cup unsalted butter, softened

½ cup lightly packed dark brown sugar

¼ cup granulated sugar

2 large eggs, lightly beaten

2 cups peeled and mashed over-ripe bananas (see sidebar)

3 Tbsp spiced dark rum

3 Tbsp sour cream (14%)

1 tsp vanilla extract

1. Preheat the oven to 350°F. Grease a 9- x 5-inch loaf pan and line the base and sides with parchment paper.

2. In a large bowl, whisk together the flour, baking powder, baking soda, cinnamon, nutmeg and salt. Set aside.

3. In a separate large bowl and using a spatula or wooden spoon, cream the butter and both sugars until smooth and creamy.

4. Add the eggs and stir to combine. Stir in the bananas, rum, sour cream and vanilla extract. Mix until thoroughly combined.

5. Add half of the flour mixture to the sugar mixture and stir until the flour is just moistened. Fold in the remaining flour until the flour is just moistened and combined with the batter. Do not overmix, or the loaf will be tough.

6. Scrape the batter into the prepared pan. Bake until a skewer inserted in the centre of the loaf comes out clean, about 1 hour.

7. Let the loaf cool in the pan for 15 minutes. Remove the loaf from the pan and let cool completely on a wire rack. (The bread can be stored at room temperature, tightly wrapped in plastic wrap, for up to 3 days.)

BAKING DAY SECRETS

Overripe, almost black bananas give banana bread the best, most intense flavour. If you don't have any overripe bananas on hand, bake yellow ones on a parchment-lined baking sheet in a 300°F oven until the skins turn black, 30 to 40 minutes.

Glazed Lemon Loaf

This light loaf has a wonderful hit of lemon flavour, and the creamy glaze makes it extra special.

Makes one 9- x 5-inch loaf
Prep time: 20 minutes
Cooking time: 50 to 55 minutes

Loaf

1 ½ cups all-purpose flour

2 tsp baking powder

½ tsp fine sea salt

1 cup sour cream (14%)

3 large eggs

¾ cup granulated sugar

¼ cup lightly packed golden yellow sugar

½ cup unsalted butter, melted and cooled

3 Tbsp finely grated lemon zest

2 Tbsp freshly squeezed lemon juice

2 tsp lemon extract

½ tsp vanilla extract

Sour Cream–Lemon Glaze

1 ½ cups icing sugar, sifted

½ cup sour cream (14%)

½ tsp lemon extract

Finely grated lemon zest (optional)

1. Preheat the oven to 350°F. Grease and flour a 9- x 5-inch loaf pan, or grease the pan and line the base and sides with parchment paper.

2. For the loaf, whisk together the flour, baking powder and salt in a medium bowl. Set aside.

3. In the bowl of a stand mixer fitted with the whisk attachment (or in a large bowl and using a hand-held electric mixer), beat the sour cream, eggs and both sugars on medium speed until smooth and creamy.

4. With the mixer running on medium-low speed, gradually beat in the melted butter until well combined, scraping down the sides of the bowl once or twice.

5. Whisk in the lemon zest and juice, lemon and vanilla extracts.

6. Add the flour mixture to the lemon mixture and stir until the flour is just moistened and combined with the batter. Do not overmix, or the loaf will be tough.

7. Scrape the batter into the prepared pan. Use a spatula to gently smooth the top level. Bake until a skewer inserted in the centre of the loaf comes out clean, 50 to 55 minutes.

8. Let the loaf cool in the pan for 15 minutes. Remove the loaf from the pan and let cool completely on a wire rack. (The loaf can be stored at room temperature, tightly wrapped in plastic wrap, for up to 3 days.)

9. For the sour cream–lemon glaze, whisk together the icing sugar and sour cream in a medium bowl until smooth and creamy. Add the lemon extract and whisk well. (For a thicker glaze, gradually whisk in a little more icing sugar.)

10. Drizzle or spread the glaze over the top of the loaf. Sprinkle with lemon zest (if using).

GET A HEAD START

Wrap the unglazed loaf in plastic wrap, then foil. Freeze for up to 3 months. Unwrap and defrost before spreading with the glaze.

Jelly Doughnuts

Jelly doughnuts are popular any time of the year, but these delectable fried sweets are also a traditional dessert served at Hanukkah, when they're known by their Hebrew name, sufganiyot. Like all doughnuts, they're best served immediately after frying, so be sure to have a hungry crowd around when you make these.

Makes 32 doughnuts
Prep time: 45 minutes
Rising time: 1 ½ hours
Cooking time: about 4 minutes
    per batch

¾ cup warm whole milk
    (about 110°F)

2 ¼ tsp active dry yeast

2 cups all-purpose flour

¼ cup granulated sugar

½ tsp fine sea salt

2 large egg yolks

2 Tbsp unsalted butter, melted

Vegetable oil for deep-frying

²/₃ cup seedless red fruit jam,
    such as strawberry, sour cherry
    or raspberry

Icing sugar for dusting

1. In a small bowl, whisk together the warm milk and yeast. Let stand until puffy, about 5 minutes.

2. In a large bowl, whisk together the flour, sugar and salt until well combined.

3. Make a well in the centre of the flour mixture. Pour in the milk mixture, then the egg yolks. Mix until a shaggy dough forms.

4. Add the melted butter. Mix until the dough is smooth and holds together.

5. Turn out the dough onto a lightly floured work surface and knead well until smooth, 5 to 10 minutes.

6. Place the dough in a lightly oiled large bowl, turning the dough to coat it evenly with oil. Cover the bowl with a damp towel, or loosely with plastic wrap. Let stand in a warm place until the dough has doubled in size, about 1 hour.

7. Line two large baking sheets with parchment paper. Set aside.

8. On a lightly floured work surface, punch down the dough to remove the air. Roll it out to ¼-inch thickness.

9. Using a 2-inch round cutter, cut out 32 rounds, rerolling the dough scraps once. (Rerolling the scraps more than once makes the doughnuts tough.) Place the rounds, about ½ inch apart, on the prepared baking sheets. Cover with a damp towel, or loosely with plastic wrap. Let stand in a warm place until risen, puffy and about ½ inch thick, about 30 minutes.

10. Following the manufacturer's instructions, heat the oil in a deep-fryer to 360°F to 375°F. Alternatively, pour enough oil into a deep, large, heavy-bottomed saucepan to come one-third of the way up the sides of the saucepan. Hook a candy thermometer over the side of the saucepan. Heat the oil over medium heat until the thermometer registers 360°F to 375°F.

11. Meanwhile, line a large baking sheet with paper towels. Place the jam in a piping bag fitted with a ¼-inch round tip. Set aside.

12. Using a flat spatula or tongs and working in batches, carefully slide the doughnuts, one at a time, into the hot oil. Do not crowd the deep-fryer or sauce-pan. If using a saucepan, adjust the heat, if necessary, to maintain the temperature of the oil at a constant 360°F to 375°F.

13. Fry the doughnuts until the undersides are golden brown, 1 to 2 minutes. Carefully flip the doughnuts and fry until the second side is golden brown, 1 to 2 minutes.

14. Using tongs or a slotted spoon, remove the doughnuts to the prepared baking sheet. Repeat with the remaining dough.

15. When the doughnuts are cool enough to handle, use a paring knife to puncture a hole in the side of each one. Wiggle the knife around slightly to form a pocket in the centre of each doughnut.

16. Place the tip of the piping bag into the hole of one doughnut and pipe in about 1 teaspoonful of jam. Repeat with the remaining doughnuts. Dust the doughnuts with icing sugar and serve immediately. (The doughnuts are best served the day they're made.)

Maple Potato Doughnuts

Doughnuts made from mashed potato first appeared in the mid-1900s. They're super soft and creamy on the inside, but they have a nice, crunchy crust for contrast.

Makes 8 large doughnuts
Prep time: 45 minutes
Cooking time: about 4 minutes per batch

Doughnuts

2 ½ cups all-purpose flour

1 Tbsp baking powder

1 tsp ground cinnamon

½ tsp fine sea salt

1 cup granulated sugar

¼ cup unsalted butter, melted

¾ cup cooled mashed potatoes
   (about 2 medium potatoes)

2 large eggs

½ cup whole milk

Vegetable oil for deep-frying

Glaze

1 cup icing sugar, sifted

3 Tbsp maple syrup

1 to 3 Tbsp milk or cream

Pinch of fine sea salt

Maple sugar for topping
   (optional)

1. For the doughnuts, whisk together the flour, baking powder, cinnamon and salt in a large bowl. Set aside.

2. In a separate bowl and using an electric mixer, beat the sugar and butter until pale and fluffy. Stir in the mashed potatoes and eggs.

3. Add the flour mixture to the sugar mixture, alternately with the milk, making four additions of flour and three of milk, and beginning and ending with the flour. Stir until well combined. The dough will be soft.

4. Handling the dough as little as possible (so the finished doughnuts are tender), turn out the dough onto a well-floured surface. Roll it out to ¾-inch thickness.

5. Using a 3 ½-inch doughnut cutter (or a 3 ½-inch round cutter for the doughnuts and a 1-inch round cutter for the holes), cut the dough into eight doughnuts, rerolling the dough scraps once. (Rerolling the scraps more than once makes the doughnuts tough.) Either reserve the doughnut holes for frying separately or incorporate them back into the dough.

6. Following the manufacturer's instructions, heat the oil in a deep-fryer to 360°F to 375°F. Alternatively, pour enough oil into a large, heavy-bottomed saucepan to come one-third of the way up the sides of the saucepan. Hook a candy thermometer over the side of the saucepan. Heat the oil over medium heat until the thermometer registers 360°F to 375°F. Line a large baking sheet with paper towels.

7. Using a flat spatula or tongs and working in batches, carefully slide the doughnuts, one at a time, into the hot oil. Do not crowd the deep-fryer or saucepan. If using a saucepan, adjust the heat, if necessary, to maintain the temperature of the oil at a constant 360°F to 375°F.

8. Fry the doughnuts (and the holes, if using) until the undersides are golden brown, 1 to 2 minutes (30 seconds for the holes). Carefully flip the doughnuts and fry until the second side is golden brown, 1 to 2 minutes (30 seconds for the holes).

9. Using tongs or a slotted spoon, remove the doughnuts to the prepared baking sheet. Repeat with the remaining dough. Let the doughnuts cool on the baking sheet.

10. For the glaze, combine the icing sugar, maple syrup, 1 tablespoonful of the cream and the salt in a wide bowl until well combined and smooth. If the glaze is too stiff, add a little more cream, 1 tablespoonful at a time, until the glaze is soft enough to dip the doughnuts in.

11. Dip the tops of the cooled doughnuts in the glaze. Sprinkle the glazed tops with maple sugar (if using). Serve the doughnuts immediately. (The doughnuts are best served the day they're made.)

BAKING DAY SECRETS

Look for maple sugar at your local farmer's market or in a specialty grocery store.

Baked Boston Cream Doughnuts

Like their namesake pie, these easy baked doughnuts are filled with a rich pastry cream and topped with a luscious chocolate glaze.

Makes 20 doughnuts
Prep time: 30 minutes
Rising time: 1 hour, 45 minutes
Cooking time: 5 to 7 minutes

Doughnuts

¾ cup warm whole milk (about 110°F)

2 ¼ tsp active dry yeast

⅓ cup granulated sugar

1 large egg, beaten

1 Tbsp unsalted butter, melted

½ tsp fine sea salt

2 to 3 cups all-purpose flour

Pastry Cream Filling

1 large egg

2 large egg yolks

½ cup granulated sugar

¼ cup cornstarch

2 cups whole milk

2 Tbsp unsalted butter, softened

1 tsp vanilla extract

Chocolate Glaze

¾ cup semi-sweet chocolate chips

½ cup whipping cream (35%)

Decorative sprinkles (optional)

1. For the doughnuts, whisk together the warm milk and yeast in a large bowl. Let stand until puffy, about 5 minutes.

2. Gently stir the sugar, egg, butter and salt into the milk mixture.

3. Add the flour, ½ cup at a time, mixing well after each addition, just until the dough holds together and begins to pull away from the sides of the bowl. (You may not need all of the flour.)

4. Turn out the dough onto a lightly floured work surface and knead well until smooth, 5 to 10 minutes.

5. Place the dough in a lightly oiled large bowl, turning the dough to coat it evenly with oil. Cover the bowl with a damp towel, or loosely with plastic wrap. Let stand in a warm place until the dough has doubled in size, about 1 hour.

6. On a lightly floured work surface, punch down the dough to remove the air. Roll it out to ½-inch (1 cm) thickness. Line two large baking sheets with parchment paper. Set aside.

7. Using a 2-inch round cutter, cut out 20 rounds, rerolling the dough scraps once. (Rerolling the scraps more than once makes the doughnuts tough.) Place the rounds, about ½ inch apart, on the prepared baking sheets. Cover with a damp towel, or loosely with plastic wrap. Let stand in a warm place until risen, puffy and about 1 inch thick, about 45 minutes.

8. When ready to bake, preheat the oven to 375°F.

9. Bake the doughnuts, on the parchment-lined baking sheets, until the undersides are lightly browned, 5 to 7 minutes. Transfer the doughnuts to a wire rack and let cool completely before filling them.

10. For the pastry cream filling, whisk together the egg and egg yolks in a medium bowl. Whisk in ¼ cup of the sugar and the cornstarch. Set aside.

11. In a medium, heavy-bottomed saucepan, stir together the milk and the remaining ¼ cup of sugar. Bring to a boil over medium heat.

12. Remove the saucepan from the heat and slowly whisk a few tablespoonfuls of the hot milk into the egg mixture. Slowly whisk the rest of the hot milk into the egg mixture.

13. Pour the milk-egg mixture back into the saucepan. Cook over medium heat, whisking often to prevent the mixture from scorching on the bottom of the saucepan, until the pastry cream is thick and glossy, about 3 minutes. Remove the saucepan from the heat. Stir in the butter and vanilla extract until the butter melts.

14. Place a piping bag fitted with a plain tip in a tall glass. Fold down the sides of the bag and pour in the pastry cream. Lift the bag out of the glass. Secure the open end of the bag with an elastic. Refrigerate until the pastry cream is chilled, about 30 minutes.

15. For the chocolate glaze, put the chocolate chips and cream in a heatproof bowl set over a saucepan of hot, not boiling, water. Stir often until the chocolate is melted and smooth. Remove the bowl from the heat and set aside.

16. To assemble the doughnuts, use a paring knife to puncture a hole in the side of each doughnut. Wiggle the knife around slightly to form a pocket in the centre of each doughnut.

17. Place the tip of the piping bag into the hole of one doughnut and pipe in some pastry cream. Repeat with the remaining doughnuts.

18. Once all the doughnuts have been filled, dip the top of each one into the chocolate glaze. Add a scattering of sprinkles (if using). Transfer the glazed doughnuts to a wire rack until the glaze is set, 5 to 10 minutes. (The doughnuts are best served the day they're made.)

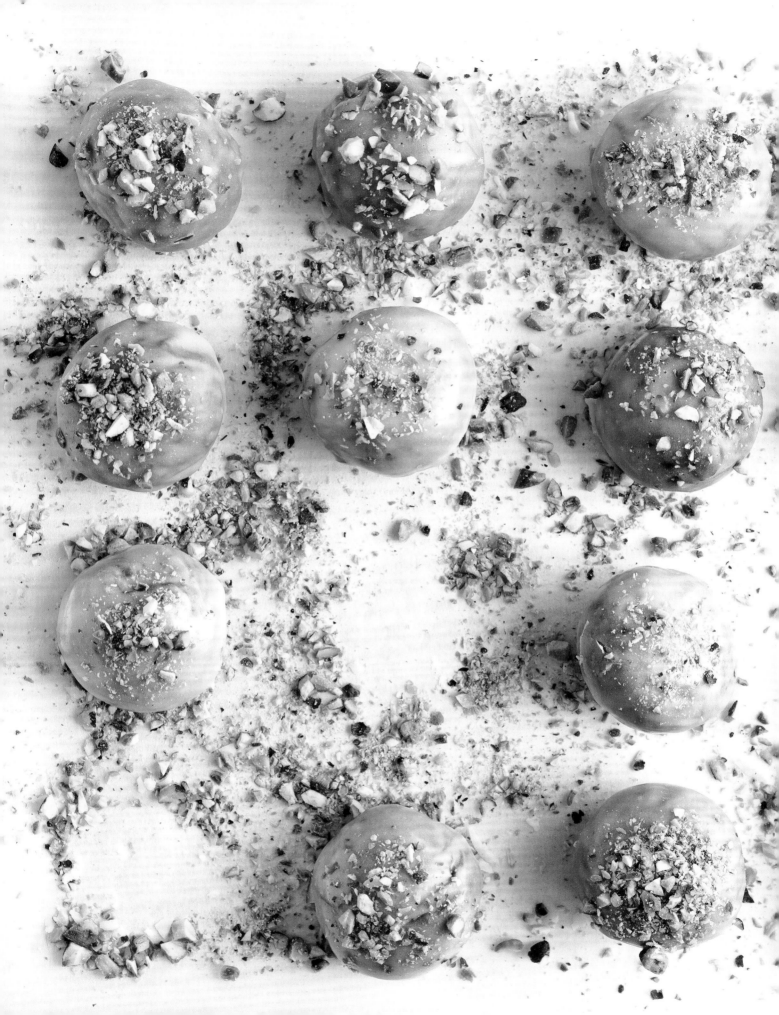

Pistachio Doughnut Holes

These bite-size doughnuts are the perfect indulgence. Their vanilla glaze and sprinkle of pistachios add just the right touch of sweetness and texture. (The doughnut holes are best served the day they're made.)

Makes 24 doughnut holes
Prep time: 45 minutes
Standing time: at least 30 minutes
Rising time: about 1 ½ hours
Cooking time: 1 minute per batch

Starter

¾ cup warm whole milk (about 110°F)

2 Tbsp active dry yeast

¾ cup all-purpose flour

Doughnut Batter

¼ cup whole milk

1 Tbsp active dry yeast

3 large egg yolks

3 Tbsp granulated sugar

1 tsp vanilla extract

½ tsp fine sea salt

2 to 3 cups all-purpose flour

¼ cup unsalted butter, softened

Vegetable oil for deep-frying

Glaze

4 cups icing sugar, sifted

⅓ cup whole milk

1 tsp vanilla extract

½ cup crushed unsalted, shelled pistachios

1. For the starter, whisk the milk and yeast in a small bowl. Stir in the flour until the mixture is smooth. Cover the bowl with plastic wrap. Let stand in a warm place until puffy, at least 30 minutes.

2. For the batter, whisk the milk and yeast in a medium bowl. Add the starter, egg yolks, sugar, vanilla and salt. Using an electric mixer, beat until combined, about 30 seconds.

3. Add ½ cup of the flour. Beat for 30 seconds just to combine. Add the butter and beat until the ingredients are well combined.

4. Continue adding the flour, ¼ cup at a time, until the dough comes together, pulls away completely from the sides of the bowl and is smooth but not too sticky. (You may not need all of the flour.)

5. Turn out the dough onto a lightly floured work surface and knead until smooth, 5 to 10 minutes.

6. Place the dough in a lightly oiled large bowl, turning the dough to coat it evenly with oil. Cover the bowl with a damp towel. Let stand in a warm place until the dough has doubled in size, about 1 hour.

7. Line a large baking sheet with parchment paper. On a lightly floured work surface, punch down the dough to remove the air. With lightly floured hands, pinch off small pieces of the dough and roll them into 1-inch balls. Place the balls on the prepared baking sheet. Cover the baking sheet with a damp towel. Let stand in a warm place until risen and puffy, 20 to 30 minutes.

8. Following the manufacturer's instructions, heat the oil in a deep-fryer to 360°F to 375°F. Alternatively, pour enough oil into a large, heavy-bottomed saucepan to come one-third of the way up the sides of the saucepan. Hook a candy thermometer over the side of the saucepan. Heat the oil over medium heat until the thermometer registers 360°F to 375°F. Line a baking sheet with paper towels.

9. Using a flat spatula or tongs and working in batches, carefully slide the doughnut holes into the hot oil. Do not crowd the deep-fryer or saucepan. If using a saucepan, adjust the heat, if necessary, to maintain the temperature of the oil at a constant 360°F to 375°F.

10. Fry the doughnut holes until the undersides are golden brown, 30 seconds. Carefully flip the doughnut holes and fry until the second side is golden brown, about 30 seconds. Using tongs or a slotted spoon, remove the doughnuts to the prepared baking sheet.

11. Repeat with the remaining dough.

12. For the glaze, whisk the icing sugar, milk and vanilla extract in a medium bowl until smooth.

13. Line another large baking sheet with parchment paper. Using two forks, toss the doughnut holes, one at a time, in the glaze to coat completely. Transfer the doughnut holes to the prepared baking sheet. Immediately sprinkle with pistachios.

Churros with Cajeta and Chocolate Sauce

Long, thin doughnuts called *churros* are popular throughout Latin America. Here they're served with chocolate sauce and *cajeta*, a luscious caramel that's similar to dulce de leche.

Makes 12 churros
Prep time: 30 minutes
Cooking time: 5 to 7 minutes per batch

Chocolate Sauce

½ cup semi-sweet chocolate chips

½ cup whipping cream (35%)

Cinnamon Sugar

½ cup granulated sugar

1 Tbsp ground cinnamon

Churros

1 cup water

½ cup unsalted butter, softened

1 Tbsp granulated sugar

¼ tsp fine sea salt

1 cup all-purpose flour

3 large eggs

Vegetable oil for deep-frying

1 batch of cajeta for serving
(recipe follows)

1. For the chocolate sauce, place the chocolate chips in a heatproof bowl and set aside.

2. In a small saucepan, bring the cream to a boil over medium-high heat. Remove from the heat and immediately pour the cream over the chocolate chips. Let stand for about 1 minute, then stir gently until all of the chocolate chips have melted and the sauce is smooth and glossy. Scrape the sauce into an airtight container and refrigerate until ready to serve. (The sauce can be refrigerated for up to 4 days.)

3. For the cinnamon sugar, whisk together the sugar and cinnamon in a small bowl. Spread the cinnamon sugar on a small rimmed baking sheet. Set aside.

4. For the churros, combine the water, butter, sugar and salt in a medium saucepan. Bring to a boil over medium-high heat, stirring to combine.

5. Turn down the heat to low and, stirring vigorously, add the flour all at once. Cook over low heat, stirring constantly, until the dough looks a little dry, 30 to 45 seconds.

6. Remove from the heat. Add the eggs one at a time, beating well after each addition. Beat the mixture until the dough is smooth. Fit a piping bag with a large open star tip and spoon the dough into it. Set aside.

7. Following the manufacturer's instructions, heat the oil in a deep-fryer to 350°F. Alternatively, pour enough oil into a large, heavy-bottomed saucepan to come one-third of the way up the sides of the saucepan. Hook a candy thermometer over the side of the saucepan. Heat the oil over medium heat until the thermometer registers 350°F. Line a large baking sheet with paper towels.

8. Carefully pipe 4- to 8-inch strips of the dough into the hot oil, using scissors to release the piped dough from the piping bag. Do not crowd the deep-fryer or saucepan. If using a saucepan, adjust the heat, if necessary, to maintain the temperature of the oil at a constant 350°F.

9. Fry the churros, using tongs to straighten them, if necessary, and prevent them sticking to each other, until golden brown, 5 to 7 minutes.

10. Using tongs or a slotted spoon, place the churros in the cinnamon sugar and toss to coat them. Transfer to the prepared baking sheet. Repeat with the remaining dough.

11. Warm the cajeta and chocolate sauce. Serve the churros immediately with cajeta and chocolate sauce for dipping. (The churros are best served the day they're made.)

Cajeta

Makes about 4 cups
Prep time: 15 minutes
Cooking time: about 2 hours

4 cups whole milk (goat's, cow's or a combination)

1 cup granulated sugar

1 vanilla bean OR 1 Tbsp vanilla extract

2 tsp water

¼ tsp baking soda

1. In a medium, heavy-bottomed saucepan, combine the milk and sugar.

2. Using a sharp knife, split the vanilla bean in half lengthwise. Scrape the seeds out into the milk, then drop in the pod. (If using vanilla extract, add it in Step 7.)

3. Cook over medium heat, stirring often, until the sugar has dissolved and the milk comes to a simmer. Remove the saucepan from the heat.

4. In a small bowl, stir together the water and baking soda. Add the baking soda mixture to the milk (it will bubble up and become frothy). When the bubbles subside, return the saucepan to the heat.

5. Turn down the heat to medium-low and bring the mixture back to a simmer. Cook, stirring occasionally, until the mixture thickens to a dip consistency and darkens in colour, 1 to 2 hours. (The longer you cook the mixture, the thicker it will become and the more intense the caramel flavour will be. But note that once the cajeta cools, it becomes even thicker.)

6. Remove the saucepan from the heat. Let the cajeta cool completely. If it's too thick for your liking, stir in a little hot water. If it's too thin, return it to the heat and continue cooking until you have the consistency you want.

7. Discard the vanilla bean. Add the vanilla extract (if using). Scrape the cajeta into an airtight container and refrigerate until ready to serve. Reheat gently until warm before serving. (The cajeta can be refrigerated for up to 1 month.)

Glazed Apple Fritters

We like crisp Granny Smith apples for these tasty fritters, but any tart apple will do. See the photo on page 301.

Makes about 28 fritters
Prep time: 30 minutes
Marinating time: 20 minutes
Cooking time: 4 to 5 minutes per batch

Apples

3 large Granny Smith apples, peeled, cored and cut into ¼-inch pieces

2 Tbsp granulated sugar

1 Tbsp freshly squeezed lemon juice

Batter

2 ¼ cups all-purpose flour

¼ cup firmly packed dark brown sugar

3 Tbsp granulated sugar

2 ½ tsp baking powder

2 tsp ground cinnamon

1 tsp ground ginger

1 tsp fine sea salt

1 ¼ cups sour cream (14%)

2 large eggs

3 Tbsp unsalted butter, melted

Vegetable oil for deep-frying

Glaze

1 ½ cups icing sugar, sifted

¼ cup apple juice

1 tsp ground ginger

1 tsp vanilla extract

1. For the apples, toss together the apples, sugar and lemon juice in a medium, nonreactive bowl. Set aside to marinate for 20 minutes.

2. For the batter, whisk together the flour, both sugars, baking powder, cinnamon, ginger and salt in a large bowl.

3. In a medium bowl, stir together the sour cream, eggs and butter until smooth.

4. Make a well in the flour mixture and add the sour cream mixture all at once. Stir until a smooth batter forms. Stir in the apples and set aside.

5. Following the manufacturer's instructions, heat the oil in a deep-fryer to 375°F. Alternatively, pour enough oil into a large, heavy-bottomed saucepan to come one-third of the way up the sides of the saucepan. Hook a candy thermometer over the side of the saucepan. Heat the oil over medium heat until the thermometer registers 375°F. Line a large baking sheet with paper towels.

6. Drop heaping tablespoonfuls of the batter into the hot oil, frying no more than six at a time. If using a saucepan, adjust the heat, if necessary, to maintain the temperature of the oil at a constant 375°F.

7. Fry the fritters, using tongs to prevent them from sticking to each other, until a deep golden brown, 4 to 5 minutes, flipping the fritters halfway through.

8. Using tongs or a slotted spoon, remove the fritters to the prepared baking sheet. Repeat with the remaining batter.

9. For the glaze, in a medium bowl, stir together the icing sugar, apple juice, ginger and vanilla extract until smooth.

10. Using two forks, dip each fritter into the glaze to coat completely. As each fritter is coated, lift it out with a fork, letting any excess glaze drip off. Place each fritter on a wire rack. Let the glaze dry slightly, then serve immediately.

PUDDINGS, CUSTARDS & SAUCES

Very Vanilla Pudding

Sometimes simplicity is best, and this comforting vanilla pudding is just that. But, if you want to make it a little bit special, layer the pudding—as we did for the photograph—with crushed chocolate wafer cookies, then garnish with softly whipped cream.

Makes 6 servings
Prep time: 15 minutes
Cooking time: about 15 minutes
Chilling time: at least 3 hours

1 vanilla bean

½ cup granulated sugar

¼ cup cornstarch

¼ tsp fine sea salt

2 ⅔ cups whole milk

1 large egg

BAKING DAY SECRETS

Sometimes, when you're cooking puddings, the mixture might start to curdle. If it does, simply scrape it into a food processor fitted with the steel blade or a blender, then process or blend until smooth.

1. Using a sharp knife, slit the vanilla bean lengthwise. Using the tip of the knife, scrape the seeds out into a large bowl. Reserve the pod.

2. Add the sugar, cornstarch and salt to the vanilla seeds and whisk well to combine. Whisk in ⅓ cup of the milk until smooth. Beat in the egg.

3. In a medium saucepan, combine the remaining 2 ⅓ cups of milk and the vanilla pod. Bring to a boil over medium-high heat.

4. Gradually whisk a little of the hot milk into the sugar mixture. Slowly add the remaining hot milk, whisking constantly, until the mixture is smooth.

5. Return the milk mixture to the saucepan. Cook over medium heat, whisking constantly, until the mixture thickens and is the consistency of mayonnaise, about 10 minutes. Don't worry if it starts to bubble, just turn down the heat a little and keep whisking.

6. Remove from the heat and discard the vanilla bean. (For a silky-smooth pudding, pour it through a fine-mesh sieve.) Spoon the pudding into six individual dishes or a large serving bowl. Lay a piece of plastic wrap directly on the surface of the puddings, then chill for at least 3 hours, or overnight. (The puddings can be covered and refrigerated for up to 3 days.)

Oh-So-Chocolatey Pudding

One taste is all it takes: this is the only chocolate pudding recipe you'll ever need. It's rich and creamy, and you only have to dirty one saucepan to make it happen.

Makes 6 servings
Prep time: 15 minutes
Cooking time: about 20 minutes
Chilling time: at least 3 hours

½ cup granulated sugar

¼ cup cornstarch

Pinch of fine sea salt

3 cups whole milk

6 oz semi-sweet or dark chocolate, coarsely chopped, OR
1 cup semi-sweet chocolate
chips

1 tsp vanilla extract

Whipped cream and crumbled
chocolate wafer cookies for
garnish (optional)

1. In a medium saucepan, whisk together the sugar, cornstarch and salt. Whisk in just enough of the milk to form a smooth paste. Whisk in the remaining milk until the mixture is smooth.

2. Cook over medium heat, whisking constantly, until the mixture thickens and is the consistency of mayonnaise, about 10 minutes. Don't worry if it starts to bubble, just turn down the heat a little and keep whisking.

3. Turn down the heat to low and add the chocolate. Cook, stirring often, until the chocolate has melted and the mixture is quite thick, about 5 minutes. Remove from the heat and stir in the vanilla extract. (For a silky-smooth pudding, pour it through a fine-mesh sieve.)

4. Spoon the pudding into six individual dishes or a large serving bowl. Lay a piece of plastic wrap directly on the surface of the puddings, then chill for at least 3 hours, or overnight. (The ungarnished puddings can be covered and refrigerated for up to 3 days.) Garnish the puddings with whipped cream and crumbled cookies (if using).

CHANGE IT UP

Chocolate Parfait: Layer the pudding with whipped cream and crumbled chocolate wafers or chocolate sandwich cookies.

Chocolate Strawberry Trifle: Layer the pudding with chunks of Simple Chocolate Cake (page 104) and sliced strawberries that have been tossed with a little granulated sugar.

Velvety Butterscotch Pudding

I t's hard to believe such a simple pudding can taste so deca-dent, but this butterscotch treat is a real crowd-pleaser. The whisky helps boost the butterscotch flavour, but you can omit it if you prefer.

Makes 6 servings

Prep time: 15 minutes

Cooking time: about 12 minutes

Chilling time: at least 3 hours

¼ cup unsalted butter, softened

1 cup firmly packed dark brown sugar

3 Tbsp cornstarch

½ tsp fine sea salt

2 ½ cups whole milk

2 large eggs

2 tsp whisky (optional)

1 tsp vanilla extract

Whipped cream and toasted chopped pecans for garnish (optional)

CHANGE IT UP

Butterscotch Parfait: Layer the pudding with chopped pecans or crushed ginger snaps, then garnish with softly whipped cream.

1. Place the butter in a large bowl. Set aside.

2. In another large bowl, whisk together the sugar, cornstarch and salt. Whisk in ¼ cup of the milk. Whisk in the eggs until smooth.

3. In a large saucepan, bring the remaining 2 ¼ cups of milk to a boil. Gradually whisk a little of the hot milk into the sugar mixture. Slowly add the remaining hot milk, whisking constantly, until the mixture is smooth.

4. Return the milk mixture to the saucepan. Cook over medium heat, whisking constantly, until the mixture thickens and is the consistency of mayonnaise, about 10 minutes. Don't worry if it starts to bubble, just turn down the heat a little and keep whisking.

5. Remove from the heat and whisk in the whisky (if using) and vanilla extract. (For a silky-smooth pudding, pour it through a fine-mesh sieve.)

6. Pour the milk mixture into the bowl with butter. Whisk until the butter melts.

7. Spoon the pudding into six individual dishes or a large serving bowl. Lay a piece of plastic wrap directly on the surface of the puddings, then chill for at least 3 hours, or overnight. (The ungarnished puddings can be covered and refrigerated for up to 3 days.) Garnish the puddings with whipped cream and chopped pecans (if using).

Decadent Chocolate Mousse

This luscious chocolate mousse has subtle notes of coffee and whisky. It's the perfect indulgence for Valentine's Day or any other special occasion. For a chocolate-peanut version, layer the mousse with chopped salted peanuts.

Makes 4 servings

Prep time: 20 minutes

Cooking time: about 7 minutes

Chilling time: at least 4 hours

Mousse

6 oz semi-sweet chocolate, coarsely chopped

¾ cup unsalted butter, softened

¼ cup brewed black coffee

4 large egg yolks

⅔ cup granulated sugar

2 Tbsp whisky (optional)

1 Tbsp water

Whipped cream and chocolate shavings (see sidebar) for garnish

Egg Whites

4 large egg whites

Pinch of fine sea salt

1 Tbsp granulated sugar

½ tsp vanilla extract

1. For the mousse, combine the chocolate, butter and coffee in a medium bowl set over a saucepan of hot, not boiling, water. Heat, stirring occasionally, until smooth. Remove from the heat and set aside.

2. Fill a large bowl with ice water and set aside.

3. In another medium bowl set over a saucepan of simmering water, whisk together the egg yolks, sugar, whisky (if using) and water until the mixture is light and begins to thicken slightly, 3 to 5 minutes.

4. Remove from the heat and set the bowl containing the egg yolk mixture in the bowl of ice water. Continue whisking until the egg yolk mixture is cooled and thickened.

5. Fold the chocolate mixture into the cooled egg yolk mixture. Set aside.

6. For the egg whites, in a large bowl and with clean beaters, beat the egg whites and salt until frothy. Beat in the sugar until stiff peaks form. Beat in the vanilla extract.

7. Using a rubber spatula, fold half of the egg whites into the mousse. Fold in the remaining egg whites just until incorporated. Do not overmix or the mousse will not be as light as it should be.

8. Spoon the mousse into four individual dishes or a large serving bowl. Chill for at least 4 hours, or overnight. (The ungarnished mousse can be covered and refrigerated for up to 3 days.) Serve garnished with whipped cream and chocolate shavings.

BAKING DAY SECRETS

To make chocolate shavings, use a wide vegetable peeler to pare shavings from a block of room-temperature chocolate.

Cinnamon Rice Pudding

Rice pudding is everything you could ever want on a chilly day: it's rich, creamy and spiced with the warming flavour of cinnamon. This recipe is oh-so-easy, too.

Makes 4 to 6 servings
Prep time: 15 minutes
Cooking time: about 1 hour
Chilling time: at least 3 hours
(optional)

½ cup short-grain white rice (such as Arborio, pearl or Valencia)

1 ½ cups water

1 cinnamon stick (3 inches)

4 cups whole milk

½ cup granulated sugar

1 tsp vanilla extract

Ground cinnamon or freshly grated nutmeg for garnish

1. Rinse the rice well under cold, running water, then drain well.

2. In a large, heavy-bottomed saucepan, combine the rice, water and cinnamon stick. Bring to a boil over medium heat. Turn down the heat to low, then simmer, covered, until all the water has been absorbed, about 15 minutes.

3. Stir in the milk, sugar and vanilla extract. Bring to a simmer over medium heat. Turn down the heat to low, then cook, uncovered and stirring occasionally, until the pudding is thick and creamy, about 45 minutes. Be sure to scrape the bottom of the saucepan as you stir to ensure the pudding doesn't burn.

4. Remove from the heat. Spoon the pudding into four to six individual dishes or a large serving bowl. Serve warm or refrigerate for at least 3 hours, or overnight, until chilled. (The puddings can be covered and refrigerated for up to 3 days.) Sprinkle with cinnamon or nutmeg before serving.

CHANGE IT UP

For a flavour twist, add the finely grated zest of 1 lemon or 1 orange when you add the vanilla extract.

For a vegan rice pudding, use 2 cups almond milk and 2 cups unsweetened coconut milk instead of regular milk.

Chai-Spiced Tapioca Pudding

You can customize this exotic-tasting pudding by substituting other spices to create different chai blends— whole black peppercorns, whole cloves and star anise are all great additions.

Makes 6 servings
Prep time: 20 minutes
Standing time: 25 minutes
Cooking time: about 15 minutes
Chilling time: at least 1 hour

1 tsp whole green cardamom pods

1 cup water

1 plain black tea bag

1 cinnamon stick (3 inches)

⅓ cup small pearl tapioca

2 large eggs

1 ½ cups whole or 2% milk

1 cup whipping cream (35%)

½ cup granulated sugar

¼ tsp ground ginger

¼ tsp freshly grated nutmeg

Pinch of fine sea salt

1 large ripe mango, peeled, pitted and cut into ½-inch pieces

Whipped cream for serving (optional)

1. Using the flat side of a large knife or the back of a spoon, crush the cardamom pods slightly. Place them in a tea ball, or wrap them in a small piece of cheesecloth and secure it with kitchen twine.

2. In a medium saucepan, bring the water to a boil over medium-high heat. Remove from the heat and add the cardamom pods, tea bag and cinnamon stick. Let steep for 5 minutes.

3. Discard the tea bag. Add the tapioca to the water. Let stand for 20 minutes.

4. Meanwhile, whisk the eggs well in a medium bowl. Set aside.

5. Add the milk, cream, sugar, ginger, nutmeg and salt to the saucepan containing the tapioca. Bring to a gentle boil over medium-low heat, stirring constantly.

6. Turn down the heat to low. Cook, stirring gently, until the mixture thickens and the tapioca pearls swell and become translucent, 8 to 10 minutes. Discard the cardamom and cinnamon stick.

7. Stir a few tablespoonfuls of the hot tapioca mixture into the eggs to temper them, then add the egg mixture to the saucepan. Cook over low heat, stirring constantly, for 3 minutes.

8. Remove from the heat. Spoon the pudding into six individual glasses or a large serving bowl. Lay a piece of plastic wrap directly on the surface of the puddings, then chill for at least 1 hour, or overnight. (The ungarnished puddings can be covered and refrigerated for up to 3 days.) Top the puddings with the mango and serve with whipped cream (if using).

Pouding Chômeur

The name of this classic Québécois recipe translates as "poor man's pudding" or "unemployment pudding." Created during the Depression, it's a simple dessert that uses affordable, everyday ingredients. In spite of its humble origins, this is one rich and decadent dessert that we just can't get enough of. As the pudding bakes, the syrup sinks to the bottom of the dish, creating a rich, gooey sauce.

Makes 8 to 12 servings
Prep time: 25 minutes
Cooking time: about 45 minutes

Cake

1 ¾ cups all-purpose flour

1 ½ tsp baking powder

½ tsp fine sea salt

1 cup granulated sugar

2 Tbsp unsalted butter, softened

1 large egg

¾ cup whole milk

Syrup

2 cups firmly packed dark brown sugar

2 cups whipping cream (35%), whole milk or water, OR a mixture (see sidebar)

¼ cup unsalted butter, softened

1 tsp vanilla extract

Vanilla ice cream, whipped cream or Greek yogurt for serving (optional)

1. Preheat the oven to 350°F. Grease a 10-cup soufflé or baking dish. Set aside.

2. For the cake, whisk together the flour, baking powder and salt in a medium bowl. Set aside.

3. In a large bowl, cream together the sugar and butter until pale and fluffy. Beat in the egg until well combined.

4. Add the flour mixture to the sugar mixture alternately with the milk, making three additions of flour and two of milk, and beginning and ending with the flour. Stir until well combined.

5. Scrape the batter into the prepared dish, spreading it evenly with an offset spatula. Set aside.

6. For the syrup, whisk together the sugar and the water, milk and/or cream in a medium saucepan. Add the butter and vanilla extract. Bring to a boil over medium-high heat, stirring just until the sugar has dissolved.

7. Remove from the heat and gently pour the syrup over the cake batter to cover it completely.

8. Bake until a wooden skewer inserted in the centre of the cake comes out clean, 30 to 40 minutes. Serve warm or at room temperature, with vanilla ice cream, whipped cream or Greek yogurt (if using). (Leftovers can be covered and refrigerated for up to 3 days.)

CHANGE IT UP

For a more traditional French-Canadian flavour, use 1 ½ cups of brown sugar and 1 ½ cups of cream, milk and/or water in the syrup and add ½ cup maple syrup.

Old-Fashioned Applesauce

S erve this thick applesauce with roast pork or potato latkes, or call it apple compote and serve it as a refreshing dessert. It's a great way to use up any apples that are starting to go soft.

Makes about 1 cup
Prep time: 10 minutes
Cooking time: about 10 minutes

2 Granny Smith apples, cored and chopped, but not peeled

½ cup water

¼ cup granulated sugar

2 tsp freshly squeezed lemon juice

BAKING DAY SECRETS

We love the tart flavour of Granny Smiths, but feel free to use your favourite apple variety in this recipe. Each type of apple has its own flavour profile, making applesauce different every time you switch varieties.

1. In a medium saucepan, stir together the apples, water, sugar and lemon juice. Bring to a simmer over medium heat. Cook, covered, until the apples are very tender, about 8 minutes.

2. Transfer the apple mixture to a food processor fitted with the steel blade or a blender. Process or blend until smooth.

3. Rub the purée through a fine-mesh sieve to remove the apple peel and make the sauce completely smooth. (The applesauce can be refrigerated in an airtight container—preferably a glass one—for up to 1 week.)

Lemon Berry Trifle

Trifle is a decadent, old-fashioned dessert made with layers of cream, cake, custard and fruit. Our version uses lemon curd, instead of custard, and fresh berries for the fruit.

Makes 6 to 8 servings
Prep time: 20 minutes
Chilling time: at least 4 hours

4 cups mixed fresh hulled whole strawberries and raspberries

2 ½ cups whipping cream (35%)

¼ cup granulated sugar

10 cups 1-inch cubes Lovely Vanilla Layer Cake (page 106) or pound cake

1 cup Zesty Lemon Curd (recipe follows)

1. Slice the strawberries, but leave the raspberries whole. In a medium bowl, gently toss the berries together.

2. In a medium bowl and using an electric mixer, whip the cream with the sugar until it holds stiff peaks.

3. In the base of a 12-cup glass serving bowl, arrange half of the cake. Top with half of the berries. Spread half of the lemon curd over the berries, then top with half of the whipped cream. Repeat the layers with the remaining ingredients.

4. Serve immediately, or cover with plastic wrap and refrigerate for at least 4 hours. (The trifle can be stored in the fridge for up to 2 days.)

CHANGE IT UP

Trifles are wonderfully versatile. Switch up the ingredients to create a whole new flavour profile.

Cookies 'n' Cream Trifle: Omit the lemon curd and berries, and layer cubes of chocolate cake with crushed chocolate wafers and whipped cream.

Traditional Trifle: Follow the recipe for Lemon Berry Trifle, but drizzle the first layer of cake cubes with 1 tablespoonful of sherry and 1 tablespoonful of cognac. Let stand for 15 minutes. Spoon 3 tablespoonfuls of strawberry jam over the cake cubes, then proceed with the recipe.

Zesty Lemon Curd

Makes about 1 cup
Prep time: 15 minutes
Cooking time: 10 to 15 minutes
Cooling time: about 40 minutes

¼ cup unsalted butter, softened

1 cup granulated sugar

⅔ cup freshly squeezed lemon juice (about 4 lemons)

2 large eggs

2 large egg yolks

BAKING DAY SECRETS

For an easy dessert in double-quick time, layer the lemon curd in individual glass dishes with Very Vanilla Pudding (page 282) and graham cracker crumbs.

1. Place the butter in a large bowl and set a fine-mesh sieve over the bowl. Set aside.

2. In a large, heavy-bottomed, nonreactive saucepan, whisk together the sugar, lemon juice, eggs and egg yolks. Cook over medium heat, whisking constantly, until the mixture just begins to thicken, 10 to 15 minutes. (Do not let the mixture boil, or the eggs will scramble.)

3. Remove from the heat, then pour the lemon mixture through the sieve into the bowl of butter.

4. Remove the sieve. Stir the lemon mixture until the butter has completely melted. Let the lemon curd cool at room temperature for about 40 minutes before spooning it into a clean jar or other airtight container. (The lemon curd can be refrigerated for up to 1 week.)

Bellissimo Tiramisu

This decidedly grown-up dessert, or its non-alcoholic version (see sidebar page 293), is delectable served with shots of espresso. For best results, use good-quality mascarpone cheese to ensure the dessert keeps its shape.

Makes 6 to 8 servings
Prep time: 40 minutes
Cooking time: about 6 minutes
Chilling time: at least 4 hours, 20 minutes

4 large egg yolks

½ cup granulated sugar

⅓ cup water

1 carton (1 lb/500 g) mascarpone cheese, at room temperature

½ cup whipping cream (35%)

1 tsp vanilla extract

1 ½ cups hot brewed black coffee

1 Tbsp instant espresso powder

¼ cup Marsala (see sidebar)

¼ cup dark rum

24 ladyfinger cookies

½ cup grated or finely chopped bittersweet or dark chocolate

2 Tbsp unsweetened cocoa powder for dusting

1. Put a medium bowl in the freezer to chill. In a large bowl and using an electric mixer, beat the egg yolks until pale.

2. In a small, heavy saucepan, combine the sugar and water. Hook a candy thermometer over the side of the saucepan. Cook the sugar mixture, without stirring, until the candy thermometer registers 240°F, about 6 minutes. (If you don't have a candy thermometer, drop a little of the mixture into a bowl of cold water. If it forms a soft ball, it's ready.)

3. With the mixer running on medium-high speed, gradually pour the hot sugar mixture into the beaten yolks. When all the syrup has been added, increase the speed to high. Beat until the mixture has doubled in volume and is cool to the touch, about 5 minutes. Set aside.

4. In a large bowl and using a rubber spatula, cream the mascarpone until smooth, about 1 minute.

5. Remove the chilled bowl from the freezer. Add the cream and vanilla and, using an electric mixer, beat until stiff peaks form.

6. Fold a small amount of the mascarpone into the egg yolk mixture. Fold all the egg yolk mixture back into the mascarpone. Fold in the whipped cream. Set aside in the fridge until ready to use.

7. In a medium bowl, stir together the coffee and instant espresso powder until the powder has dissolved. Stir in the Marsala and rum. Pour the coffee mixture into a shallow dish and let cool to room temperature, about 20 minutes.

8. To assemble the tiramisu, spoon 3 or 4 tablespoonfuls of the mascarpone mixture over the base of a 9-inch square glass baking dish or pan. (If using a metal pan, line the base and sides with parchment paper, leaving an overhang of paper on two facing sides to help you remove the tiramisu from the pan.)

9. One at a time, quickly immerse half of the ladyfingers in the coffee mixture, being careful not to soak them (or the dessert will be soggy). Arrange the dipped ladyfingers, side by side, over the mascarpone layer, trimming the cookies, if necessary, to fit the dish. Alternatively, arrange half of the ladyfingers in a single layer over the mascarpone. Brush generously with the coffee mixture.

10. Spoon half of the remaining mascarpone over the ladyfingers. Using an offset spatula, smooth the mixture evenly over the cookies, right to the edges of the dish. Sprinkle generously with half of the grated chocolate.

11. Dip the remaining ladyfingers in the coffee mixture and arrange on top of the mascarpone, trimming to fit. Top the ladyfingers with half of the remaining mascarpone, spreading right to the edges of the dish.

12. Fit a piping bag with a round tip and spoon the remaining mascarpone mixture into it. Pipe lines or kisses in rows over the tiramisu. Chill the tiramisu in the fridge for at least 4 hours, or preferably overnight.

13. When ready to serve, generously dust the surface of the tiramisu with cocoa powder, then sprinkle with the remaining chocolate.

14. To serve, spoon or cut portions straight from the dish, if using a glass dish. If using a metal pan, use the parchment paper overhang to carefully lift the tiramisu from the pan to a serving plate. Cut into portions to serve.

CHANGE IT UP

For an alcohol-free tiramisu, omit the Marsala and rum and stir ¼ cup firmly packed dark brown or demerara-style sugar into the hot coffee until dissolved.

For individual servings of tiramisu, spoon about 2 tablespoonfuls of the mascarpone mixture into each of 6 to 8 individual dishes. Layer the ladyfingers, mascarpone and chocolate in the dishes, cutting the dipped ladyfingers into thirds or quarters to fit into the dishes. Garnish as for the large tiramisu.

BAKING DAY SECRETS

Marsala is a dessert wine produced in Sicily. If you can't find it, substitute brandy, or a coffee, amaretto or Irish cream liqueur.

Québécois Dumplings
with Maple Caramel

Known as *grand-pères* in their native Quebec, these fluffy dumplings in a rich syrup are a comforting dessert on a cold winter's day.

Makes 6 to 8 servings
Prep time: 20 minutes
Cooking time: about 25 minutes

Maple-Caramel Syrup

1 ¼ cups water

1 cup maple syrup

¾ cup lightly packed dark brown sugar

½ tsp fine sea salt

Dumplings

2 cups all-purpose flour

¼ cup granulated sugar

1 Tbsp baking powder

½ tsp fine sea salt

¼ cup unsalted butter, frozen

1 cup whole milk

1 tsp vanilla extract

Chopped toasted almonds, hazelnuts or pecans for garnish

Vanilla ice cream for serving (optional)

1. For the maple-caramel syrup, stir together the water, maple syrup, brown sugar and salt in a large saucepan. Cook over medium heat, stirring often, until the sugar has dissolved and the mixture comes to a boil. Remove from the heat and set aside.

2. For the dumplings, whisk together the flour, sugar, baking powder and salt in a large bowl.

3. Using the large holes on a box grater, grate the frozen butter into the flour mixture. Toss to coat the butter with the flour mixture. Make a well in the centre of the flour mixture.

4. In a measuring cup or jug, stir together the milk and vanilla extract. Pour the milk into the well in the flour mixture. Using a wooden spoon or spatula, stir just until the dry ingredients are moistened. Do not overmix.

5. Return the saucepan containing the syrup to medium heat and bring the syrup to a boil.

6. Have ready a bowl of cold water. Using a 2-tablespoonful ice cream scoop, scoop the dumpling batter into the boiling syrup, holding the scoop close to the surface of the syrup before releasing the batter. Dip the scoop into the bowl of water before scooping more batter.

7. When all the batter has been scooped into the syrup, turn down the heat to low. Simmer the syrup, covered, until the dumplings are tender and cooked through, 15 to 20 minutes.

8. Using a slotted spoon, divide the dumplings among six to eight shallow dessert bowls. Spoon the syrup over the dumplings and sprinkle with nuts. Serve immediately with vanilla ice cream (if using).

CHANGE IT UP

Spice up the dumplings by adding ½ teaspoonful of ground cinnamon to the flour mixture.

Classic Crème Brûlée

Perfect crème brûlées are super creamy with crisp amber tops—like these! A butane kitchen torch works best for caramelizing the sugar, but if you don't have one, broil the sugar-topped crème brûlées as close to the element as possible until the sugar caramelizes.

Makes 4 servings
Prep time: 20 minutes
Cooking time: about 50 minutes
Chilling time: at least 2 hours

6 large egg yolks

¼ cup granulated sugar

¾ tsp vanilla extract

1 ½ cups whipping cream (35%)

Pinch of fine sea salt

Additional granulated sugar
   for topping

1. Preheat the oven to 300°F. In a large bowl, whisk the egg yolks well. Add the sugar, then whisk really vigorously. (Whisking hard allows the sugar crystals to break down the eggs and results in extra-creamy crème brûlées.)

2. Add the vanilla extract and continue to whisk vigorously.

3. Add the cream to the egg mixture and stir in gently until the ingredients are combined. Add the salt and stir gently. (Gentle stirring at this point minimizes the number of bubbles in the crème brûlées.)

4. Strain the egg mixture through a fine-mesh sieve into a pitcher. Put four ¾-cup ramekins or custard cups in a shallow roasting pan. Pour the egg mixture into the ramekins.

5. Pull the oven rack partway out of the oven and put the roasting pan containing the ramekins on the rack. Pour hot, not boiling, water into the roasting pan to come halfway up the sides of the ramekins. Carefully slide the oven rack back into the oven.

6. Bake until the custards are set around the edges but not in the centres, about 50 minutes. Carefully remove the roasting pan from the oven.

7. Leave the custards in the roasting pan until the ramekins are cool enough to handle. Remove the ramekins from the roasting pan and let cool completely on a wire rack. Cover each

ramekin with plastic wrap, then refrigerate for at least 2 hours, or overnight.

8. Sprinkle about 1 teaspoonful of additional sugar over each custard to cover the surface completely.

9. Following the manufacturer's instructions, light a butane kitchen torch. (See sidebar on page 213 if you don't have a butane torch.) Using small, circular motions, torch the sugar on top of each custard so it melts gently without darkening too quickly (or catching fire!). If the sugar darkens too quickly, hold the torch further away; if the sugar isn't darkening, hold the torch closer to it. Refrigerate the crème brûlées, uncovered, for 5 minutes before serving.

Vanilla Panna Cotta
with Grilled Peaches

Panna cotta—the name means "cooked cream"—is a decadent Italian dessert that's a cinch to make. Our version, with its hint of bourbon, is the perfect summer dessert for an adult party. With juicy grilled peaches on the side, it's sure to delight your guests.

Makes 6 servings
Prep time: 20 minutes
Standing time: 5 to 10 minutes
Cooking time: about 20 minutes
Chilling time: at least 2 hours

Vanilla Panna Cotta

⅓ cup cold water

4 ½ tsp unflavoured powdered gelatin

4 cups whipping cream (35%) or half-and-half cream (10%)

½ cup granulated sugar

1 vanilla bean

2 tsp bourbon (optional)

Grilled Peaches

6 peaches, pitted and cut into 1-inch pieces

½ cup granulated sugar

1 tsp ground cinnamon

Mint sprigs for garnish

1. For the vanilla panna cotta, pour the water into a medium bowl. Sprinkle the gelatin over the water and let stand until puffy, 5 to 10 minutes.

2. In a medium saucepan, combine the cream and sugar. Using a sharp knife, slit the vanilla bean lengthwise. Using the tip of the knife, scrape the seeds out into the saucepan. Drop in the vanilla pod.

3. Stir the cream mixture over medium heat until the sugar has dissolved. Remove from the heat.

4. Strain the hot cream into the bowl containing the gelatin. Stir until the gelatin has completely dissolved. Stir in the bourbon (if using). Discard the vanilla pod.

5. Pour the cream mixture into six individual glasses or ¾-cup ramekins or custard cups. Refrigerate, uncovered, until set, at least 2 hours.

6. For the grilled peaches, preheat the barbecue to medium. In a medium bowl, toss the peaches with the sugar and cinnamon, making sure all the peach pieces are evenly coated.

7. Cut a piece of heavy-duty foil large enough to enclose the peaches. Tip the peaches out onto the foil and crimp the edges together tightly to enclose them completely. Place the foil package on the warming shelf of the barbecue. Grill, turning the package often, until the peaches are bubbly and warm, about 10 minutes.

8. Remove the foil package from the grill and open it up. Let the peaches cool to room temperature.

9. Serve the panna cottas topped with the grilled peaches. Garnish with mint.

BAKING DAY SECRETS

If you want to test your presentation skills, pour the cream mixture into lightly oiled tea cups or custard cups. Once the panna cottas are set, run a slim knife around the edges of each one, then turn them out onto individual dessert plates. Spoon the grilled peaches over the panna cottas and garnish with mint.

Delectable Caramel Sauce

This easy sauce goes with practically anything. Try it with Flourless Chocolate-Hazelnut Cake (page 120), drizzled over bananas or grilled peaches, or simply as a topping for vanilla or chocolate ice cream.

Makes about 1 ¾ cups
Prep time: 10 minutes
Cooking time: 25 minutes

1 ¼ cups granulated sugar

¼ cup water

½ tsp apple cider vinegar or freshly squeezed lemon juice

1 ¼ cups whipping cream (35%)

2 tsp vanilla extract

½ tsp fine sea salt

¼ cup unsalted butter, softened

1. Have ready a clean pastry brush and a small bowl of cold water.

2. Put the sugar in a medium, heavy-bottomed saucepan. Stir in the water and vinegar so the sugar is completely moistened.

3. Cook over medium heat, stirring often, until the sugar has dissolved and the mixture comes to a boil. Stop stirring.

4. Dip the pastry brush in the water and brush down the sides of the saucepan to dislodge any

sugar crystals. Boil until the mixture begins to turn a caramel colour, 8 to 10 minutes, brushing down the sides of the saucepan as necessary. Do not stir.

5. Meanwhile, stir together the cream, vanilla extract and salt in a small saucepan. Bring to a simmer over medium heat. Remove from the heat and set aside.

6. Once the sugar mixture begins to darken, gently swirl the saucepan a few times to even out the colour. Cook until the

mixture is deep amber (350°F on a candy thermometer), about 10 minutes.

7. Remove from the heat and, stirring constantly, carefully pour in hot cream (the mixture will bubble up). Return the saucepan to medium-low heat. Cook, stirring, until smooth.

8. Remove from the heat and stir in the butter until it melts. Let the caramel sauce cool slightly before serving. (The sauce can be refrigerated in an airtight container for up to 1 month.)

CHANGE IT UP

You'll love how easy it is to tweak Delectable Caramel Sauce. Try these variations.

Butterscotch Sauce: Replace the granulated sugar with firmly packed dark brown sugar.

Chocolate Caramel Sauce: After adding the butter, stir in ½ cup chopped dark chocolate until it melts (return the saucepan to low heat if necessary).

Whisky Caramel Sauce: Replace 2 tablespoons of the cream with 2 tablespoons of whisky.

Mixed Berry Coulis

Make this lovely fruit sauce with fresh berries in the summer or with thawed and drained frozen berries the rest of the year. It's tasty over ice cream, with your favourite pudding or on pancakes. We also love it alongside slices of our Lemon–White Chocolate Cheesecake Mousse Cake (page 116).

Makes about 1 ½ cups
Prep time: 10 minutes
Cooking time: about 2 minutes

2 cups mixed berries, fresh or thawed and drained

⅓ cup granulated sugar (or more to taste; see sidebar)

3 Tbsp water

Pinch of fine sea salt

1 Tbsp freshly squeezed lemon juice

1. In a medium saucepan, combine the berries, ⅓ cup sugar, water and salt. Bring to a simmer over medium heat, then simmer for 1 minute.

2. Remove from the heat and let cool slightly. In a food processor fitted with the steel blade or a blender, process or blend the fruit mixture until smooth.

3. Rub the fruit purée through a fine-mesh sieve into a medium bowl, pressing firmly down with a flexible spatula to extract as much liquid as possible. Discard the pulp in the sieve.

4. Stir the lemon juice into the berry coulis. Taste and add more sugar, if necessary. (The coulis can be refrigerated in an airtight container for up to 4 days.)

BAKING DAY SECRETS

You may need to add a little more sugar to the finished coulis, depending on the types of berries you use. Sweet berries, like blueberries and strawberries, will likely not need extra sugar, whereas more tart ones, such as raspberries and blackberries, may need a little.

Crème Anglaise

This rich, creamy custard is delectable with all kinds of desserts and cakes. Try it drizzled over Vanilla-Chocolate Marble Slab Cake (page 114) or Glazed Apple Fritters (photo opposite, recipe page 280).

Makes about 1 ½ cups
Prep time: 10 minutes
Cooking time: 8 minutes

4 large egg yolks

⅓ cup granulated sugar

1 cup whole milk

½ cup whipping cream (35%)

2 tsp vanilla extract

BAKING DAY SECRETS

Make sure to pour the hot milk mixture very slowly into the egg mixture. Add it too quickly and you may end up with scrambled eggs!

1. In a medium bowl, whisk together the egg yolks and sugar until slightly thickened, about 3 minutes.

2. In a medium, heavy-bottomed saucepan, combine the milk and cream. Stirring gently, bring just to a simmer over medium heat (bubbles will form around the edge, with a few forming in the centre).

3. Whisking continuously, slowly pour the hot milk mixture into the egg mixture. After the first few tablespoonfuls have been added, the milk mixture can be added more quickly.

4. Once all the milk has been added, pour the custard back into the saucepan. Cook, stirring continuously, over medium-low heat, until the mixture coats the back of a spoon and holds a clear trail when you run a finger through it, 4 to 5 minutes (an instant-read thermometer will read 175°F).

5. Immediately pour the custard through a fine-mesh sieve into a clean bowl. Stir in the vanilla extract. Serve immediately. (Alternatively, lay a piece of plastic wrap directly on the surface of the custard and let cool completely. It can be refrigerated in this way for up to 3 days.)

Glazed Apple Fritters
(recipe page 280)

Easy Chocolate Syrup

This chocolate syrup may be simple, but it's full of flavour. The perfect topping for ice cream, it's a made-in-heaven sensation poured over a slice of chocolate cake, such as Simple Chocolate Cake (page 104) or Chocolate Genoise Cake (page 119). Try it as a dip with Churros with Cajeta (page 278).

Makes 1 ½ cups
Prep time: 5 minutes
Cooking time: about 5 minutes

1 ½ cups granulated sugar

¾ cup unsweetened cocoa powder

Pinch of fine sea salt

1 cup water

1 tsp vanilla extract

1. In a small saucepan, gently whisk together the sugar, cocoa powder and salt. Whisk in the water until the mixture is smooth.

2. Bring to a boil over medium-high heat, whisking occasionally. Turn down the heat to medium-low. Cook, whisking constantly, for 3 minutes.

3. Remove from the heat and whisk in the vanilla extract. Let cool completely. (The syrup can be refrigerated in an airtight container for up to 1 month.)

CANDIES

Chocolate Fudge

Our favourite holiday gifts are always homemade, and this traditional chocolate fudge is no exception. It's a must for the chocoholic on your list.

Makes 64 pieces
Prep time: about 45 minutes
Cooking time: about 20 minutes
Chilling time: at least 6 hours

2 ½ cups granulated sugar

1 cup whole milk

½ cup unsweetened cocoa powder

¼ cup unsalted butter, softened

1 tsp vanilla extract

½ cup chopped white chocolate

¼ cup chopped unblanched almonds, toasted

1. Line the base and sides of an 8-inch square baking pan with parchment paper, leaving an overhang of paper on two facing sides. (This will help you remove the fudge from the pan.) Set aside.

2. In a medium saucepan, whisk together the sugar, milk and cocoa. Bring to a boil over medium-high heat, whisking constantly.

3. Turn down the heat to medium. Hook a candy thermometer over the side of the saucepan. Cook the sugar mixture, without stirring, until the candy thermometer registers 235°F, about 20 minutes. (If you don't have a candy thermometer, drop a little of the mixture into a bowl of cold water. If it forms a soft ball, it's ready.)

4. Immediately remove the saucepan from the heat and stir in the butter and vanilla extract.

5. Pour the mixture into a heatproof bowl and let cool, without stirring, until the candy thermometer registers 120°F.

6. Using a wooden spoon, beat the fudge until it loses its sheen and starts to thicken, 5 to 8 minutes. Scrape the fudge into the prepared pan, smooth the top level with an offset spatula and let cool completely. Refrigerate for at least 6 hours.

7. Melt the chocolate in a heatproof bowl set over a saucepan of hot, not boiling, water. Remove from the heat and stir until smooth.

8. Spread the chocolate evenly over the fudge in the pan. Sprinkle with almonds. Set aside until the chocolate has set.

9. Using the parchment paper overhang, remove the fudge from the pan to a cutting board. Cut into 1-inch squares. (The fudge can be refrigerated in an airtight container for up to 1 week, or frozen for up to 2 months.)

CHANGE IT UP

Substitute sprinkles or crushed candy canes for the almonds.

Sucre à la Crème

The ingredient list for this traditional French-Canadian fudge may be simple, but the taste is amazing. Smooth and creamy with notes of caramel, this is a melt-in-the mouth decadent treat.

Makes 24 pieces
Prep time: 15 minutes
Cooking time: about 8 minutes
Chilling time: 30 minutes

1 cup granulated sugar

1 cup lightly packed golden yellow sugar

1 cup whipping cream (35%)

1 Tbsp unsalted butter, softened

1 tsp vanilla extract

BAKING DAY SECRETS

Be sure to use an electric mixer when beating the fudge. This incorporates lots of air into the mixture and results in the perfect soft texture.

1. Line the base and sides of an 8-inch square baking pan with parchment paper, leaving an overhang of paper on two facing sides. (This will help you remove the fudge from the pan.) Set aside.

2. In a large microwaveable bowl, stir together both sugars and the cream.

3. Microwave the sugar mixture on medium-high for 4 minutes. Stir well, then microwave on medium-high for another 4 minutes, or until the sugars are completely dissolved. (The cooking time may vary depending on the wattage of your microwave oven.)

4. Add the butter and vanilla extract. Using an electric mixer on high speed, beat the mixture until it thickens and loses its sheen, about 2 minutes.

5. Scrape the fudge into the prepared pan, smoothing the top level with an offset spatula. Cover with plastic wrap and refrigerate until firm, about 30 minutes.

6. Using the parchment paper overhang, lift the fudge from the pan to a cutting board. Cut into 24 pieces. (This fudge gets better with time so, for best flavour, store it in an airtight container at room temperature for at least 2 days, or refrigerate for up to 2 weeks.)

Pecan Fudge

A batch of homemade fudge makes the perfect hostess gift or an after-dinner sweet treat. Talk about versatile!

Makes 16 pieces

Prep time: 20 minutes

Cooking time: about 8 minutes

Setting time: 1 hour, 15 minutes

3 ¼ cups lightly packed golden yellow sugar

1 cup sour cream (14%)

Pinch of fine sea salt

¼ cup unsalted butter, softened

1 tsp vanilla extract

1 cup chopped pecans

16 Glazed Pecans (recipe follows)

1. Line the base and sides of an 8-inch square baking pan with parchment paper, leaving an overhang of paper on two facing sides. (This will help you remove the fudge from the pan.) Set aside.

2. In a large saucepan, combine the sugar, sour cream and salt. Bring to a full, rolling boil over medium heat, stirring until the sugar dissolves.

3. Hook a candy thermometer over the side of the saucepan. Continue boiling, without stirring, until the candy thermometer registers 240°F, about 8 minutes. (If you don't have a candy thermometer, drop a little of the mixture into a bowl of cold water. If it forms a soft ball, it's ready.)

4. Immediately remove from the heat. Add the butter, but don't stir. Let the fudge cool until the candy thermometer registers 110°F. Stir in the vanilla extract.

5. Using an electric mixer, beat the fudge on low speed until it just begins to thicken and lose its sheen, about 5 minutes.

6. Stir in the chopped pecans. Scrape the fudge into the prepared pan, smoothing the top level with an offset spatula. Let stand at room temperature until set, about 15 minutes.

7. Score the fudge into 16 pieces, and press a glazed pecan into each piece. Let the fudge cool completely at room temperature, about 1 hour. Cut into pieces. (The fudge can be stored in an airtight container at room temperature, with wax paper between the layers, for up to 2 weeks.)

Glazed Pecans

Makes 2 cups

Prep time: 5 minutes

Cooking time: 13 minutes

¼ cup lightly packed golden yellow or dark brown sugar

¼ cup unsalted butter, softened

2 cups pecan halves

1. Preheat the oven to 350°F. Line a large rimmed baking sheet with parchment paper, then set aside.

2. In a medium saucepan, stir together the sugar and butter over medium heat until the sugar has dissolved and the butter has melted, about 3 minutes.

3. Remove from the heat. Stir in the pecans until well combined.

4. Spread the pecan mixture out on the prepared baking sheet. Bake until golden and fragrant, about 10 minutes, stirring halfway through baking time.

5. Separate the pecans on the baking sheet so they're not touching, then let cool completely.

Nut Brittle

Homemade gifts are always welcome, and this crunchy nut brittle is a particular favourite of ours. Choose a combination of peanuts, pecans, hazelnuts and/or cashews for the nut mixture, choosing nuts of a similar size so they toast evenly.

Makes about 30 pieces
Prep time: 15 minutes
Cooking time: 25 minutes
Setting time: about 30 minutes

3 cups mixed nuts (see above)

2 cups granulated sugar

½ cup unsalted butter, softened

½ cup water

⅓ cup liquid honey

½ tsp baking soda

Fleur de sel or coarse sea salt for garnish

1. Preheat the oven to 300°F. Spread the nuts out on a large rimmed baking sheet. Toast in the oven, stirring occasionally, just until the nuts are golden and fragrant, 7 to 10 minutes. Set aside.

2. Line a second large baking sheet with parchment paper. Set aside.

3. In a large, heavy-bottomed saucepan, combine the sugar, butter, water and honey. Cook over medium-low heat, stirring until the sugar has dissolved and the butter has melted.

4. Hook a candy thermometer over the side of the saucepan. Keeping the heat at medium-low, bring the sugar mixture to a boil, then boil, without stirring, until the caramel is golden brown and the candy thermometer registers 310°F, about 12 minutes. (If you don't have a candy thermometer, drop a little of the mixture into a bowl of cold water. If it forms a hard ball, it's ready.)

5. Immediately stir in the baking soda (the caramel will foam up). Moving quickly, stir in the nuts then scrape the mixture out onto the prepared baking sheet.

6. Using the back of a large spoon, spread the nut mixture out as thinly as you can. Sprinkle generously with fleur de sel.

7. Let stand at room temperature until cool and hardened, about 30 minutes. Break the brittle into small chunks. (The nut brittle can be stored in an airtight container at room temperature, with wax paper between the layers, for several weeks.)

BAKING DAY SECRETS

To save time, use roasted, salted nuts for the Nut Brittle and skip Step 1 of the recipe. Sprinkle the finished brittle sparingly with salt to compensate for the extra salt in the nuts.

Chic & Simple Chocolate Truffles

Rich and indulgent, these truffles are simple to make and can be customized to your taste with different flavours and coatings.

Makes 18 large or 36 mini truffles
Prep time: 15 minutes
Cooking time: 5 minutes
Chilling time: at least 2 hours

Truffles

1 ¼ cups bittersweet or semi-sweet chocolate chips

¾ cup plus 3 Tbsp whipping cream (35%)

⅓ cup lightly packed dark brown sugar

Pinch of fine sea salt

2 Tbsp unsalted butter, softened

Coatings

Turbinado sugar, finely chopped nuts, icing sugar and/or unsweetened cocoa powder

Chopped dark chocolate, melted (optional)

1. For the truffles, place the chocolate chips in a medium bowl. Set aside.

2. In a small saucepan, combine the cream, sugar and salt. Heat over medium-low heat, stirring occasionally, until the sugar has dissolved and the cream starts to simmer, about 5 minutes. Do not boil.

3. Pour half of the hot cream over the chocolate chips. Let stand for 30 seconds, then stir until the chocolate chips have melted.

4. Pour the rest of the cream over the chocolate. Add the butter. Stir until well combined, smooth and glossy. Let cool to room temperature, then refrigerate for at least 2 hours, or overnight.

5. Line two large baking sheets with parchment paper. Using a small ice cream scoop or melon baller, scoop the chocolate mixture into individual mounds on one of the prepared baking sheets.

6. On the other baking sheet, spread out your chosen dry coating or have ready a bowl of melted chocolate (if using).

7. With clean hands, roll each scoop into a neat ball. Roll each ball in your chosen dry coating. Alternatively, use two forks to dip the truffles, one at a time, into the melted chocolate.

8. Place each truffle in a foil or paper candy case. Sprinkle the chocolate-dipped truffles with more turbinado sugar, if liked. (The truffles can be refrigerated in an airtight container for up to 1 week. Bring to room temperature before serving.)

BAKING DAY SECRETS

Rolling the truffles into balls is easier if your hands are cool. Have a bowl of ice water and a towel nearby and, as your hands warm up, dip them in the ice water for a few seconds, then dry before continuing to roll the truffles.

CHANGE IT UP

Earl Grey Truffles: Add 2 Earl Grey tea bags to the cream mixture in Step 2. Heat the cream as instructed, then remove from the heat and let steep for 5 minutes. Press the tea bags with the back of a spoon, then discard. Pour the infused cream over the chocolate chips and continue with the recipe as above.

Peppermint Truffles: Follow the instructions for Earl Grey Truffles, but use peppermint tea bags.

Mocha Truffles: Add 2 teaspoonfuls of instant espresso powder in Step 2.

Rosemary Truffles: Add 2 teaspoonfuls of dried rosemary in Step 2. Heat the cream as instructed, then remove from the heat and let steep for 5 minutes. Strain the cream, then pour it over the chocolate chips and continue with the recipe.

Boozy Truffles: Add 1 tablespoonful of your favourite liqueur or spirit when adding the butter in Step 4. Stir well.

Dark Chocolate Peanut Butter Cups

The marriage of peanut butter and chocolate is a match made in heaven, so you'll know what we mean when we say these treats are little bites of bliss.

Makes 36 peanut butter cups
Prep time: 30 minutes
Cooking time: about 5 minutes
Setting time: 1 hour
Chilling time: about 1 hour

½ cup smooth peanut butter

¼ cup graham cracker crumbs

¼ cup brick-style cream cheese, at room temperature

3 Tbsp icing sugar

1 Tbsp vanilla extract

8 oz dark chocolate, finely chopped

1. In a medium bowl, stir together the peanut butter, graham cracker crumbs, cream cheese, icing sugar and vanilla extract until well combined and smooth. Set aside.

2. In a heatproof bowl set over a saucepan of gently simmering water, melt the chocolate until smooth. Remove from the heat.

3. Line the wells of a mini muffin pan with paper liners, if you have one. Otherwise, arrange 36 mini paper liners on a large baking sheet.

4. Spoon about 2 teaspoonfuls of the melted chocolate into the bottom of each paper liner, tilting them so the chocolate coats three-quarters of the way up the sides. Let stand until the chocolate has almost set.

5. Spoon about 1 teaspoonful of the peanut-butter mixture into the centre of each chocolate-filled paper liner. Pour a thick layer of melted chocolate over the peanut butter mixture so the edges of the two layers of chocolate match up and seal in the filling.

6. Chill the cups in the fridge until set, about 1 hour. Peel the paper liners away from the cups before serving. (The cups can be refrigerated in an airtight container for up to 1 week.)

Homemade Marshmallows

Homemade marshmallows are a real treat. Your campfire s'mores never tasted so good!

Makes 16 to 24 marshmallows
Prep time: 30 minutes
Cooking time: about 10 minutes
Setting time: at least 6 hours

Icing sugar for dusting

1 cup cold water

3 envelopes (3 Tbsp) unflavoured powered gelatin

1 ½ cups granulated sugar

1 cup white corn syrup

¼ tsp fine sea salt

1 Tbsp vanilla extract

1. Grease an 8-inch square baking pan (for thick marshmallows) or a 13- x 9-inch baking pan (for thinner marshmallows). Dust the pan generously with icing sugar.

2. Pour ½ cup of the water into a large bowl. Sprinkle with the gelatin. Set aside.

3. In a large, heavy-bottomed saucepan, combine the remaining ½ cup of water with the granulated sugar, corn syrup and salt. Cook on medium-low heat, stirring until the sugar has dissolved. Hook a candy thermometer over the side of the saucepan. Increase the heat to medium-high. Cook, without stirring, until the candy thermometer registers 240°F, about 10 minutes.

4. Using an electric mixer on low speed, gradually beat the sugar mixture into the gelatin mixture, drizzling the sugar mixture in slowly. Gradually increase the speed to high and beat until the mixture is thick and very sticky, about 10 minutes. Beat in the vanilla extract.

5. Scrape the mixture into the prepared pan, spreading it level. Dust the top with icing sugar.

6. Let stand, uncovered, at room temperature until the marshmallow is firm enough to cut, at least 6 hours or preferably overnight.

7. Invert the pan onto a large cutting board and unmould the marshmallow. Grease a large knife or pizza wheel and cut 16 to 24 pieces.

8. Toss the marshmallows in additional icing sugar to prevent them from sticking together. (The marshmallows can be stored in an airtight container, with parchment paper between the layers, for up to 1 month.)

BAKING DAY SECRETS

Homemade marshmallows hate sticky summer weather, so avoid prepping these on especially humid days. The moisture in the air can affect the cooking time and even prevent the candy from setting properly.

Creamy Orange Bites

These snack-size cakes taste just like orange ice cream bars. The hit of nostalgia makes them perfect for parties, but best make sure you taste-test them along the way, because they'll be gone in a flash.

Makes 72 bites
Prep time: 1 hour
Cooking time: about 40 minutes
Chilling time: about 20 minutes

Cake

2 cups carbonated orange soft drink

4 cups cake-and-pastry flour OR 3 ½ cups all-purpose flour sifted with ½ cup cornstarch

2 tsp baking powder

1 ½ tsp baking soda

1 tsp fine sea salt

1 cup unsalted butter, softened

2 cups granulated sugar

4 large eggs

2 tsp vanilla extract

Frosting

1 ½ cups unsalted butter, softened

4 cups icing sugar, sifted

1 Tbsp whipping cream (35%)

1 tsp vanilla extract

Orange gel food colouring

Orange sprinkles for garnish

1. Preheat the oven to 350°F. Grease two 9-inch round baking pans with butter, then dust them lightly with flour.

2. For the cake, pour the orange drink into a pitcher and stir until the bubbles disappear and the drink is no longer fizzy. Set aside.

3. In a medium bowl, whisk together the flour (or the flour and cornstarch), baking powder, baking soda and salt. Set aside.

4. In a large bowl and using an electric mixer, beat the butter with the sugar until pale and fluffy.

5. Beat in the eggs one at a time, beating well and scraping down the bowl after each addition. Beat in the vanilla extract. Beat in the orange drink until well combined.

6. Add the flour mixture to the sugar mixture, stirring just until incorporated (do not overmix).

7. Divide the batter evenly between the prepared baking pans. Tap the pans lightly on the counter a couple of times to release any air bubbles.

8. Bake until the cakes are golden brown and a toothpick inserted in the centre of each cake comes out clean, 35 to 40 minutes.

9. Let the cakes cool in the pans for 15 minutes. Run a knife around the edges of the cakes to loosen them. Carefully remove the cakes from the pans and let cool completely on a wire rack.

10. When cool, break the cakes into coarse crumbs and place them in a large bowl.

11. For the frosting, cream the butter with ½ cup of the icing sugar in a medium microwaveable bowl. Gradually add the remaining icing sugar, beating until the mixture is smooth. Beat in the cream and vanilla extract.

12. Scrape half of the frosting into a second medium bowl. Add enough food colouring to this second bowl of frosting to tint it bright orange.

13. Add the orange frosting to the cake crumbs, stirring until well combined. Form the cake mixture into seventy-two 1-inch balls.

14. Line a large baking sheet with parchment paper.

15. Microwave the bowl of white frosting on high power for 10-second intervals, stirring after each interval, until the frosting is the consistency of very thick pancake batter and coats the back of a spoon.

16. Using two forks, dip each cake ball into the warm white frosting to coat completely. As each ball is coated, lift it out with a fork, letting any excess frosting drip off. Place each ball on the prepared baking sheet and garnish with orange sprinkles.

17. When all the balls are coated and garnished, refrigerate them until the frosting is set. Place the balls in paper liners before serving.

BAKING DAY SECRETS

If the white frosting begins to set while you're dipping the cake balls, warm it in the microwave on high power for 5-second intervals until it melts a little.

Chocolate-Covered Sponge Toffee

Make a maple version of this old-fashioned treat by substituting maple syrup for the honey.

Makes about 40 small pieces
Prep time: 30 minutes
Cooking time: about 10 minutes
Cooling time: 2 hours

2 cups granulated sugar

½ cup water

½ cup golden corn syrup

¼ cup liquid honey

1 Tbsp vanilla extract

1 Tbsp baking soda, sifted

1 cup dark chocolate chips

1. Line a rimmed baking sheet with parchment paper. Set aside.

2. In a large, deep saucepan, combine the sugar, water, corn syrup, honey and vanilla extract. Cook over medium heat, stirring gently, until the sugar has dissolved.

3. Increase the heat to medium-high. Hook a candy thermometer over the side of the saucepan. Cook the sugar mixture, without stirring, until the candy thermometer registers 300°F, 8 to 10 minutes. (If you don't have a candy thermometer, drop a little of the mixture into a bowl of cold water. If it forms a hard ball, it's ready.)

4. Immediately remove from the heat and, stirring constantly, add the baking soda. The mixture will bubble up. Pour the toffee onto the prepared baking sheet. Let cool at room temperature for 2 hours.

5. In a medium heatproof bowl set over a saucepan of gently simmering water, melt the chocolate until smooth. Pour the chocolate over the toffee, spreading to cover the toffee completely. Let cool until the chocolate is set.

6. Use a large, sharp knife to cut the toffee into pieces. (The toffee can be stored in an airtight container, with wax paper between the layers, for up to 1 month.)

Pretzel Bonbons
with Pecans and Salted Vanilla Caramel

Resembling a famous Christmas chocolate candy, these homemade treats are a snap to prepare and make a great hostess gift at holiday time.

Makes: 24 bonbons
Prep time: 20 minutes
Chilling time: at least 40 minutes
Cooking time: 5 minutes

24 whole mini pretzels

24 Salted Vanilla Caramels (page 316)

¼ cup smooth or crunchy peanut butter

24 pecan halves, toasted

1 ½ cups bittersweet or semi-sweet chocolate chips

Sea salt flakes for garnish

CHANGE IT UP

Try using other nuts, instead of the pecans— walnuts, almonds or hazelnuts all work well.

1. Line a large baking sheet with parchment paper. Arrange the pretzels, about 1 ½ inches apart, on the baking sheet.

2. Place a caramel on top of each pretzel and gently press down. Spoon ½ teaspoonful of peanut butter on top of each caramel.

3. Press a pecan half into the peanut butter on each candy. Refrigerate until chilled, about 10 minutes.

4. Meanwhile, melt the chocolate in a medium heatproof bowl set over a saucepan of gently simmering water. Stir until smooth.

5. Carefully spoon the melted chocolate over each candy, covering the pecans, caramel and pretzels. Sprinkle the tops with sea salt flakes.

6. Let cool at room temperature for 2 hours or refrigerate until chilled, about 30 minutes. Put the bonbons in paper or foil candy cases. (The bonbons can be refrigerated in an airtight container for up to 2 weeks or frozen for up to 2 months.)

Salted Vanilla Caramels

Salted caramels have never been easier to make: this recipe takes just a few minutes in your microwave.

Makes about 25 caramels

Prep time: 15 minutes

Cooking time: about 6 minutes

Cooling time: at least 2 hours

½ cup granulated sugar

½ cup lightly packed dark brown sugar

½ cup golden corn syrup

½ cup sweetened condensed milk

¼ cup unsalted butter, softened

1 ½ tsp vanilla extract

½ tsp fine sea salt

Sea salt flakes for garnish

1. Line the base and sides of an 8-inch square baking pan with parchment paper, leaving an overhang of paper on two facing sides. (This will help you remove the caramels from the pan.) Set aside.

2. In a large microwaveable bowl, combine both sugars, the corn syrup, condensed milk, butter, vanilla extract and salt.

3. Microwave on high power for 6 minutes, stirring every 2 minutes.

4. Check the temperature with a candy thermometer: it should register 250°F. If the mixture is too cool, heat for 30-second intervals until it reaches 250°F.

5. Carefully pour the caramel into the prepared pan and sprinkle with sea salt flakes. Let cool at room temperature for at least 2 hours.

6. Using the parchment paper overhang, lift the caramel from the pan to a cutting board. With a large, sharp knife, cut into 25 pieces. (The caramels can be stored in an airtight container, individually wrapped in wax paper or cellophane, for up to 1 month.)

Peppermint Patties

T his classic candy is always a crowd-pleaser and, since the patties keep well, you can keep them on hand for whenever the urge strikes.

Makes about 30 patties
Prep time: about 30 minutes
Chilling time: at least 2 ½ hours
Cooking time: 5 minutes

Filling

2 ½ cups icing sugar, sifted

2 Tbsp white corn syrup

2 Tbsp whipping cream (35%)

2 Tbsp coconut oil, melted

1 tsp peppermint extract

½ tsp vanilla extract

Blue gel food colouring (optional)

Green gel food colouring (optional)

Additional icing sugar for dusting

Coating

2 cups bittersweet chocolate chips

1 Tbsp coconut oil

Icing

½ cup icing sugar, sifted

2 ½ tsp water

1. For the filling, stir together the icing sugar, corn syrup, cream and coconut oil in a large bowl. Using an electric mixer, beat on low speed for 1 minute. Stir in the peppermint extract and vanilla extract.

2. Tint the filling an icy blue-green by beating in 2 drops of blue colouring for every 1 drop of green (if using) until the desired colour is reached.

3. Shape the filling into a disc. Wrap it tightly in plastic wrap and refrigerate for 30 minutes.

4. Line a large baking sheet with parchment paper and set aside. Generously sprinkle a clean work surface with icing sugar.

5. Roll out the filling on the prepared work surface to ¼-inch thickness, dusting with more icing sugar as necessary. Cut out patties using a 1 ½-inch cookie cutter, rerolling the scraps until all the filling is used. Place the patties on the prepared baking sheet. Put the baking sheet in the freezer for at least 1 hour.

6. For the coating, melt the chocolate and coconut oil in a medium bowl set over a saucepan of gently simmering water. Stir until smooth.

7. Using two forks, dip each patty in the melted chocolate. As each patty is coated, lift it out with a fork, letting any excess chocolate drip off. Slide the coated patty back onto the baking sheet, scraping chocolate from the base of the patty with the fork. Let cool at room temperature for at least 1 hour or until set.

8. For the icing, whisk together the icing sugar and water in a small bowl until smooth. Using the tines of a fork or a piping bag fitted with a fine tip, drizzle the icing decoratively over the patties. Let the patties stand at room temperature until the icing is set. (The peppermint patties can be refrigerated in an airtight container for up to 2 weeks.)

BAKING DAY SECRETS

Leave the bowl of chocolate over the simmering water as you dip the patties to prevent the chocolate from thickening too much.

Pistachio-Cranberry Nougat

The flavour of the honey really shines through in this pillowy-soft homemade nougat, so use your favourite variety.

Makes 36 pieces
Prep time: 30 minutes
Cooking time: 15 minutes
Cooling time: 6 hours

2 cups granulated sugar

1 ½ cups liquid honey

1 Tbsp water

4 large egg whites

Pinch of fine sea salt

Pinch of cream of tartar

1 ½ cups unsalted pistachios, shelled

1 cup dried cranberries

Additional shelled pistachios and/ or dried cranberries for garnish (optional)

1. Line a 13- x 9-inch baking pan with parchment paper. Set aside.

2. In a large, heavy-bottomed saucepan, stir together the sugar, honey and water. Hook a candy thermometer over the side of the saucepan.

3. Cook the sugar mixture over medium-high heat until the candy thermometer registers 315°F, about 15 minutes. Stir every 5 minutes at first, then more often once the temperature exceeds 250°F. The hotter the mixture gets, the foamier and bubblier it will be on top.

4. Once the mixture reaches 315°F, immediately remove the saucepan from the heat. Carefully pour the hot sugar mixture into a clean saucepan to prevent it from cooking further. Hook the candy thermometer over the side of this second saucepan and let the mixture cool to 300°F. This won't take long, so watch carefully.

5. While the sugar mixture is cooling, in a large bowl and using an electric mixer, beat the egg whites, salt and cream of tartar until stiff peaks form.

6. With the mixer running on medium-high speed, gradually beat the cooled sugar mixture into the egg whites, drizzling it in a thin but continuous stream. It should take 4 to 5 minutes to add all the sugar mixture, so take your time.

7. Continue beating on medium-high speed until the mixture has roughly tripled in volume. At first the colour will be golden, but it will gradually turn to ivory as you beat.

8. Turn down the mixer speed to low. Add the pistachios and dried cranberries, beating just until incorporated.

9. Scrape the mixture into the prepared pan. (The mixture will be very thick and sticky.) Sprinkle the top with additional pistachios and/or dried cranberries (if using).

10. Place a sheet of parchment paper on top of the nougat and use a rolling pin to smooth out the nougat evenly in the pan. Let stand at room temperature until cool, about 3 hours. Invert the pan onto a large cutting board and unmould the nougat. Cool at room temperature for a further 3 hours.

11. Using a sharp knife, cut the nougat into pieces, running the knife under hot water between each cut. (The nougat can be refrigerated in an airtight container, with parchment paper between the layers, for up to 2 weeks.)

Nutty Divinity

This chewy, nougat-like confection lends itself to all kinds of flavour variations. We like this nutty version, but check out the sidebar for some of our other favourite flavours. See photo on page iv.

Makes 16 pieces
Prep time: 10 minutes
Cooking time: about 15 minutes
Cooling time: 3 hours

½ cup sliced almonds, toasted

1 large egg white

1 cup granulated sugar

¼ cup white corn syrup

2 Tbsp brewed black coffee

2 Tbsp water

Pinch of fine sea salt

½ tsp almond extract

¼ tsp vanilla extract

1. Line a baking sheet with parchment paper. Reserve about 16 almond slices. Sprinkle the remaining almonds evenly over the baking sheet. Fit a piping bag with a large-holed round tip. Set aside.

2. Put the egg white in a large bowl and have an electric mixer ready. Set aside.

3. In a large saucepan, combine the sugar, corn syrup, coffee, water and salt. Cook over medium heat, stirring just until the sugar has dissolved.

4. Hook a candy thermometer over the side of the saucepan. Cook the sugar mixture over medium heat, without stirring, until the candy thermometer registers 250°F, about 15 minutes. (If you don't have a candy thermometer, drop a little of the mixture into a bowl of cold water. If it forms a soft ball, it's ready.)

5. Meanwhile, using the electric mixer, beat the egg white until stiff peaks form. As soon as the candy thermometer reaches 250°F, remove from the heat. Beat the syrup into the egg white in a slow, steady stream.

6. Add the almond and vanilla extracts and continue beating until stiff peaks form and the meringue becomes slightly dull-looking.

7. Immediately spoon the mixture into the prepared piping bag. Pipe the mixture into "kisses" or swirls onto the sliced almonds on the baking sheet.

8. Decorate the candies with the reserved almond slices, gently pressing them in. Let cool at room temperature for several hours. (The divinity can be stored in an airtight container for up to 2 weeks.)

BAKING DAY SECRETS

To prevent the meringue mixture from sticking, dip your spatula in cold water before spooning the meringue into the piping bag.

Stop beating the meringue as soon as it becomes dull-looking. It becomes more difficult to work with as it cools.

Have all your utensils to hand—the baking sheet lined with parchment and toasted almonds, piping bag fitted with its tip, cold water for the spatula, electric mixer ready— before starting to make the divinity.

CHANGE IT UP

Traditional Divinity: Replace the coffee with an extra 2 table-spoonfuls of water. Increase the vanilla extract to ½ teaspoon-ful, and omit the almonds and almond extract.

Mocha Divinity: Replace the water with an extra 2 table-spoonfuls of brewed coffee. Add ¼ cup semi-sweet chocolate chips along with the almond and vanilla extracts in Step 6.

Tropical Divinity: Stir 2 tablespoonfuls of toasted unsweetened shredded coconut and 2 tablespoonfuls of finely chopped dried pineapple into the mixture before beating in Step 6.

Peppermint Divinity: Replace the coffee with an extra 2 table-spoonfuls of water. Substitute peppermint extract for the almond extract, and omit the almonds.

Metric Conversion Table

WEIGHT	
⅛ oz	4 g
½ oz	15 g
1 oz	30 g
2 oz	60 g
3 oz	85 g
4 oz/¼ lb	110 g
5 oz	140 g
6 oz	170 g
7 oz	200 g
8 oz/½ lb	225 g
12 oz/¾ lb	340 g
1 lb	450 g

VOLUME	
¼ tsp	1.25 mL
½ tsp	2.5 mL
1 tsp	5 mL
1 Tbsp	15 mL
1½ Tbsp	22 mL
2 Tbsp	30 mL
3 Tbsp	45 mL
¼ cup	60 mL
⅓ cup	80 mL
½ cup	120 mL
⅔ cup	160 mL
¾ cup	185 mL
1 cup	240 mL
1¼ cups	300 mL
1⅓ cups	320 mL
1½ cups	360 mL
2 cups	480 mL

LENGTH	
¼ inch	6 mm
½ inch	1.2 cm
¾ inch	2 cm
1 inch	2.5 cm
1¼ inches	3 cm
1½ inches	4 cm
2 inches	5 cm
3 inches	8 cm
4 inches	10 cm
5 inches	13 cm
6 inches	15 cm
7 inches	18 cm
8 inches	20 cm
9 inches	23 cm
10 inches	25 cm
11 inches	27 cm
12 inches	30 cm

OVEN TEMPERATURE	
160°F	70°C
275°F	135°C
300°F	150°C
325°F	160°C
350°F	175°C
400°F	200°C
425°F	220°C
450°F	230°C

Acknowledgements

Whenever a project of this scope is undertaken, it involves a team who commits to spending an incredible amount of effort and time to bring all of the pieces together.

We would like to thank Julia Aitken for all her tremendous work in taking our recipes that we have collected over the years, as well as the new ones, and putting a consistent voice to them for us. Her breadth of experience and skills were greatly appreciated.

Nancy Gavin, Brand Development Manager at Redpath Sugar, for bringing the project forward and keeping all the balls in the air to ensure that each section of the book embodied the essence of the Redpath tradition.

Richard Feltoe, Curator and Corporate Archivist at the Redpath Sugar Museum, for his insight and wealth of knowledge and information for the historical aspects of the book.

Alexa Bosshardt, Corporate Research Chef at ASR Group, for her patience as she reviewed all of the recipes to ensure that they were precise and for offering invaluable tips.

Evelyn Hopkins, Corporate Counsel ASR Group, for her astute advice and support throughout the entire project.

For the whole Nourish Food Marketing team whose creativity and enthusiasm was instrumental in developing the book. Their team was led by Andreas Düss, Head of Creative and Innovation, whose numerous talents helped to bring the idea to life. This team also consisted of Magenta Piroska and Alexandra Yue in culinary development, Danika Zandboer for photography and styling, and Laura Zahody as project manager.

Of course, we would not have this book if it wasn't for our publisher, Robert McCullough, who understood our vision for a book based on such an iconic brand, and who provided guidance as we undertook this project. We would also like to thank the whole team at Appetite by Random House, including Zoe Maslow, our editor; Kelly Hill, our designer; Bonnie Maitland, our sales director; and Carla Kean and the entire production department.

Carrot Cake, page 110

Index

THE
END

Black & White Cookies, page 35

Summer Peach Pie, page 205

Lemon–White Chocolate Cupcakes, page 139

Morning Glory Muffins, page 87

Orange-Scented Brioche, page 256

Chocolate Brandy Snaps, page 50